—————————————— ▼ ——————————————

Direct Democracy

A Twentieth Century Fund Book

The Twentieth Century Fund is a research foundation undertaking timely analyses of economic, political, and social issues. Not-for-profit and nonpartisan, the Fund was founded in 1919 and endowed by Edward A. Filene.

Direct Democracy

*The Politics of Initiative,
Referendum, and Recall*

Thomas E. Cronin

A TWENTIETH CENTURY FUND BOOK

HARVARD UNIVERSITY PRESS
Cambridge, Massachusetts, and London, England
1989

Library of Congress Cataloging-in-Publication Data

Cronin, Thomas E.
    Direct democracy : the politics of initiative, referendum, and recall /
Thomas E. Cronin.
        p. cm.
    " A Twentieth Century Fund book."
    Bibliography: p.
    Includes index.
    ISBN 0-674-21025-5 (alk. paper)
    1. Referendum—United States—History—20th century. 2. Recall—
—United States—History—20th century.   3. Populism—United States—
—History—20th century.   I. Title.
JF493.U6C76   1989   88-14859
328'.2—dc19   CIP

CONTENTS

▼

Foreword

▼

AMERICANS have grown increasingly restive when dissatisfied with legislation or elected officials between elections. As a result, public interest in and use of the devices created to give voters a greater direct voice in our democracy—referendum, recall, and initiative—have proliferated in recent years.

These devices, which gained popularity during the Progressive era, had been used only selectively since. The first indications that Americans were turning once again to the tools of direct democracy as a means of increasing their influence over government came in the late 1970s, perhaps most notably in 1978, when Californians collected enough signatures in a grass-roots petition drive to place Proposition 13 on the ballot.

This awakening of interest did not pass unnoticed at the Twentieth Century Fund. In the belief that this was a subject that would only grow in importance, the Trustees and staff sought a project to examine it. At our suggestion, Thomas E. Cronin, McHugh Professor of American Institutions and Leadership at The Colorado College, began a survey and review of participatory democracy in America. Cronin has himself been an active participant in American politics: at one point he took time to campaign for public office, an effort that enhanced his understanding of the reasons citizens have turned to devices that give them a direct voice in government. Cronin has thoroughly examined the development of recall petitions, local initiatives, and referenda and interviewed those involved in the recent growth of the direct democracy movement. He finds that there are difficulties with direct democracy devices, yet he concludes that these procedures have been a lasting, and generally a positive, part of the American political landscape.

Finally, we are particularly grateful to Cronin because he went further than his original mandate. He went on to consider the feasibility and pitfalls of a national referendum and to propose a set of safeguards that are needed to ensure that the initiative, referendum, and recall are used in a manner compatible with representative government.

M. J. Rossant, Director
The Twentieth Century Fund
June 1988

PREFACE

▼

SEVERAL events and concerns inspired this book. First, while helping to direct a signature petition drive by a civic interest group in the late 1970s, I was impressed by the workings of grass-roots democracy and the impact such a drive could have on an unresponsive legislature. Yet I was also troubled by the ways in which signatures were solicited and the inevitable temptations to collect as many signatures as possible in whatever way they could be collected—and how, in the rush to obtain signatures, certain abuses of democratic process could also occur. This intensive participation in the process persuaded me that ballot democracy was yet another imperfect, if useful, institution in a world of imperfect political institutions.

Second, as a student of national leadership and the American presidency, I became concerned about the possible impact of proposed national referenda and national recalls. How would these devices help or hinder the complicated governing responsibilities we assign to the president and Congress? Who would be hurt and who would benefit? Could we predict what kinds of policies or partisan interests might be promoted or diminished?

Finally, I was struck by the outburst of alarm—among public officials and their friends, who generally view themselves as defenders of an activist government and participatory politics—when Proposition 13 won such strong approval in California in 1978. In the years immediately following, it was apparent that many modern-day progressives champion strong representative government yet vigorously campaign against the spread of populist-style direct democracy. An apparent fear of majority rule and populist devices has developed among many of the very people who once supported them.

For a long while, I have generally sympathized with the Jeffersonian-inspired populist persuasion that trusts the good sense of the common citizen—especially if there are good newspapers and good schools. According to this optimistic perspective, a country willing to share more political power with its citizens will find a citizenry willing to participate in the workings of government. I reject the verdict that most citizens must be passive spectators. I also hold that we need better and more-involved citizens more than we need larger-than-life, charismatic leaders.

More than any other form of government, democracy requires a healthy blend of faith and skepticism: faith that if people are informed and caring, they can be trusted with self-government; and a persistent questioning of leaders and majorities. A system as large as ours also requires wise and gifted leaders who will promote, shape, and help guide public opinion on transcendent issues, and leadership institutions with resources and prerogatives equal to the demands facing the system. This necessary tension between the quest for political equality and the requirements for statecraft is apparent in the following chapters.

This is not an advocacy book. I have tried throughout to provide a balanced evaluation. Although my heart tends to side with populism, my head is skeptical about the workability and desirability of many direct democracy devices. My own ambivalence is amply reinforced by the reality that most Americans are also of two minds about populist democracy. They want more of it in the abstract, yet they are often cautious and concerned about its excesses in practice. America is a nation of countless paradoxes; its citizens' ideas about democracy and governance are merely one of them.

I have also tried to be comprehensive. In addition to reading nearly all available studies, reports, hearings, and polls on the subject, since 1980 I have interviewed more than 200 political activists and elected officials in ten states from Maine to Oregon, conducted a poll of Colorado citizens, and, in 1987, commissioned the Gallup Organization to survey a national sample of adult Americans on their attitudes toward direct democracy. The results of this research confirm that these populist devices are here to stay, have worked better at the state and local levels than most people realize, need further safeguard regulation to ensure they serve the larger and longer-term public interest, and are not now needed or desirable at the national level. This book provides ample evidence that there are problems associated with their use in most states permitting them. Only when these instruments of democracy can be made to work better than they currently do should we even consider them seriously at the federal level.

Many of the imperfections can be eliminated through incremental improvements of the kind states have made in recent years. I am less optimistic about the problem of how election issues are funded. The Supreme Court has prohibited state restrictions on spending in initiative and referendum campaigns. In the name of defending everyone's First Amendment rights, the Court is perhaps encouraging a different form of corruption. These flaws will have to be addressed by anyone who wishes to encourage and extend populist democracy.

I am indebted to a number of institutions and people who assisted me in the research for and writing of this book. I am grateful to The Twentieth Century Fund, its board of trustees, its director, the late Murray J. Rossant, and its staff, especially Beverly Goldberg, for their financial support and encouragement. Alex Holzman provided helpful editorial assistance for the Fund and the book.

Dr. Aida Donald and Elizabeth Suttell at the Harvard University Press helped improve the manuscript in important ways. My research was made easier at every stage by the assistance of several excellent students at The Colorado College, especially Jean Anderson, Paul Hudnut, Robert S. Lackner, Tom Ori, Holly Ornstein, and Jeff Weill.

The staffs at the Tutt Library of The Colorado College, the Firestone Library at Princeton University, and the Institute for Advanced Study at Princeton all provided valuable help. I am grateful too to the people at the Gallup Organization, especially its president, Andy Kohut, for their general advice and assistance with a national poll designed for this study.

Several colleagues around the country—Benjamin R. Barber, Robert C. Benedict, Larry L. Berg, Eugene Lee, Daniel H. Lowenstein, David B. Magleby, Patrick B. McGuigan, Austin Ranney, David Schmidt, John S. Shockley, and Betty H. Zisk—have shared their advice or research on various aspects of direct democracy, and my debt to them and their work is evident throughout this book. Many of them joined with me several years ago to form the Direct Democracy Research Group, a working group of the American Political Science Association, and its sessions have informed this research at nearly every stage. I also thank Professor Jerry B. Briscoe for sharing his unpublished research on California recall elections.

Finally, I thank the hundreds of officials and political observers who talked with me about the workings of the initiative, referendum, and recall in their states and communities. As I record my gratitude to all of these people for their help in making this a better book, I also hereby absolve them of responsibility for what I have written and recommended.

Direct Democracy

▼

Introduction

▼

FOR ABOUT a hundred years Americans have been saying that voting occasionally for public officials is not enough. Political reformers contend that more democracy is needed and that the American people are mature enough and deserve the right to vote on critical issues facing their states and the nation. During the twentieth century, American voters in many parts of the country have indeed won the right to write new laws and repeal old ones through the initiative and referendum. They have also thrown hundreds of state and local officials out of office in recall elections.

Although the framers of the Constitution deliberately designed a republic, or indirect democracy, the practice of direct democracy and the debate over its desirability are as old as English settlements in America. Public debate and popular voting on issues go back to early seventeenth-century town assemblies and persist today in New England town meetings.

Populist democracy in America has produced conspicuous assets and conspicuous liabilities. It has won the support and admiration of many enthusiasts, yet it is also fraught with disturbing implications. Its most important contributions came early in this century in the form of the initiative, referendum, and recall, as a reaction to corrupt and unresponsive state legislatures throughout the country. Most of us would not recognize what then passed for representative government. "Bills that the machine and its backers do not desire are smothered in committee; measures which they do desire are brought out and hurried through their passage," said Governor Woodrow Wilson at the time. "It happens again and again that great groups of such bills are rushed through in the hurried hours that mark the close of the legislative sessions, when everyone is withheld from vigilance by fatigue and when it is possible to do secret things."[1] The threat, if not the reality, of the initiative, referendum, and recall helped to encourage a more responsible, civic-minded breed of state legislator. These measures were not intended to subvert or alter the basic character of American government. "Their intention," as Wilson saw it, was "to restore, not to destroy, representative government."[2]

The *initiative* allows voters to propose a legislative measure (statutory initiative) or a constitutional amendment (constitutional initiative) by filing a petition bearing a required number of valid citizen signatures.

The *referendum* refers a proposed or existing law or statute to voters for their approval or rejection. Some state constitutions require referenda; in other states, the legislature may decide to refer a measure to the voters. Measures referred by legislatures (statutes, constitutional amendments, bonds, or advisory questions) are the most common ballot propositions. A *popular* or *petition referendum* (a less frequently used device) refers an already enacted measure to the voters before it can go into effect. States allowing the petition referendum require a minimum number of valid citizen signatures within a specified time. There is confusion about the difference between the initiative and referendum because *referendum* is frequently used in a casual or generic way to describe all ballot measures.

The *recall* allows voters to remove or discharge a public official from office by filing a petition bearing a specified number of valid signatures demanding a vote on the official's continued tenure in office. Recall procedures typically require that the petition be signed by 25 percent of those who voted in the last election, after which a special election is almost always required. The recall differs from impeachment in that the people, not the legislature, initiate the election and determine the outcome with their votes. It is a purely political and not even a semijudicial process.

American voters today admire and respect the virtues of representative government, yet most of them also yearn for an even greater voice in how their laws are made. They understand the defects of both representative and direct democracy and prefer, on balance, to have a mixture of the two. Sensible or sound democracy is their aspiration.

Although Americans cannot cast votes on critical national issues, voters in twenty-six states, the District of Columbia, and hundreds of localities do have the right to put measures on their ballots. Legislatures can also refer measures to the public for a general vote. And constitutional changes in every state except Delaware must be approved by voters before becoming law. Voters in fifteen states and the District of Columbia can also recall elected state officials, and thirty-six states permit the recall of various local officials.

When Americans think of their right to vote, they think primarily of their right to nominate and elect legislators, members of school boards and of city councils, and the American president. Yet California's famous Proposition 13 in June 1978 focused nationwide attention on the public's right to participate in controversial tax decision making, as Californians voted to cut their property taxes by at least half. More voters participated in this issue contest than in the same day's gubernatorial primaries.

California's Proposition 13 had two additional effects. It triggered similar tax-slashing measures (both as bills and as direct legislation by the people) in numerous other states, and it encouraged conservative interest groups to use the initiative and referendum processes to achieve some of their goals. In the past decade conservative interests have placed on state and local ballots scores of measures favoring the death penalty, victims' rights, English-only regulations, and prayer in schools, and opposing taxation or spending, pornography, abortion, and homosexuality. Several states have regularly conducted referenda on issues ranging from a nuclear freeze to seat-belt laws. Citizens are now voting on hundreds of initiatives and referenda at state and local levels. In 1982, 1984, and 1986 more than 225 issues were put to the voters for decisions; 42 initiatives alone were voted on in fifteen states in 1986. In 1988 voters voted on at least 50 citizen-initiated measures in about eighteen states. And scores of recall elections have also taken place. Several state and local officials have been recalled for either raising taxes or failing to curb government spending.

Since Proposition 13, governors and legislative leaders in several states, mostly Republicans, have led efforts to get the initiative and referendum enacted in their jurisdictions. Major discussions on both have taken place in Alabama, Georgia, Hawaii, Minnesota, New Jersey, New York, Rhode Island, and Texas. In 1980, 53 percent of Minnesota voters approved adoption of the initiative and referendum, but their constitution required an absolute majority of all those coming to the polls that day to approve it, and because some voters refrained from voting on this ballot question it failed to satisfy this requirement. In 1986, 48 percent of Rhode Island voters approved an initiative process—not enough to get it into their constitution, but a significant show of support nonetheless. Republican Governor Thomas Kean in New Jersey strongly endorsed it in his 1986 state of the state address, saying, "We have good government in New Jersey, but we can make it better—more responsive—more efficient. The people of most states have the right to directly change their laws. People in New Jersey deserve the same right."[3]

In 1987, two-thirds of a nationwide sample of 1,009 American adults, in a telephone survey conducted by the Gallup Organization and commissioned for this book, said that citizens should be able to vote directly on some state and local laws, implying that elected officials should not have a monopoly over the making of laws. Three-quarters of those responding to the survey believed that voters are able to cast informed votes in state and local ballot issue elections. An impressive number of those who were not registered to vote said they would probably vote if they were able to do so on a few proposed state and national laws on election day.

The United States is one of very few democracies that do not permit a national referendum. Leaders in several other nations have often put issues before the voters at large. President Corazon Aquino submitted the 1986 Philippine constitution to the people for ratification, and the constitution provides for both the initiative and referendum. Spanish citizens voted to remain in the North Atlantic Treaty Organization. The Irish and Italians have voted on the divorce issue. The Swiss vote with frequency on both major and mundane issues. Charles de Gaulle put before French voters the issue of whether France should give up Algeria and won their support for his policy. The British have voted in a national referendum on whether to remain in the European Common Market. Polish authorities recently placed two important economic issues on the national ballot and suffered embarrassing defeats. And several nations have settled border or boundary disputes by putting these matters to the people.

More Americans favor than oppose the idea of a national referendum; and 58 percent of those surveyed in a Gallup poll I commissioned in 1987 favored having a national advisory referendum on a few proposed laws every two years at the time of the national elections. Congressman Richard Gephardt, a 1988 presidential candidate, noted a few years ago that American voters seldom trust their politicians to respond to their legitimate concerns. They stay home on election day, but they would participate if they had a better way to make themselves heard. "A national referendum," Gephardt added, could "provide the vehicle for the re-expression of public sentiment for or against critical issues facing the nation."[4] Political theorist Benjamin R. Barber acknowledges in a similar vein that a strong democracy cannot be government by all the people all the time on public matters. "But it can and must be government by all the people some of the time in at least some public matters," says Barber. "To remain free we will have to remain democratic; and to remain democratic we will have to acknowledge that voting presidents in and out of office is not enough."[5]

What are the politics and consequences of recall elections? Voters in Omaha in 1987 turned their two-term mayor out of office because of his alleged arrogance. Back in 1921 voters in North Dakota removed their governor in a recall election. Voters in Louisiana and Michigan mounted efforts to recall their governors in the 1980s. Arizona's Republican governor, Evan Mecham, most likely would have been recalled by the citizens in that state had not the legislature, a few weeks before the scheduled recall election in the spring of 1988, removed him by convicting him after he had been impeached. This much-discussed direct democracy device has been little studied. Yet my 1987 survey showed that 55 percent of adult Americans would like to be able to recall presidents who prove inadequate to their job, and that 67 percent favor giving themselves the right to recall members of Congress.

Skeptics, however, worry about tyranny by the majority and fear voters are seldom well enough informed to cast votes on complicated, technical national laws. People also worry, and justifiably, about the way well-financed special interest groups might use these procedures. Corruption at the state level is much less common today than it was early in the century, but special interests are surely just as involved as ever. The power of campaign contributions is clear. The advantages to those who can afford campaign and political consultants, direct mail firms, and widespread television and media appeals are very real. Although in theory Americans are politically equal, in practice there remain enormous disparities in individuals' and groups' capacities to influence the direction of government. And although the direct democracy devices of the initiative, referendum, and recall type are widely available, the evidence suggests it is generally the organized interests that can afford to put them to use. The idealistic notion that populist democracy devices can make every citizen a citizen-legislator and move us closer to political and egalitarian democracy is plainly an unrealized aspiration.

The initiative, referendum, and recall were born in an era of real grievances. They made for a different kind of democracy in those areas that permitted them. At the very least, they signaled the unacceptability of some of the most corrupt and irresponsible political practices of that earlier era. It is fashionable among political analysts today to say that although they have rarely lived up to their promises, neither have they resulted in the dire outcomes feared by critics. Yet they have had both good and questionable consequences. This book examines how we came to supplement representative government with these populist devices and assesses their direct and indirect effects. The central questions addressed in the following chapters are:

Do voters know what they are signing when they sign petitions?
Do voters cast an informed vote when the issues are put to them in initiative, referendum, and recall elections?
Does majority rule come at the expense of minority rights?
What is the influence of those who are willing and able to spend large sums of money to support or block ballot measures?
What are the assets and liabilities of the recall election?
What are the prospects for and the desirability of a national initiative and referendum?
What is the overall record of direct democracy in America? What have we learned about voting in these elections at the state and local levels? Who wins and who loses? What does it mean?

By examining direct democracy practices we can learn about the strengths and weaknesses of a neglected aspect of American politics, as well as the workings of representative democracy. We seek to understand it so we can improve it, and to improve it so it can better supplement rather than replace our institutions of representative government.

CHAPTER 1

▼

To Govern Ourselves Wisely

▼

Governments are instituted among men deriving their just powers from the consent of the governed.

> —Declaration of
> Independence, 1776

Men love power . . . Give all power to the many, they will oppress the few. Give all power to the few, they will oppress the many. Both therefore ought to have power, that each may defend itself against the other.

> —Alexander Hamilton, 1787

AMERICANS of the Revolutionary era were profoundly ambivalent about democracy. About one-third would gladly have continued as loyal subjects of the king; another third did not want to be bothered by tedious debates about forms of government, representation, and election schemes: they wanted to be left alone and to leave what limited governing was necessary to those who were willing to do it. A positive embrace of democracy in any real sense came well after the writing of the Constitution.

When democracy, even in its limited forms, did evolve, it did so too quickly for many people. The very notion of direct and frequent popular participation in state or national decision making frightened many of those in privileged positions. Many worried about tyranny by the majority and held the protection of the minority to be of equal if not superior importance to majority rule. The purpose of elections, most people then believed, was to select leaders—not to get the public wholly involved in the affairs of government. Once basic rules of constitutionalism could be agreed on, political leaders would govern and the governed would obey. Even the desirability of a representative government with the suffrage limited to white males was debated well into the nineteenth century.

Yet the reasonable voice of the people has always been accorded a special significance in theories of American governance. And the impetus for the American Revolution surely emerged from the protests of the common people as much as, if not more than, from the well bred, well read, and well fed. In urging American unity in the war effort, Thomas Jefferson emphasized the fundamental right of a people to rebel and end the illegitimate rule of unreasonable and unresponsive leaders. Even Alexander Hamilton, whom one could hardly accuse of being a professional democrat, later wrote that the fabric of the new American republic ought to rest on the solid basis of the consent of the people. "The streams of national power ought to flow immediately from that pure original foundation of all legitimate authority."[1] James Madison emphasized it was essential for the new republic to derive its legitimacy from "the great body of the society, not from any inconsiderable portion, or a favored class of it."[2] But although Madison and his peers conceded that government should be carried on with steady attention to the expectations and preferences of the American voter, they opposed widespread and continuous public participation in the conduct and operations of government decision making. Regular elections would be sufficient to render elected officials sensitive to the public's wishes.

A hundred years later, populists and progressives began to call for more direct participation in the democratic process. The cure for the ills of representative democracy, they argued, was more democracy, and three of the proposed cures were the initiative, referendum, and recall. Today we hear similar calls for more direct democracy, including the direct election of the American president, easier voter registration procedures at all levels, and even, occasionally, two-way interactive, electronic town meetings and teledemocracy technologies. Certain writers and reformers in American politics say it is time to consider bolder, more innovative forms of citizen education and citizen involvement if we want to become a robust, healthy, and strong democracy.[3]

If we have learned anything about democracy in the twentieth century, it is that the slogan "The cure for democracy is more democracy" is only a partial truth. A democracy requires more than popular majority rule and a system of democratic procedures to flatter the voters. A vital democracy puts faith not only in the people but also in their ability to select representatives who will provide a heightened sense of the best aspirations for the whole country and who can make sense of the key issues.

In practice, Americans are torn between wanting responsible leaders to make decisions and wanting the general public to be consulted (see Table 1.1). There exists in America both an uncertainty about the ability of the average voter to make policy and about the desirability of having elected officials make unilateral decisions.

Democracy American style is fraught with paradox. Most Americans believe that majority rule is both their right and "what democracy is all about." Although most Americans realize they do not have all the answers, they believe that on important issues the voting public can be trusted to do what is right just about as often as their elected public officials (see Chapter 4).

Most Americans are not inclined to exercise their political rights fully. But the right they exercise most often is the right to choose elected officials. They believe that representative assemblies are better

Table 1.1. **Informed leadership vs. democratic values (%) (N = 1026)**

1. To be realistic about it, our elected officials:	
—know much more than the voters about issues, and should be allowed to make whatever decisions they think best	8
—would badly misuse their power if they weren't watched and guided by the voters	68
—Decline to choose	23
2. When making new laws, the government should pay most attention to:	
—the opinion of the people who really know something about the subject	53
—the opinions of average citizens, regardless of how little they know	22
—Decline to choose	25
3. Should people with more intelligence and character have greater influence over the country's decisions than other people?	
—Yes, because they have more to offer and can do more to benefit society.	39
—No, because every citizen must have an equal right to decide what's best for the country.	45
—Decline to choose	16

Source: Civil liberties national survey, 1978–79, reported in Herbert McClosky and John Zaller, *The American Ethos: Public Attitudes toward Capitalism and Democracy* (Cambridge, Mass.: Harvard University Press, 1984), p. 79.

suited than ordinary citizens to decide technical and legal policy matters. They believe, too, that legislative bodies provide an opportunity for the views and concerns of minorities to be expressed and balanced against the interests of majorities.

Americans' ambivalence toward procedural democracy is explained in large measure by their general satisfaction with the capacity of elected officials to reconcile their objective needs with their expectations. Perhaps, though, Americans have for too long underestimated the potential of a citizenry that is well educated and informed. Such a citizenry would be motivated to participate more vigorously in the political process. Ironically, public leadership of a major kind would be needed to implement programs to heighten citizen interest in more fully exercising their democratic rights!

A populist impulse, incorporating notions of "power to the people" and skepticism about the system has always existed in America. Americans seldom abide quietly the failings and deficiencies of capitalism, the welfare state, or the political decision rules by which we live. We are, as historian Richard Hofstadter wrote, "forever restlessly pitting ourselves against them, demanding changes, improvements, remedies."[4] Demand for more democracy occurs when there is growing distrust of legislative bodies and when there is a growing suspicion that privileged interests exert far greater influences on the typical politician than does the common voter.

Direct democracy, especially as embodied in the referendum, initiative, and recall, is sometimes viewed as a typically American political response to perceived abuses of the public trust. Voters periodically become frustrated with taxes, regulations, inefficiency in government programs, the inequalities or injustices of the system, the arms race, environmental hazards, and countless other irritations. This frustration arises in part because more public policy decisions are now made in distant capitals, by remote agencies or private yet unaccountable entities—such as regulatory bodies, the Federal Reserve Board, foreign governments, multinational alliances, or foreign trading combines—instead of at the local or county level as once was the case, or as perhaps we like to remember.

Champions of populist democracy claim many benefits will accrue from their reforms. Here are some:

Citizen initiatives will promote government responsiveness and accountability. If officials ignore the voice of the people, the people will have an available means to make needed law.

Initiatives are freer from special interest domination than the legislative branches of most states, and so provide a desirable safeguard that can be called into use when legislators are corrupt, irresponsible, or dominated by privileged special interests.

The initiative and referendum will produce open, educational debate on critical issues that otherwise might be inadequately discussed.

Referendum, initiative, and recall are nonviolent means of political participation that fulfill a citizen's right to petition the government for redress of grievances.

Direct democracy increases voter interest and election-day turnout. Perhaps, too, giving the citizen more of a role in governmental processes might lessen alienation and apathy.

Finally (although this hardly exhausts the claims), citizen initiatives are needed because legislators often evade the tough issues. Fearing to be ahead of their time, they frequently adopt a zero-risk mentality. Concern with staying in office often makes them timid and perhaps too wedded to the status quo. One result is that controversial social issues frequently have to be resolved in the judicial branch. But who elected the judges?

For every claim put forward on behalf of direct democracy, however, there is an almost equally compelling criticism. Many opponents believe the ordinary citizen usually is not well enough informed about complicated matters to arrive at sound public policy judgments. They also fear the influence of slick television advertisements or bumper sticker messages.

Some critics of direct democracy contend the best way to restore faith in representative institutions is to find better people to run for office. They prefer the deliberations and the collective judgment of elected representatives who have the time to study complicated public policy matters, matters that should be decided within the give-and-take process of politics. That process, they say, takes better account of civil liberties.

Critics also contend that in normal times initiative and referendum voter turnout is often a small proportion of the general population and so the results are unduly influenced by special interests: big money will win eight out of ten times.

A paradox runs throughout this debate. As the United States has aged, we have extended the suffrage in an impressive way. The older the country, the more we have preached the gospel of civic participation. Yet we also have experienced centralization of power in the national government and the development of the professional politician. The citizen-politician has become an endangered species.

Representative government is always in the process of development and decay. Its fortunes rise and fall depending upon various factors, not least the quality of people involved and the resources devoted to making it work effectively. When the slumps come, proposals that would reform and change the character of representative government soon follow. Direct democracy notions have never been entirely foreign to our country—countless proponents from Benjamin Franklin to Jesse Jackson, Jack Kemp, and Richard Gephardt have urged us to listen more to the common citizen.

The Doctrine of the Consent of the Governed

An animating principle of the American Revolution and the Declaration of Independence was that a just government must derive its powers from the consent of the people. The legitimacy of popular consent was widely acknowledged in America in the 1770s and 1780s. Participatory government of a limited kind had already taken hold in pre-Revolutionary communities. Indeed decision making by referendum can be traced back in Massachusetts to at least 1640. Town meetings and countless kindred consultative forums flourished in seventeenth-century America, and experience in these workshops of democracy bred a self-confidence and a civic culture that generally whetted the appetite for more. Majority rule became, if somewhat grudgingly, an accepted way of conducting community affairs. The Revolution added enormously to the quest for democratic procedures, heightening yearnings of ordinary people for suffrage as well as for more self-rule.

Still, the patriots fought not to establish a democracy but to establish a republic, which in Enlightenment thought had many definitions. But generally it embodied three principles: initial consent of the governed, rule by law, and representation of the people. People come together for mutual protection. Beyond this they create government for the purpose of securing and enhancing their natural rights. The rights come first. People are primary, governments secondary. Government's coercive authority is derived from the consent or approval of the people. The doctrine of the consent of the governed as it evolved in the 1780s stipulated, at least implicitly, that a government would be evaluated largely on the basis of how it improved the well-being and protected the natural rights of its citizens.

Thomas Hobbes (1588–1679) had defined the notion of consent narrowly: "For Hobbes, representative government is by consent, but it is not elective after that consent. The sovereign must have absolute power or he is no sovereign, and the people may not vote him out. They might elect representatives to a Parliament, but only to advise the sovereign and only if he permits it."[5] In contrast, John Locke (1632–1704) and other Enlightenment theorists believed that the original consent granted a government could also be withdrawn. Locke claimed that even if an earlier generation did "sign a contract" and thereby give its consent to certain governmental authorities, this consent was not necessarily binding on the next generation: when they reached maturity, they could either stay and hence give their consent or move elsewhere and thereby withdraw it. Of course, too, they could rebel, but this would not be practical, he noted, if they were decidedly in the minority.

However, most Revolutionary leaders and thinkers were profoundly skeptical of direct or pure democracy on a large scale. They had read about the rise and decline of Athens and other ancient city-states that preached and practiced early versions of democracy, and they accepted the widely held view that the follies of such kinds of democracy easily outweighed their virtues. Had not Athens declined in large part because, as it grew, it failed to move from direct democracy to a representative one? These republican forms might have permitted them to govern effectively on a substantially larger territorial basis. The founders rejected the idea of direct democracy beyond the neighborhood or community level as impractical for a sprawling country of 4 million people.

John Adams carefully analyzed previous models of government in an effort to construct a science of politics based on enduring laws of human behavior. Adams saw the need for the consent of the governed. He was doubtless pleased that his own Massachusetts submitted its 1780 constitution (which he had largely drafted) for popular debate and consideration at the open town meetings throughout the commonwealth. He could readily agree with the framers of the Constitution that a republic was a government deriving all its powers directly or indirectly from the great body of the people. But he rejected universal suffrage and equal participation in government by all the citizens. The frailties and passions of ordinary men made them incapable of responsible participation in government. Thus power should be delegated from the many to the prudent and virtuous few.

Unlike many other Enlightenment theorists, Adams saw humanity as inherently corrupt and base. People might have been "created equal," but this did not mean they had equal or identical abilities or talent. Like Aristotle, he believed people are naturally divided into "gentlemen" and "simple men," the former destined to rule, the latter destined to be ruled. Accordingly, everything must be done to educate and take advantage of the superior qualities of gentlemen. For Adams, a society without caste or class was neither likely nor desirable. Further, these aristocratic elements in society must play a vital role in countering the popular storms and passions of the ordinary people.

Adams contended that only those who owned property and thus could be trusted to behave in a responsible way should vote. He did not so much emphasize restricting the vote as extending property ownership, "giving the humblest citizen material stake in his society and thus nipping any impulse to treat lightly the property of his more prosperous neighbor; for by doing so he would imperil his own."[6] Adams, always the realist, thus shared what might be called an incentive theory of citizenship and suffrage.

Although Adams clearly recognized the desirability of representative institutions, he also recognized a problem:

> In a large society, inhabiting an extensive country, it is impossible that the whole should assemble to make laws. The first necessary step, then, is to delegate power from the many to a few of the most wise and good.
>
> The principal difficulty lies, and the greatest care should be employed, in constituting this representative assembly. It should be in miniature an exact portrait of the people at large. It should think, feel, reason, and act like them. That it may be the interest of this assembly to do strict justice at all times, it should be equal representation, or, in other words, equal interests among the people should have equal interests in it.[7]

Adams stressed the need for more than one legislative assembly. A single assembly, he said, was liable to all the views, foibles, and frailties of an individual, subject to fits and starts of passion, flights of enthusiasm, and likely to produce hasty and sometimes regrettable judgments. Thus he called for a second house or council, to be elected by the first assembly. Members of this second chamber could come from the assembly or from the public at large, yet it would be kept reasonably small. Adams thought twenty to thirty would suffice. Each chamber, together with independent judges and governor, would have, in effect, a veto upon the actions of the other.

Both during and after his presidency, Adams was regarded as a champion of property and of semiaristocratic tendencies. Yet his political ideas typified the exhilarating, if cautious, Revolutionary era search for governmental forms that would steer a path between the no-longer-acceptable monarchy and the much-feared excesses of pure or direct democracy. For Adams "the consent of the governed" usually meant that the people should have "an essential share in the sovereignty," not an exclusive claim on it. He supported "the traditional Whig notion of balancing the interests of the few and the many by requiring the explicit consent of both camps."[8]

A few Americans in the 1780s believed in political equality and at least envisaged a broad interpretation of the phrase "consent of the governed." This small band of early democrats viewed consolidated large-scale government as an invitation to oppression. Public opinion, they held, must be the basis of political lawmaking. Though not advocating direct democracy, they viewed a form of explicit representative democracy as vital. They challenged Adams's notion that "enlightened" representatives should use their own judgment to replace the views of their constituents. Representatives ought to be bound by the dictates of the governed. Further, a large House of Representatives was desirable. They also urged short terms, rotation in office, and the option to recall unresponsive legislators. They believed the only way to ensure liberty and to secure natural rights would be to keep legislators constantly accountable to their constituents. Two states even experimented with elections every six months as a means of keeping state officials truly "representative."

A few early democrats continued to hold that the best or the only way to preserve rights was to organize into small republics, where accountability could be maximized. They were especially apprehensive that the new constitution would encourage a system of representation in which only the privileged classes would regularly participate in the operations of government. Under the proposed election system and size of Congress, they contended, "men of the elevated rank in life will alone be chosen. The other orders in the society, such as farmers, traders, and mechanics, who all ought to have a competent number of their best informed men in the legislature, shall be totally unrepresented . . . Congress will consist of the lordly and high minded; of men who will have no congenial feelings with people, but a perfect indifference for, and contempt for them."[9]

In short, what about the "respectable yoemanry"? Perhaps they were not better than elites, yet surely they had not been corrupted.

Carrying this notion to its logical conclusion, one might put it this way: give the ordinary people the facts and they will see the rational and reasonable way to act. But give the elite classes the sole right to be the lawmakers and give them two- and six-year terms with indefinite reeligibility, and the "consent of the governed" will soon be forgotten.

During and immediately after the Revolution the rights to vote and to ratify state constitutions were broadened. There was a general easing of property requirements for voting: in many states, 70 percent of white males who paid property taxes were eligible; in some places, such as Vermont, just about every adult male could vote. Apportionment also took place in an attempt to equalize voting-district populations. There were, in addition, increased demands that representation in state legislatures should mirror the views of the people. A veritable "delegate theory" of democracy took hold in certain states. As political scientist Donald Lutz suggests, people were beginning to redefine "consent of the governed" in novel ways: "Implausible as it sounds, there was a serious and reasonably successful effort to create legislatures which would produce legislation indistinguishable from that passed by the people at large gathered in one room. There were three mechanisms available for furthering this end: frequent elections, reduced requirements for officeholding, and petitions and instructions to the legislature."[10]

But the centralizing nationalists, later called Federalists, who shaped the U.S. Constitution were less idealistic and perhaps more realistic about a direct participatory role for the average voter. Planning for a government that would serve a large territory and large populations, they opted time and again for more indirect ways to realize the consent of the governed. The framers believed the consent of the people would be manifest, if not directly conveyed, through open debate and regularly scheduled fair elections, first to select those who would ratify the Constitution, second to select representatives to state and national legislatures, and finally to choose electors, directly or indirectly, who would help select the new national executive. "The Federalists chose a version of republican government different from that which had developed during the 1780s . . . part of the Federalist legacy is a doctrine of consent with contradictions and ambiguities."[11]

No one tried or even dreamed of trying to put forward a set of arrangements for a pure democracy "town meeting" style for the new nation. Still, some were disappointed that the new national government was somehow taking a step back from the exhilarating if imperfect experiments in self-government at the state and local levels. There was a certain brooding among a few radicals "that just possibly a means could be found for taking the vote of a sizable and scattered population on some questions."[12] The idea of a plebiscitary or referendum democracy was still alien to the existing political thought. Yet what else could explain the repeated Federalist arguments against direct democracy? What else could account for this plea by Fisher Ames in the 1788 Massachusetts convention, called to consider ratification of the proposed U.S. Constitution?

> Much has been said about the people's divesting themselves of power when they delegate it to representatives, and that all representation is to their disadvantage because it is but an image, a copy fainter and more imperfect than the original . . . It has been said that a pure democracy is the best government for a small people, who may assemble in person. It is of small consequence to discuss it, as it would be inapplicable to the great country we inhabit. It may be of some use in this argument, however, to consider that it [pure democracy] would be very burdensome, subject to factions and violence; decisions would often be made by surprise, in the precipitancy of passion . . . It would be a government not by laws but by men.[13]

The overriding challenge to the framers was to devise a constitution that could win approval at state ratifying conventions and gain the acceptance of the public at large. A central participant in this exercise was James Madison. Madison, who in effect served as the campaign manager for ratification, was a leading exponent of a middle-of-the-road strategy. He sought to devise a representative democracy that could win acceptance from procedural conservatives and democrats alike. He clearly rejected direct democracy and searched for a means to place public power in the hands of the wise and virtuous few. In effect, Madison embraced a watered-down version of "consent of the governed."

James Madison: Champion of Representative Government

The scholarly, frail, well-read Madison staked out a political position between Thomas Jefferson, Thomas Paine, and Patrick Henry on the left and John Adams, George Washington, and Alexander Hamilton on the establishment or nationalist side. He would not, for example, go so far as Jefferson, who sometimes insisted the whole adult population had the right and the wisdom to govern themselves. Nor, on the other hand, would he side with Hamilton, who initially favored a modified form of the British monarchy and who sometimes referred to the mass of common people as a "Beast," believing that only "experts"—the well-born, the rich, and people like himself—should control the government. Hamilton also wanted such restrictions on suffrage as proof of land ownership.

Madison hoped public opinion, properly harnessed, would serve, at least in normal times, as one of the prime guides for government lawmaking and leadership. Yet because of his profound concern to avoid all forms of tyranny—including tyranny by both the government and the majority—he emphatically wanted public opinion to be filtered and modified. "I go on the great republican principle," he told the 1788 Virginia ratifying convention, "that the people will have the virtue and intelligence to select men of virtue and wisdom."[14]

Like Adams, Madison sought a set of governmental arrangements that would achieve stability as well as secure natural rights. Multiple checks would be needed on the popular authority. "If men were angels, no government would be necessary. If angels were to govern men, neither external nor internal controls on government would be necessary."[15] But since neither was the case, the framers of the Constitution had to devise a republic that could temper human imperfections and protect people from one another.

Near the top of Madison's suggested list of checks and balances was the notion of "enlarging the sphere." For him the cure for irresponsible majority dominance was the formation of an extended republic in which the continual interplay and exchange among a multiplicity of diverse interest groups would stifle the formation of the only majority to be feared, the one that would be adverse to the general good and the rights of the minority.[16] "The only remedy is to enlarge the sphere and thereby divide the community into so great a number of interests and parties, that in the first place a majority will not be likely at the same moment to have a common interest separate from that of the whole or of the minority; secondly, that in case they should have such an interest, they might not be apt to unite in pursuit of it."[17]

The device of representation was also central to Madison's design. He did not question that the consent of the people was a valid concept and that power "flowed" from the people to those temporarily in power. Yet the "people" could not govern wisely and involve themselves on a regular basis in government operations. How could citizens express their consent? The solution was the representational device. Through prudent representation the public voice would be tempered. Fears of "unpropertied masses" gaining control of the government would be mitigated by restrictions on the vote (such as property or acreage ownership and taxpayer status) and by qualifications for officeholding. Moreover, Madison argued that U.S. senators should be men of wealth and enjoy long terms of office. Wise and virtuous representatives would provide the indispensable ingredients of debate, discussion, and judgment.

Fear of injudicious majority rule was widespread. The electorate in the new republic was far broader than any that had ever attempted to elect a nation's decisionmakers. The tumult of revolution, fear of the unknown, and earlier excesses of legislative rule in some states all prompted many an initial champion of human rights to caution in the 1780s. Even Jefferson's faith in the mass of the people was tempered by at least two considerations. First, he recognized the existence of a natural aristocracy, an aristocracy of merit and self-earned excellence, and thought the best of governmental forms would of necessity enable these naturally talented individuals to rise to positions of leadership. Second, although he romanticized about small farmers as God's chosen people, his faith in the urban masses was decidedly less exalted, and he worried that mobs in the large cities would be easily corrupted.

Thomas Paine also championed indirect democracy. "By ingrafting representation upon democracy, we arrive at a system of government capable of embracing and confederating all the various interests and every extent of territory and population." Like Adams and Madison, Paine praised the new arrangement and its strengths: "Our new system has settled the form by a scale parallel in all cases to the extent of the principle. What Athens was in miniature, America will be in magnitude. The one was of the ancient world—the other is becoming the admiration and model of the present. It is the easiest of all the forms of government to be understood and the most eligible in practice; and excludes at once the ignorance and insecurity of the hereditary mode and the inconvenience of the simple democracy."[18]

Most Americans at the time, as they do today, supported the relatively indirect form of "consent of the governed" devised by the Federalists. Gradually the political system has been opened up in the direction of more direct democracy: the direct election of U.S. senators;

the vote for women, blacks, and younger people; the direct primary for nominating party candidates; sustained efforts to revise and even abolish the Electoral College; more representative jury participation; and even experiments at workplace democracy. From time to time we witness movements such as "populism," "power to the people," participatory politics, decentralized school boards, and workers' councils.[19]

In a century of centralization and complexity we are rarely far removed from the debates over how and how much to reconnect the leaders and the led. Indeed, technological inventions now make possible various forms of teledemocracy, and interactive two-way communication and feedback response processes may lead future reformers to propose yet further notions for involving people in the governing process. Definitional and political debates over "consent of the governed" are a constant of our political culture.

CHAPTER 2

▼

Representative Democracy

▼

What are the true boundaries of the people's power? The answer cannot be simple. But for a rough beginning let us say that the people are able to give and to withhold their consent to being governed— their consent to what the government asks of them, proposes to them, and has done in the conduct of their affairs. They can approve and disapprove its performance. But they cannot administer the government . . . They cannot normally initiate and propose necessary legislation. A mass cannot govern.

—Walter Lippmann, 1955

The people are not supposed to govern; they are not supposed to decide issues. They are supposed to decide who will decide.

—George F. Will, 1977

THE enduring challenge of American politics since 1787 has been the reconciliation of effective government with personal liberty and individual rights. The task is one of making government serve the preferences of the people and not the reverse. To this end, the Constitution grants, disperses, and restrains the powers of government. Politics at its best in the American republic is a process of diffusing power and enabling citizens to achieve a nobility that is rarely attainable elsewhere. This is the empowerment of citizens to think and act together in deciding what kinds of communities, states, and nation they want to have. The American political system at its best enables large numbers both to have a say in the laws that regulate them and to participate in the great debates about crucial public policy decisions.

Americans, however, have never quite been able to make up their minds about whether the will of the majority should prevail in all cases. If it should, even the Jeffersonians insisted that it had to be "reasonable." Yet who was to decide what was reasonable—majority sentiment filtered through the legislative bodies, or through other executive and court authorities? Invariably the main response to these questions has been to call upon representative institutions to provide the major say in defining the majority's reasonable will. As a result, legislatures and executive officials exercise considerable power in shaping priorities and public policy. This power is at once obvious, ambiguous, and paradoxical.

We commonly refer to our governmental arrangements as a representative democracy. Our states and even most of our cities are too large to allow for direct government by the people. Few believe a continuous do-it-yourself town meeting form of self-governance is sensible even if they might fancy that ideal. Instead American voters elect approximately 550,000 officials to a wide array of governmental bodies.

Representative democracy was never intended to be the equivalent of direct or pure democracy. The nation's founders viewed the latter as impractical, undesirable, and downright dangerous, especially because it might threaten minority rights. Although its representative processes are one of the most durable and sturdy features of the Republic, Americans seldom have been fully satisfied by them. Why is this so? And why have would-be reformers seldom been of one mind?

The concept of representation has had a complicated lineage in the history of political discourse. It can be traced back at least to the Middle Ages. Popes were sometimes viewed as the representatives of Christ and the apostles; kings were viewed as the representatives of the people; and, later, parliaments were thought to represent the people, even before election processes were developed. The consent of the parliament was viewed as the consent of the people as a whole. After the English Civil War, the concept of representation as a political right of the citizen developed further, but not until the late eighteenth and early nineteenth centuries did institutional inventions and a more refined political philosophy translate that right into a reality.

The American colonists, like nine-tenths of the people in Britain in the 1760s and 1770s, did not choose any representatives to the House of Commons. Yet when various tea and war taxes were imposed, Americans protested taxation without representation. The debate over representation broadened, and the right to participate in one's government became the galvanizing cause of the American Revolution.

British leaders tried to persuade the colonists that they did not actually have to vote for members of Parliament in order to be represented there. They presumed a single autonomous public interest, so that the consent of the majority of the House of Commons became a binding decision on the whole population. The assumption was that the English people, despite class differences or geographic distance, were essentially a homogeneous people with common interests. What affected nonelectors was presumed to affect electors eventually, and what affected Englishmen elsewhere in the empire ultimately affected every Englishman.[1] According to what has been called the doctrine of virtual representation, residents of the colonies were *virtually*, if not *actually*, represented in Parliament. (The framers of the Constitution used similar reasoning to defend the exclusion of women, blacks, the poor, and, in many instances, those who did not own substantial acreage or regularly pay taxes.)

Americans objected to virtual representation because they believed their interests were now different from those of the mother country. They had different ideas about where, when, and how to market their exports. And they had clashing notions about self-government and settlement policies. Given these different interests, they could not, no matter what the form of representation, be represented there. Even if they had been granted the right to elect members of Parliament, they still would have had grounds to seek separation. The time had come to establish their own government, in which their own interests would be central.

Colonial leaders knew they wanted a more representative system. Yet they were of mixed minds about what kind of representative system would serve them best. Out of the uncertainty came a turning point in history. Americans would pioneer a new governmental form—something substantially different from monarchy, from aristocracy, and from pure democracy. Yet clarity of terms was seldom present.

Although the colonists wanted a greater say in governing themselves, the American Revolution was in many ways a conservative revolution. The powerless did not instigate it and wrest democratic rights from a privileged local aristocracy. Indeed, Massachusetts in the 1760s and 1770s has been aptly described as a middle-class society in which property was easily acquired and the vast majority of people farmed their own land.[2] According to one twentieth-century historian the common man in the colonial era enjoyed more economic democracy and "had a government more responsive to the popular will than we have at the present time. There were far more representatives in proportion to the population than we now have, and the representatives were more responsible to their constituents for their actions than are legislators at present."[3]

The Doctrine of Instructed Representatives

The development of representative government involved considerable debate over the right of the people or of a legislature to instruct its representatives. Several of the colonies, and, under the Articles of Confederation, several states—including Massachusetts, North Carolina, Pennsylvania, and Vermont—at one time or another provided in their constitutions for instructing their representatives explicitly on how to vote. This approach derived from a belief that the right of the people to participate and be represented in a legislature was the primary means of securing liberty. Whenever a clear expression of the will of the majority was present, the representative was obliged to vote according to that mandate. The commanding power of instructions, they said, is the grand pivot upon which our political system should turn. Representation was to be the foundation of free government. Binding instructions compelled a legislator to represent in rather explicit terms the people who had elected him. In some ways this system resembled the current procedures used by the president and secretary of state to instruct our ambassadors to the United Nations on how they ought to vote on major issues.

In the states the right of instruction applied primarily to the directly elected and more populous houses in the legislatures. Members of the state senate usually were elected indirectly. However, even the independence of senators was challenged by those who contended that all legislators were representatives and hence were using delegated powers that ultimately belonged to the people. And if the senate was to be guided by binding instructions, why should the governor not be held accountable too? Notions of accountable government unfolded rapidly, though not necessarily in a coherent or wholly settled fashion.

Not until the late 1780s did Americans begin to challenge the doctrine of binding instructions. Hamilton and Madison led the charge. They were concerned, especially at the national level, that a representative exercise independent judgment in deciding critical policy matters. A concern for the whole, the *res publica* (literally, the public's matter), was necessary, lest the nation's longer-term interests be sacrificed constantly to local views, just as intense localism often sacrificed individual states' general interests to the counties and towns.

The right to instruct representatives was originally included in the proposed amendments to the Constitution that became the Bill of Rights. But the majority sentiment held, with Madison, that the people's right to petition Congress in essence gave them the right to offer advice, and that the right to compel a representative to weigh and reflect the precise attitude of the majority was impractical and undesirable. The amendment was defeated forty-one to ten in the House of Representatives.

The intent of the framers and the leaders in the first Congress was to free America from the vices of localism, to overcome the defects of a narrow, short-term, special-interest representation, and at the same time to encourage voters to select as their representatives persons of ability, integrity, and patriotism. A congressman from Pennsylvania argued against the practice of instruction on the grounds that the people's view is sometimes emotional and rallied by partisan or faction leaders. Although public opinion is generally respectable, there are "moments it has been known to be often wrong; and happy is the Government composed of men of firmness and wisdom to discover and resist popular error."[4]

Still, some states continued to require their U.S. senators to vote according to a state legislature's majority view; the state legislators believed that their right to elect senators to Congress conveyed also a right to instruct. The right of instruction was justified not by any provisions in the Constitution, but by the then-accepted theories of representative government. States supporting Jeffersonian Republicans or Jacksonian Democrats in the years 1800–1840 were the most inclined to practice it. Federalists and Whigs, with their more elitist and "Burkean" views about representation, typically protested the practice. Regionally, legislative instructions were used mainly in the South, although New Jersey and Ohio instructed their senators to support Andrew Jackson's presidential initiatives, and Vermont instructed its senators and requested its representatives "to present anti-slavery resolutions to Congress and to work toward their fulfillment."[5]

Many senators simply ignored these instructions. Others, however, including a few distinguished senators, were forced to resign when they disobeyed their legislatures. In some ways, such forced resignations anticipated the populist and progressive movements' demands for recall.

After 1840 the practice of instructing representatives declined, in part as a result of its blatantly partisan use in abolitionist and states' rights issues, in part as a result of mounting objections to the removal of respected senators who had voted according to their best judgment. By 1860 the practice was obsolete.[6]

Conflicting Theories of Representation

The precise meaning of the term *representation* has never been clear, in large part because definitions are never entirely separate either from conceptions of its ideal form or from policies and political objectives. Still, the word generally connotes to make present, to symbolize or to stand for something absent; thus it implies presenting the views of those who cannot be present, or a "re-presentation." To represent someone politically, in short, is to serve on behalf of another person and somehow to be held accountable to that person.

Representative government, in its early versions, sometimes meant the periodic election of "typical" or representative persons, and the periodic election of people who would, in general, speak and vote for those who elected them. More recently, most citizens have come to view their representatives as persons who will continually "make present" the voters' views in the halls of government. Public opinion polls show that large numbers of citizens, sometimes by nearly a two-to-one margin, believe legislators today should vote against measures when a majority of the people they represent oppose such measures.

Yet herein lies the puzzle or dilemma: to what extent can one represent the views or interests of others? Precisely how is the relationship authorized, defined, carried out, and terminated? Political scientist Hanna Pitkin has summed up "the paradoxical requirement" of representation, "that a thing be simultaneously present and not present" in terms of a conflict between mandate and independence.

> The *mandate theorists* keep trying to tell us that nothing will count as representative unless the absent thing is really made present in some meaningful sense. If the representative's actions bear no relationship to his constituents' needs, interests, wishes, or welfare, or even conflict with these, then he is not making them present by his actions. The *independence theorists* keep

trying to tell us that nothing will count as representative if the absent thing is literally present, acting for itself. It must be present through an intermediary, must remain absent in some meaningful sense. Unless the representative is sufficiently independent so that he hardly acts, his constituents are not represented, but simply present in the action.[7]

The dilemma is ancient and perhaps irresolvable.

This debate between mandate and independence positions is sometimes discussed as a delegate-versus-trustee dispute. The delegate view requires the representative to mirror the views of the district's or state's voters. While recognizing that representatives should be concerned for the best interest of the state or nation as a whole, delegate advocates contend that the prime obligations are to constituents. Some critics label such representatives "errand boys," but defenders claim that a broadened use of positive instructions on central questions of public interest allows the people at large to participate in the exercise of legislative authority. Consider the common sense of the common person, say these defenders. The people, when consulted, know their own mind and are the legitimate source of government instructions. To make self-government work, they argue, we must find ways to keep representatives explicitly accountable.

The intellectual godfather of the trustee or independence position is Edmund Burke. Burke thought of proper governance as an elite representing not individual voters or people but the great, stable central interests that, taken together, make up the national interest. Representatives must be free to exercise their own best judgment and accountable to constituents only at certain intervals. Their decisions would be made on the basis of wise deliberation and debate, with an eye toward constituents' best interests, but not toward slavishly obeying unrefined public sentiment. Representatives owed their constituents their mature judgment and enlightened conscience, which ought not be sacrificed to serving opinion. In short, representatives' first loyalty was to the longer-term interests of the country, especially when such interests differed from parochial moods of the moment: "Parliament is not a congress of ambassadors from different and hostile interests; which interests each must maintain, as an agent and advocate, against other agents and advocates; but parliament is a deliberative assembly of one nation, with one interest, that of the whole; where not local purposes, not local prejudices ought to guide, but the general good resulting from the general reason of the whole."[8]

Burke also viewed pure democracy as uncontrolled popular power under which, among other undesirable things, minorities, including especially the minority that held substantial property, would be suppressed or oppressed.

Burke's views influenced the founders of the American republic, especially John Adams and James Madison. Madison came close in the late 1780s to developing a comprehensive theory of representation and republican government, and the resulting pro-independence position remains the dominant view of the role of the representative in the United States. As a practical matter, representatives, especially in the larger states and in Congress, can seldom consult constituents before voting on measures. On the one hand, legislators rarely can know accurately the views of the hundreds of thousands or millions, whose interests are enormously diverse, and whose comprehension of policy trade-offs is limited. "At the same time, and for very much the same reasons, it is increasingly impossible to hold the representative responsible for his decisions," writes Heinz Eulau; "it is evident that the electorate is chiefly guided by rather vague and often confused moods about the drift of public policy in general rather than by a clear perception as to whether the individual representative has acted responsibly or not within his discretionary capabilities."[9]

The framers proposed several safeguards against the excessive influences of localism, factions, and imprudent majoritarianism. The notion of an *extended republic* came first. Democracy could work only in a small community. Yet a representative democracy could embrace a vast number of citizens and a greater, enlarged sphere of country. Madison knew factions and class interests would inevitably arise as political forces in any political system. Yet he predicted, hoped, and gambled that the defects of democracy could be overcome in a large republic. "Extend the sphere, and you take in a greater variety of parties and interests; you make it less probable that a majority of the whole will have a common motive to invade the rights of other citizens."[10]

The larger the republic, Madison reasoned, the greater the number of groupings. To develop majority support in an extended republic, an ambitious politician would have to mobilize so many different groups—across regional, religious, commercial, and other lines—that straight economic class rule was nearly impossible. Moreover, such coalition-building efforts should have the effect of moderating these majorities. The results would be a politics of moderation and policies responsive to minorities as well as to majorities.

This concept of majority-by-coalition was central to Madison's theory of the workings of representative democracy. Martin Diamond offers this clarification:

> Often the spokesman for the interest groups dominant in his state or district, the representative may be loyally prepared to sacrifice the national interest on behalf of their extreme demands. But he and those he represents soon learn that they simply do not have the votes. In order to secure congressional majorities for desired legislation or to win the Presidency, cooperation with other groups proves necessary. Thus ensues the coalescing process. As the coalition enlarges to form the necessary majority, an enormous number of conflicting selfish interests must be taken into account. The groups within the emerging coalition must at least make concessions to each other's needs.
>
> Thus, in terms of the narrowest selfishness, multiplicity and the coalition process tend to moderate the worst effects of that selfishness. But something more valuable than that can happen. The discovery that one's grossest demands are absurdly impossible to achieve can lead to an enlightened kind of self-interest, a habitual recognition of the indisputable needs of others and a sobriety about the general requirements of society. And something still worthier can happen. As the extremes of selfishness are moderated the representative can become free to consider questions affecting the national interest on their merits. The jostling of innumerable interests gives him a margin of freedom from any single interest group. He is thereby enabled, to some extent, to pursue the national interest as he comes to see it in the instructive national arena.[11]

Madison and many of the other framers also believed in the separation of powers and balanced government. The preservation of liberty and the promotion of the public good required three separate departments, each designed to check and balance the others. And since each was designed in its own way to represent the people, the entire system would be representative. To be sure, the members of the populous House of Representatives by virtue of direct election would be the more immediate representatives; yet senators, the president, and even members of the Supreme Court ultimately derived their authority from elections, and thus from the people. Hence they too were to act as the people's deputies, the people's representatives. As Madison wrote in *The Federalist* No. 63, representation was the pivot on which the whole American system moved.[12] Virtually everything in Madison's scheme of government was intended to contain or curtail public power and thereby filter the voice of the people.

Bicameralism vs. Unicameralism

The framers of our state and national constitutions were overwhelmingly of British heritage and thus understandably based many of their ideas for their own legislative structures on British precedents. Bicameralism developed in England as an expedient to attain practical ends of certain interests at the expense of others. The theory justifying the expedient developed after the system evolved. Only later did a number of theorists, including John Stuart Mill, provide a reasoned and vigorous theoretical defense of bicameral legislatures.

Bicameralism was not initially a feature of American government. The Articles of Confederation provided for just one legislative chamber; and Georgia (1777–1789), Pennsylvania (1701–1789), and Vermont (1776–1836) experimented with unicameral state legislatures. Benjamin Franklin advocated a unicameral legislature on the grounds that bicameralism would promote delays and factions and that a bicameral legislature might be more easily dominated by a chief executive. Any legislature could make mistakes, he conceded, but a one-house legislature could remedy such a situation more quickly and easily. Some critics of the American preference for bicameralism say its adoption was merely a historical accident, that we merely copied without much consideration the then-evolving British model. Had England had a one-house or a three-house legislature, we could just as well have established one of those.

Adoption of two legislative chambers at the national level came about in part as a result of the need to accommodate the interests of both the large and small states. The small states understandably feared their views would be swamped by a federal legislature based solely on population. But a more powerful motive was a prevailing desire, based on a general belief in governmental checks and balances, to balance the aristocratic against the popular interest.[13]

One of the chief architects of the Constitution, Pennsylvania's James Wilson, made the case against unicameralism by saying a single-house legislature is calculated to unite in it "all the pernicious qualities of the different extremes of bad government. It produces general weakness, inactivity, and confusion; and these are intermixed with sudden and violent fits of despotism, injustice, and cruelty . . ." A unicameral legislature could too hastily get carried away and violate the Constitution and its basic principles. "Different will be the case when the legislature consists of two branches. If one of them should depart, or attempt to depart, from the principles of the constitution, it will be drawn back by the other. The very apprehension of the event will prevent the departure or the attempt."[14]

James Madison insisted that a double legislature was a necessary check on representatives who might be misled or unresponsive. Madison worried that even in a republican government there would be those who might forget their obligations and prove unfaithful to their important responsibilities. A second chamber less numerous than the first and enjoying a tenure of considerable duration would, Madison believed, be less tempted by factious movements and would be "a salutary check on the government."[15] Madison also believed the Senate would attract wiser, more informed men, devoted to the study of the laws, the affairs, and the comprehensive interests of the country, whereas many members of the popularly elected chamber would probably be drawn from farming or business and be less able to focus on the long-term national interest.

Madison believed that the elder statesmen who would doubtless be appointed to the Senate could veto or at least delay lamentable or intemperate measures passed by the House. In doing so, they would enable the people to rethink what they were doing and permit reason and enlightened views to prevail. The Senate's chief virtue was to consist in its proceeding with more calmness, more system, and more wisdom than a popularly elected House of Representatives. It would also be a much smaller body and designed to be as isolated from corruption as possible.

Whether the framers employed bicameralism as an antipopulist device or used it to reduce the chances of hasty, ill-considered, or dangerous legislation is difficult to determine. In public debates, they downplayed it as a means to resist majority rule or to protect the property holdings of the privileged. The benefits of bicameralism, the framers contended, were that a two-house legislature would make it more difficult to enact rash, arbitrary, or emotional legislation, would help prevent error, and would help provide for more expertise. It would do this by providing for more deliberation and debate, thereby slowing down the legislative process, and by making it more difficult for any one person, group, or region to dominate the lawmaking process.

Plainly, too, the equal vote given each state in the Senate acknowledged the semisovereignty of the states. No law could be passed without the agreement first of the majority of the people and then of the majority of the states. Madison reminded people in *The Federalist* No. 62 that those who govern may sometimes forget their obligations to their constituents. The Senate would, he wrote, double "the security of the people by requiring the concurrence of two distinct bodies in the schemes of usurpation or perfidy, where the ambition or corruption of one would otherwise be sufficient."[16] It would as well help safeguard against any yielding to the impulse of sudden and violent passions and appeals for demagogic, factious leaders.

Because senators were to be the impartial umpires and guardians of the general good, Madison urged that they be elected by the House and suggested nine-year terms, with one-third retiring every three years. Although Madison's views were modified both at the time and later, bicameralism soon became the established pattern in the United States, not only at the state and national levels, but for a long time as well at the city and sometimes even at the county levels. In the cities, the two-chamber system, with a large common council and a smaller select council, typically prevailed until the widespread municipal reforms of the early twentieth century.

Early in the twentieth century there was also some renewed interest in state-level unicameralism. A few governors and civic groups recommended it, and Oregon and Oklahoma put it on the ballot— through the initiative process—only to have it voted down by substantial majorities. The National Socialist Convention in 1912 adopted a plan calling for the abolition of the U.S. Senate, and the National Municipal League's 1921 Model Constitution favored a unicameral legislature to be elected under a proportional representation system. A Democratic governor of Kansas, George H. Hodges, championed a single-house state legislature in 1913, saying, "We should now concern ourselves in devising a system for legislating that will give us more efficiency and quicker response to the demands of our economic and social conditions and to the will of the people."[17] Yet only one state has shifted to unicameralism in this century, although all major cities adopted it. Under the crusading leadership of U.S. Senator George W. Norris, Nebraska voters in 1934 adopted a citizen-initiated constitutional amendment establishing a unicameral legislature.[18]

Contemporary supporters of unicameralism advance the following arguments for its adoption:

1. It has worked well in Nebraska, in our cities, and in the Canadian provinces.

2. The added prestige and importance of membership in a single house encourages a higher caliber of members, concentrates responsibility, and allows voters greater knowledge about their legislators' performance.

3. Deception of the public by "passing the buck" is reduced. Both the public and the press can watch the legislature more easily, making it more difficult for lobbyists to kill measures or delay popular legislation.

4. A unicameral legislature more directly represents the views of the people and more directly responds to needed and desired changes in public policy. The governor's veto, judicial review by the courts, the mood of the people at the next election, better press and media coverage of legislature sessions, and, in those states where available, the initiative, referendum, and recall all readily provide needed checks and balances. Put simply, a one-house legislature is more democratic because "upper houses" have in fact perpetuated aristocracy and government by the privileged.

But some of the undemocratic effects of bicameralism have been eliminated. During the first decades of our republic, the requirements to vote for senator and the qualifications to serve in the state senate were stricter than those for the more populous house. Today the two houses represent the same people, though usually in districts of different sizes. Reapportionment, extension of the suffrage, and elimination of most qualifications to serve in state senates have made legislatures reasonably democratic. Although the debate over bicameralism continues, the tradition of two houses appears to be here to stay.[19]

Bicameralism undeniably cuts against the populist or direct democracy grain. It complicates rather than simplifies representation. It promotes access for elites and special interests and makes it difficult for popular majorities to obtain public policy changes.[20] These were, for the most part, intended effects.

The Guarantee Clause Debate

Article IV, Section 4 of the Constitution, known as the "guarantee clause," states: "The United States shall guarantee to every State in this Union a Republican Form of Government, and shall protect each of them against invasion." Yet what exactly constitutes a republican form of government remains a source of controversy. The precise meaning of the clause has never been wholly determined, in large part because the Supreme Court has consistently refused to decide questions that have arisen under it.[21] Still, a state government is considered to be republican in form if Congress accepts its elected representative. This, in effect, is a recognition and acceptance of a suitable form of government.

The controversy arises when opponents of direct democracy devices contend that only a representative legislature acting as the sole lawmaking branch of a state can qualify the state as having a republican form. The gist of their argument is that voter initiatives violate the guarantee clause. In a landmark Oregon court case, they contended that the Constitution made no provision for overt action by the people in lawmaking, and further, that the "Republican Form of Government" clause was meant to establish the states as republics, whereas the initiative process in the states in effect transferred power away from the representative legislature to the people at large and hence converted republics into pure or at least quasi-pure democracies. Finally, some argue that the guarantee clause was explicitly placed in the Constitution as a safeguard against tyranny by majorities. Hence, go the arguments, the initiative and referendum are unconstitutional because they undermine republicanism.

State supreme courts have responded to such contentions by denying that direct democracy devices such as the initiative violate the principle of a republican form of government. They have ruled that a republican government is one administered by representatives chosen or appointed by the people or by their authority. The initiative and referendum merely reserve to the people a certain share of the legislative power. Government is still divided into legislative, executive, and judicial departments, and their duties are still discharged by representatives selected by the people. There remains, in effect, only one leg-islative department, but now with two subdivisions. The Oregon supreme court ruled: "The purpose of this provision [the guarantee clause] of the Constitution is to protect the people of the several states against aristocratic and monarchical invasions, and against insurrec-tions and domestic violence, and to prevent them from abolishing a republican form of government. But it does not forbid them from amending or changing their constitution in any way they may seé fit as long as none of these results is accomplished. No particular style of government is designated in the constitution as republican, nor is its exact form in any way prescribed."[22]

The guarantee providing for a republican form of government came about because of the insistence of men such as Madison and Jefferson who saw in monarchy the greatest threat to the life of the republic. "It would be strange indeed," writes one analyst, that a "guaranty made at the insistence of the party whose leaders are still recognized as the most pronounced advocates of democratic principles should be construed to forbid rather than to support a reform whereby the will of the people may be made more effectual in government."[23]

Perhaps this states the framers' view, although it is indeed likely that they feared a monarchical or demagogic threat to representative democracy. Court decisions and congressional actions over the years have adhered to a loose or inclusive rather than narrow definition of representative government, and, on the basis of their broader inter-pretations, direct democracy procedures have been viewed as simply one more method of making representative government more repre-sentative, more responsive, and more accountable. Few people, how-ever, ever anticipated that the bulk or even a considerable portion of the lawmaking function would be shifted from elected legislatures to the people at large. A reliance on direct legislative processes was and is viewed as an exception to the rule—as applying to less than one percent of lawmaking.

The Case for Representative Democracy

For most Americans, and for most theorists of representative government, representative democracy has never been an end in itself, but the best means of promoting liberty and personal happiness and of providing for the national security. This means providing for the rights of minorities as well as those of majorities.

Representative democracy, say its proponents, tempers conflict and encourages a refined view of the public's interest by limiting the ordinary citizen's role to the periodic election of leaders who almost always represent and defend citizens' interests more prudently than the citizens can themselves.[24]

Exactly how do legislatures succeed in these virtuous objectives? In theory by attracting persons of broad rather than narrow interests, and by permitting adequate information and time to such persons for high-quality debate, deliberation, and discussion and the possibility for revising or reversing their opinions. In an ideal representative chamber, according to some theorists, no one would arrive with predetermined policy choices, and everyone would look upon the representative institution as a forum for considering all options and examining the diverse consequences of major options for public policy choices.

The effective representative of the people, then, is not an unthinking mouthpiece for parochial interests or for each shifting breeze of opinion. On the contrary, he or she is the agent of personal insights, conscience, and judgment and will weigh these against passions of the moment in arriving at decisions. "Their one proper concern is the interest of the whole body politic, and the true democratic representative is not the cringing, fawning tool of the caucus or of the mob, but he who, rising to the full stature of political manhood, does not take orders, but offers guidance."[25]

Fear of tyranny by the majority haunted the founders from the beginning; they hoped to guard the society not only against oppression by its rulers, but also against any one part disposed to act unjustly toward any other part. At various times, American majorities would have abridged free speech, voting rights, and fair treatment in housing and employment to certain minorities; and research on the public dimensions of tolerance finds that a sizable percentage of contemporary Americans are willing to deny people the right to express unpopular views.[26] Accordingly, the founders instituted constitutional and political checks and balances, different lengths of term for different offices, and a reasonably independent judiciary as further safeguards for minority rights. Advocates also often cite three other purposes of representative democracy: (1) to protect against demagogues and to provide safeguards against unwanted and irresponsible tyrants, and the abuse of political powers; (2) to provide for stability of policy and orderly change of policies and personnel; and (3) to provide both for as much popular participation as is practical and for the necessary energy and authority without which governments could not discharge their functions.

Clearly, representative democracy involves more than simply ascertaining and applying the statistical will of the people. It is a more complicated and often untidy process by which the people and their agents inform themselves, debate and compromise, and arrive at a decision only after thoughtful consideration.

There has always been, however, a tradition of dissent, expressed by those who place greater trust in the common sense of the common citizen. In a muted way, Franklin and Jefferson sometimes suggested such notions in the founding generation. Later it would be the populists, then the progressives, and, most recently, those who champion such devices as the initiative, referendum, and recall.[27]

CHAPTER 3

▼

Direct Democracy

▼

We seek to restore the government of the Republic to the hands of the "plain people," with which class it originated.

—Populist party platform,
1892

For twenty years I preached to the students of Princeton that the Referendum and the Recall was bosh. I have since investigated and I want to apologize to those students. It is the safeguard of politics. It takes power from the boss and places it in the hands of the people.

—Woodrow Wilson, 1911

THE Levellers in mid-seventeenth-century England were probably the first modern direct democrats. They demanded that political officials, justices, and even their local ministers be popularly elected and subject to recall.[1] Their notions of representation implied the common people should have more direct control over their leaders.

Later, in his *Social Contract* (1762), Jean-Jacques Rousseau described an ideal community of free citizens living in a small city-state in which democracy could be practiced directly by the people. In this setting, citizens developed a sense of freedom that went beyond a search for personal enjoyment and advantage, one that fostered a sense of shared responsibility for the whole of the community.[2]

Rousseau, often called the patron saint of government by the people, knew there never had been and never would be a comprehensive or complete democracy. It was against the natural order of things, he wrote, for the many to govern and the few to be governed. Obviously, people could not remain continuously assembled, devoting all their time and energy to hammering out every public policy decision. Still, Rousseau invented the notion of a general will arrived at through educating people to the possibilities of lawmaking in the public interest. Rousseau was in effect saying: give democracy a chance; citizens can become free if they belong to a loving, caring, organic community.

The common good arises, or at least should arise, out of conflict and the expression of partial interests by individuals who may not be very skilled at calculating the interests of the whole. Rousseau's general will thus appears as a kind of residue of the conflict of private interests, those shared goods and values that remain after private interests cancel each other out through adversarial processes and politics. The collective conscience embodies something other, and presumably better, than the totality of the individuals who compose it.

The central idea of Rousseau's political theories is that the people, being subject to the laws, ought to be their authors. The moment people allow themselves to be represented, they surrender their freedom. Thus, every law that the people have not ratified directly is invalid; it is not a true law. In line with these views, later thinkers have argued that once a distance is placed between citizens and their delegates, the representatives will become oligarchic and the citizens will grow more and more alienated. The ideal community is small enough that its citizens can make laws reflecting the general will through face-to-face discussions. But Rousseau, when forced to think as a pragmatist, did not believe a large country such as the United States could realize this kind of deliberative democracy. A large nation would need checks and balances and centralized leadership institutions. These leaders, however, would be charged with discovering and acting in accord with the general will. The general will would still be the voice of reason. Executives would be responsible for discerning it, developing it, and, in response to it, presenting major initiatives to the people.

Rousseau's attack on representative processes and his belief that educational and community development efforts could yield a citizenry that could help fashion their own laws doubtless encouraged American populists and progressives to view him, at the very least, as a kindred spirit as they crusaded for direct democracy devices to help remedy the deficiencies of representative government in the 1890s and early twentieth century.

The Jeffersonian Persuasion

Thomas Jefferson (1743–1826) is the founding father most frequently quoted by proponents of direct democracy. Though not a proponent of direct democracy, he was more willing than most of his celebrated contemporaries to place his trust in the wisdom and goodness of the numerical majority, while maintaining a deep suspicion of government. Writing to James Madison from Paris in 1787, Jefferson admitted, "I own, I am not a friend to a very energetic government. It is always oppressive. It places the governors indeed more at their ease, at the expense of the people."[3]

Unlike most of the founders, Jefferson was only moderately alarmed by a series of rebellions in western Massachusetts in 1786–87, the most prominent of which was Shays's Rebellion. Captain Daniel Shays, a former officer in the Revolution, led a band of armed farmers seeking relief from debts and mortgage foreclosures. Their revolt prevented judges from hearing such cases, and they later attempted in vain to capture an arsenal. Eventually they were suppressed by the local militia, but not before some deaths and widely reported violence. Alexander Hamilton and George Washington cited these uprisings as examples of what happens when power passes to the common people, but Jefferson was not especially alarmed. Though not altogether pleased, he said that this was nonetheless proof that the people were enjoying liberty. A little rebellion now and then was a good thing. It kept government officials on their toes.

Jefferson held that the will of the people is the only legitimate foundation of any government; even a deficient popular government was preferable to the most glorious autocratic one. Of course, people who rule themselves may commit errors, but they have means of correcting them. He had enormous confidence in the common sense of mankind in general. As long as citizens were informed, they could be trusted with their own governance. Without education, freedom could not last. "If a nation expects to be ignorant and free, in a state of civilization, it expects what never was and never will be."[4] In his later years Jefferson claimed it was his earnest wish to see the republican principle of popular control pushed to its fullest exercise. Only then would he know that "our government may be pure and perpetual."[5]

The "Will of the People"

Americans are not the first to have engaged in a continual struggle to exert effective popular control over an ever-increasing range of governmental activity. Efforts at direct governance go back at least as far as ancient Athens, the assemblies of the Saxon tribes, and the plebiscite in the Roman Republic. The Roman plebiscite enabled the *plebs* (enfranchised commoners) to vote on repealing or enacting laws over the opposition of the senate, and optional referenda or plebiscites were also occasionally held in medieval Europe. Various forms of direct popular governance have also been in use in Swiss cantons since the twelfth and thirteenth centuries.

Direct legislation expressing the "will of the people" has had a certain legitimacy in America since the 1640s, when all or most of the freemen in New England villages assembled to make the laws by which they would be regulated. Notions of popular government or self-government animated New England town meetings and also prompted public votes on the ratification of state constitutions and state constitutional changes. A new framework of government drafted by the Massachusetts legislature in 1778 and submitted to the people for approval failed to receive a necessary two-thirds majority at least partly because it was the work of the already sitting legislature rather than a popularly elected constitutional convention. Only after a convention was established, and after its improved constitution was submitted to town meetings throughout the state, was a new constitution finally approved in 1780. New Hampshire town assemblies voted down a proposed constitution in 1778 but approved a redrafted constitution submitted for popular ratification a few years later.

Most other state constitutions were not submitted for popular ratification before 1801. However, at the end of the nineteenth century only a handful of states were governed by constitutions that had not been approved by popular referendum.

In 1818 Connecticut instituted the requirement that amendments to the state constitution be submitted automatically to voters for ratification following approval by the state legislature. Iowa and Texas (1845), Wisconsin (1846), and California (1856) submitted their draft constitutions to the people within their boundaries before becoming accepted as states. By the 1850s it had become accepted practice for admission to the Union that state constitutions first be approved by the people.

Gradually, states also began to confer upon the people the right to legislate directly upon subjects other than constitutional questions. After 1821 the Massachusetts constitution forbade the legislature to incorporate any new town as a city without the consent of the town's majority. Maryland in 1826 made the establishment of primary schools contingent upon a positive majority vote by the people in the county affected. In its 1842 constitution, Rhode Island required popular consent to allow the state to incur debts above $50,000. A referendum was held in Texas in 1850 to resolve the location of the state capital. Referenda on the location of state universities and charitable institutions became common. And "it was only a short time until the field of popular submission was extended to include statutes respecting limitations of state debts, taxation and finance, and such questions as the regulation of intoxicating liquors."[6]

The recall also appeared early in America. The 1780 Massachusetts constitution stipulated that delegates to the Congress of the United States could be recalled at any time within their one-year term, and others chosen and commissioned in their place. The Articles of Confederation in 1781 granted state legislatures rather than voters the right to recall congressional delegates.

The recall was proposed and briefly discussed in 1787 at the Constitutional Convention, and a few critics opposed ratification of the Constitution because no provision for a recall was included. Luther Martin, for example, reported back to his state legislature in Maryland that the absence of the recall, especially with six-year terms for U.S. senators, failed to ensure adequate accountability. "The *representative* ought to be *dependent* on his *constituents* and *answerable* to them; that the connection between the *representative* and the represented ought to be as *near* and as *close* as *possible*." Under this new arrangement, "for six years the senators are rendered totally and absolutely *independent* of *their States* . . . During *that time,* they may join in measures *ruinous* and *destructive* to *their States,* even such as should *totally* annihilate their *State governments,* and their States *cannot recall* them, *nor exercise any control* over them."[7]

Recall was thus a familiar concept to officials and political theorists in America's formative period. The need for the recall device in post-Revolutionary America was largely obviated by the then-widespread support for short terms and rotation in office for all public officials—especially at the state level. Terms limited to one or two years achieved much the same goal—keeping elected officials reasonably in touch with the will of the people.

The Populist Impulse

A pronounced populist impulse has always existed in the United States, from the Jeffersonian belief in a self-governing democracy of yeoman farmers, through the populist movement of the 1880s and 1890s, and in various manifestations—right- as well as left-wing—to the present. It was—and is—a quest for self-respect, equality, and a restoration of economic and social opportunity.

The more radical strains of populism have favored explicit economic remedies to penalize the financial giants of business, industry, and commerce, who were thought to be exploiting the struggling farmers. Thus the populists of the 1880s favored government ownership of the railroads, elimination of monopolies, a graduated income tax, free coinage of silver, a vastly expanded supply of money, and other efforts expected to improve the credit and social betterment of hard-pressed rural farm families.

Debtors on the frontiers, who were largely equal in financial status, frequently promoted a practical philosophy of political equality. The "boom-and-bust" cycles affecting frontier farmers and miners helped foment resentment toward elites in times of economic distress, sparking cries for economic and political reform. Such was the case with Daniel Shays's farmers and some Antifederalists and, later, Jeffersonian Republicans and Jacksonian Democrats.

The Grangers, Farmers' Alliance, single-taxers of the Henry George school, and the People's (Populist) party were all populist-minded groups that became prominent from 1875 to 1895. During this time, prices for farm commodities dropped so low that in certain sections of the country farming was carried on at an actual loss. Despite arduous work and abundant crop yields, one discouraged Texas farmer summed up the plight this way: "Cotton gone, the money is all gone too. One great discouraging fact here is so many Farmers don't own their own farms. Every agent, pedler and Every profession of man is Fleecing out the Farmers, and by the time the World Gets their Living out of the Farmer as we have to Feed the World We the Farmer has nothing Left, but a Bear Hard Living."[8]

This feeling of helplessness stood in sharp contrast to the Jeffersonian dream for the new republic. These farmers and others suffering from economic hard times looked back to an earlier age when they believed they had been less exploited—a time when there were few millionaires and no beggars, few monopolies and no recessions. In short, the populist spirit was born of both nostalgia and genuine hope for a restoration of conditions prevailing before industrialism, large-scale corporate capitalism, and the commercialization of agriculture. Although their problems were mainly the result of overproduction, farmers believed that certain greedy influences—bankers, railroaders, land speculators, and the tax structure—were at work like thieves, robbing farmers of their fair share.

In the late 1880s and early 1890s the number of farm foreclosures skyrocketed. In some counties in Kansas, for example, 90 percent of the farms passed into the ownership of loan companies. The combination of denied credit, deeper debt, harsh taxation, and rising rail rates led the discontented to suspect a conspiracy by the moneyed interests of the country to enslave them in a web of economic servitude. It was, the have-nots said, a struggle between the robbers and the robbed: "On the one side are the allied hosts of monopolies, the money power, great trusts and railroad corporations, who seek the enactment of laws to benefit them and impoverish the people. On the other are the farmers, laborers, merchants, and all other people who produce wealth and bear the burdens of taxation."[9]

Where could they turn for redress? Populists first looked to co-operatives, but they seldom worked because the commercial world possessed a near monopoly of the money supply and thus could effectively dry up credit. They then looked to government for assistance in what they considered a life-and-death situation. Populist organizers believed they had little choice but to enter politics, build coalitions, and try to bring about some measures that could regulate the moneyed interests and provide assistance for those farmers.

Government officials and state and national legislatures at the time, however, were often controlled by the special interests that were threatening to strangle the people in economic distress. Moreover, the two main political parties were largely, and sometimes entirely, under the influence of the railroads, trusts, and monopolies. It was not long before the Farmers' Alliance groups and similar advocates of change called for the creation of a new party that would be both independent of the establishment and could do the essential job of correcting the perceived ills of the country.

The People's, or Populist, party grew out of the nonpartisan Farmers' Alliance. There were branches of the party through the South, the West, and Midwest. Clearly, farmers' alliances were especially strong in Texas, the Dakotas, Kansas, Oklahoma, Alabama, California, Colorado, and elsewhere in the South and West.[10] In some areas of the country, socialist or semisocialist movements preceded the emergence of the Populist party. In California the Nationalists, a short-lived socialist evangelist movement inspired by Edward Bellamy's *Looking Backward* (1888), shifted their allegiance to the new People's party in the early 1890s. Elsewhere the single-taxers, followers of Henry George's ideas, were ready for the coming of a consciousness-raising new party. In *Progress and Poverty* (1879) George had preached the need for a substantial tax on unearned income and on any financial gain resulting from land speculation. This measure alone would restrain the speculators and enable the landless "plain people" to acquire homes and farms and thereby have a decent stake in society, free from exploitation.

By the late 1880s these varied alliances, consisting mainly of farmers, joined in some areas by miners, day laborers, and other workers, began holding political action meetings and ran candidates for office. After preliminary conventions in 1889, 1890, and 1891, the Populists held their first national convention in Omaha in July 1892, where they formally recognized the need for a political party to achieve their goals. The Populist platform supported free silver, public ownership of railroads, a graduated income tax, and other measures to increase the power and benefits of the plain people. The People's party convention also passed several resolutions that called for a restructuring of the political system. Two of these were:

> That we commend to the favorable consideration of the people and the reform press the legislative system known as the initiative and referendum.
>
> That we form a Constitutional provision limiting the Office of President and Vice President to one term, and providing for the election of Senators of the United States by a direct vote of the people.[11]

For most populists these direct democracy devices were a means of temporarily bypassing their legislatures and enacting needed laws on behalf of the downtrodden farmer, debtor, or laborer. Direct democracy became especially appealing as populists saw legislature after legislature defeat the proposals a majority of their members favored. A majority of the people, they believed, could never be corruptly influenced.

For some populists, especially the better-educated, middle-of-the-road factions, direct democracy devices became an obsession. North

Dakota farmer Lars A. Ueland, for example, was a lifelong Republican who became an activist in the Farmers' Alliance. Elected to the North Dakota legislature as a Republican in 1889, he grew disillusioned by the domination of his party by corporations, trusts, and moneyed interests. By 1892 Ueland had switched to the Populist party, which represented "the producing masses," whereas the Republican party represented "the machine in politics—the old gang." He attended the Omaha Populist convention in the summer of 1892 and instantly embraced the initiative and referendum.

> When I first became familiar with the principles of the initiative and referendum I was impressed with a sense of their value. The more I study these principles the more I am convinced that they will furnish us the missing link—the means needed—to make popular self-government do its best. Programs and reforms will then come as fast as the people need them, as fast as these changes are safe—only when a majority of the people are behind them. I would rather have the complete initiative and referendum adopted in state and nation than the most ideal political party that could be made, put into power, if one or the other could be secured.[12]

Ueland returned home and soon ran for the state legislature as a Populist (called the Independent Party in North Dakota). He won his campaign, immediately introduced legislation calling for the initiative and referendum, and within a few years his measures won approval.

At the same time that the Populist party emerged, a number of books and pamphlets began to circulate that advocated the initiative and referendum and brought them further attention as reforms worth striving toward. One such advocacy tract, *Direct Legislation by the People* (1892), by Nathan Cree, proposed a national initiative and referendum process as the necessary next step in the development of government. Cree predicted it would be a conservative influence, indeed it might act as a check on the excessive mutual backscratching by the two main political parties.

The only way to train a people for self-government, Cree argued, was to practice it. He liked the idea of "government by discussion" and viewed the majority of the people as the wisest, most just, and most conservative political power in the country. Direct popular legislation would "break the crushing and stifling power of our great party machines, and give freer play to the political ideas, aspirations,

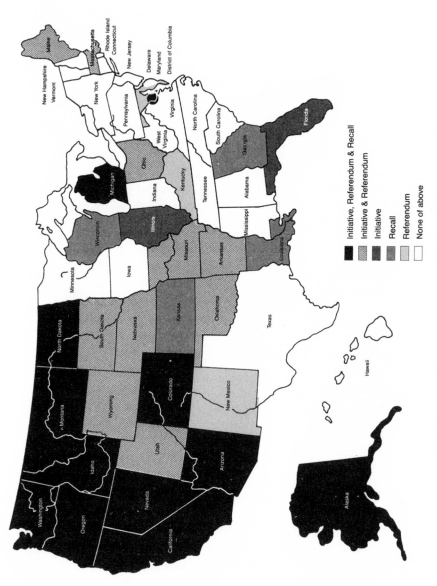

Citizen-initiated initiative, referendum, and recall at the state level.

opinions and feelings of the people. It will tend to relieve us from the dominance of partisan passions, and have an elevating and educative influence upon voters."[13] Representative processes would still be necessary, and legislatures would always remain a notable invention of modern politics and a practical necessity for large nations. Yet now was the time, Cree wrote, to combine legislature with a modified form of an ancient, primitive direct governance arrangement—the earliest and most natural for free persons. Representation alone would stifle rather than educate the people. Inviting the whole people to directly participate directly in government would be the best possible education in public affairs, the best possible antidote to apathy, and the only way to provide for democratic control over the government.

In 1893, J. W. Sullivan's *Direct Legislation by the Citizenship through the Initiative and Referendum* influenced the spread of direct democracy. A labor leader, journalist, and social reform editor, Sullivan traveled to Switzerland, observed its system of direct legislation for several months, and returned to write a series of articles about the initiative and referendum in 1889 and the early 1890s.

Sullivan was convinced by what he had observed in Switzerland that direct legislation was not an impractical, utopian scheme—it worked there, and he believed it would work well in the United States. He believed there was a radical difference between a democracy and a representative government, and he plainly preferred a democracy. In a democracy, Sullivan said, citizens themselves make the law, and sovereignty remains uninterruptedly with the citizenry. Democracy is direct rule by a changing majority of the citizens, whereas representative government is rule by a succession of "quasi-oligarchies," only indirectly and remotely responsible to the people.[14] Along with many critics of contemporary government at the time, Sullivan believed that direct legislation could enrich citizenship and replace distrust of government with respect and healthy participation. With direct legislation, "the sphere of every citizen would be enlarged; each would consequently acquire education in his role, and develop a lively interest in the public affairs in part under his own management."[15]

Sullivan overstated the success of the Swiss initiative and referendum, yet in doing so he stirred the imaginations of would-be reformers in America. For the Swiss, according to Sullivan, had thrown off the privileges of the ruler and turned their legislators into mere servants. They had "rendered bureaucracy impossible . . . and shown the parliamentary system not essential to lawmaking." If this was not enough, "they have written their laws in language so plain that a layman may be judged in the highest court. They have forestalled monopolies, improved and reduced taxation, avoided incurring heavy public debts, and made a better distribution of their land than any other European country."[16]

The writings of Cree, Sullivan, and others attracted attention from those who were groping for strategies to make legislatures responsive and responsible. An example was William S. U'Ren of Oregon, later known as a blacksmith, lawyer, spiritualist, religious mystic, and disciple of the dietician Horace Fletcher ("Never eat when you are sad or mad, only when you are glad"). He had read Henry George's bestselling *Progress and Poverty* in 1882 and became an instant convert. He and his fellow populists in other states soon learned, however, that state legislatures were highly unlikely to give even a fair hearing to George's radical and, in their view, highly confiscatory scheme.

Single-taxers and Farmers' Alliance members learned that they had to do something about the governmental processes before they could implement programs. U'Ren put it this way:

> Blacksmithing is my trade. And it has always given colour to my view of things. For example, when I was very young, I saw some of the evils in the conditions of life and I wanted to fix them. I couldn't. There were no tools. We had tools to do almost anything within the shop, beautiful tools, wonderful. And so in other trades, arts and professions; in everything but government. In government, the common trade of all men and the basis of all social life, men worked still with old tools, with old laws, with constitutions and charters which hindered more than they helped. Men suffered from this. There were lawyers enough; many of our ablest men were lawyers. Why didn't some of them invent legislative implements to help the people govern themselves? Why had we no tool makers for democracy?[17]

It was around this time that U'Ren read a leaflet about the initiative and referendum, then Sullivan's book. After thoroughly digesting Sullivan's analysis, U'Ren became a populist organizer and helped form Oregon's Direct Legislation League. "I forgot, for the time, all about Henry George and the single tax," he later recalled. "The one important thing was to restore the lawmaking power where it belonged—in the hands of the people. Once give us that, we could get anything we wanted—single tax, anything."[18] Representatives of the state Grange, Oregon Knights of Labor, Portland Federated Trades, and the Farmers' Alliance all became allies in U'Ren's campaign. To win support for his prized procedural reforms in the Oregon legislature, he decided deliberately to wheel and deal and compromise, and before long he had become an accomplished lobbyist, pamphleteer, and political horse trader. After an almost seven-year crusade, the initiative and referendum were approved in the 1899 and 1901 legislatures (as required for an amendment to the state's constitution), and Oregon voters approved it by an impressive eleven-to-one margin in 1902. Since then, Oregon has been among the most frequent users of these direct democracy devices.

Adoption of the Initiative and Referendum in the States

Because direct democracy or direct legislation measures in the 1880s and early 1890s were promoted by groups regarded as cranks—socialists and single-issue groups, most notably the single-taxers—incumbent legislators tended to dismiss both the groups and measures as too radical. By the late 1890s, however, converts to these measures were gradually increasing throughout the West. A National Direct Legislation League had been formed in the early 1890s. Its periodicals, such as the *Direct Legislation Record,* as well as other friendly journals, such as *The Arena,* heightened public interest in direct democracy. Evangelists for direct democracy, including single-tax champions Eltweed Pomeroy, U'Ren, and Ohio clergyman Herbert S. Bigelow, traveled throughout the nation singing its praises. A prosperous physician, John R. Haynes, performed this role in California, while U.S. Senator Jonathan Bourne of Oregon, Robert M. La Follette of Wisconsin, Missouri governor Joseph Folk, and George Norris of Nebraska all took up the campaign at one time or another. Eventually, after a few states had passed these measures (see Table 3.1) and their "crank" image had faded, even Theodore Roosevelt and Woodrow Wilson would embrace direct democracy devices. Wilson typified many of the progressives who were slow to join the cause but whose support, once they gave it, was complete and uncritical.

In state after state, though, the first proponents had been the leftist factions—the socialists and the People's party. In rural states the Farmers' Alliance typically was in the forefront. Thousands of labor federations, notably the miners, joined the campaign. So did the Women's Suffrage Association. Measures that would have given

Table 3.1. **State adoptions of initiative and referendum, 1898–1977**

Year	State
1898	South Dakota
1900	Utah
1902	Oregon
1904	Nevada (referendum only)
1906	Montana
1907	Oklahoma
1908	Maine, Missouri
1910	Arkansas, Colorado
1911	Arizona, California, New Mexico (referendum only)
1912	Idaho, Nebraska, Nevada (initiative only), Ohio, Washington
1913	Michigan
1914	North Dakota
1915	Kentucky (referendum only), Maryland (referendum only)
1918	Massachusetts
1959	Alaska
1968	Florida (constitutional initiative only), Wyoming
1970	Illinois (constitutional initiative only)
1977	District of Columbia

Note: During the past 20 years Alabama, Connecticut, Delaware, Georgia, Hawaii, Kentucky, Minnesota, New Jersey, New York, Pennsylvania, Rhode Island, and Texas have considered direct legislation devices at constitutional conventions or in legislative debates and hearings. Governors in Alabama, Minnesota, New Jersey, and Texas have endorsed these measures. Voters in both Minnesota and Rhode Island came very close to adding the initiative and referendum to their constitutions in the 1980s.

women the right to vote had been defeated in numerous state legislatures—often on three or four occasions—and strategists for women's suffrage now saw the initiative and referendum as a possible new means to overcome this intransigence.

In several states, prohibitionists and temperance organizations also endorsed and worked for the adoption of these popular lawmaking devices. In the midst of Colorado's battle over these measures, H. G. Fisher, president of the temperance-minded Christian Citizenship Union, allowed that "the only way in which the liquor evil can be abolished is through the adoption of the initiative, referendum and recall."[19] The National Prohibition party also endorsed direct democracy devices, although in North Dakota, where the constitution already contained a prohibition measure, local temperance forces viewed the constitutional initiative as a threat to prohibition; their political lobbying delayed adoption of the initiative in North Dakota for several years.[20] In Missouri single-taxers led the movement for initiatives, with coalition-building help from organized labor and prohibitionists.[21] In Washington State support came first from the Socialist Labor party (as early as 1885), later from labor and Grange conventions, and finally from Progressives and Democrats.[22] Arizona saw a coalition of labor, socialists, prohibitionists, women suffragists, and Democrats allied against most Republicans, the mining interests, the railroads, and President William Howard Taft.[23]

Newspapers got involved on both sides of the issue. The *Los Angeles Times* was a strong opponent of the initiative and referendum in California, asserting that the "ignorance and caprice and irresponsibility of the multitudes" would be substituted for "the learning and judgment of the Legislature";[24] radical legislation would result, and business and property rights would be subject to constant turmoil at the hands of agitators. For the *Arizona Daily Star,* on the other hand, the adoption of the initiative and referendum meant "the elimination of superstition, bigotry, intolerance and ignorance from American politics . . . an end to boss rule and . . . to grafting from the public crib; and an end of fraud, pomposities and political fakers."[25]

In many states the final battles over direct democracy devices pitted Democrats, who had been converted to the cause by labor unions, against Republicans, who generally held a more traditional view of representative government. Colorado and Massachusetts exemplified these partisan splits. Colorado's Democratic governor John F. Shafroth said that if he could have only one reform, it would be one incorporating a provision for direct legislation. "This one law would be the solution" for honest legislation in Colorado.[26] Such a measure, Shafroth believed, would put a stop to attempts to improperly influence state legislatures and would make legislators more careful and more accountable. Colorado opponents of direct democracy, especially the Republican party and the state medical society, said these procedures would be alien to representative government and harmful to the financial and social welfare and even the health and well-being of the state. According to the *Denver Republican,* "The initiative and referendum both conflict directly with the representative principle, and to the extent to which they may be applied representative government will be overthrown . . . Cannot the people of Colorado do a little sober thinking for themselves and on their own account? Must they adopt every new fangled notion which may be adopted or experimented with in some other state? Let Oregon be foolish if it wants to, but let Colorado always be sober and sane."[27]

Although the populist movement played an agitational role in incubating these notions of direct democracy devices, much of their basic development in the United States reflects the sociology, psychology, and politics of American progressivism. Their development and actual passage progressed furthest in states in which the later progressive movement was a strong force. Woodrow Wilson's conversion to the cause, especially his endorsement of the progressives' challenge of party bossism, was illustrative. His and the progressives' support for the initiative, referendum, and recall were vital to the adoption of the initiative and referendum in several states. Thus, although Massachusetts populists had embraced the idea of the initiative and referendum as early as 1895, the real fight for these procedural reforms did not come until 1916 and 1917.

The Massachusetts legislature was viewed as a reasonably responsive legislature in the early years of the twentieth century. It was still elected annually. Its record for pioneering legislation in the fields of health, education, the protection of working women and children, civil service reform, and the regulation of corporations was one of the best in the country. But social reformers, labor interests, and others were dissatisfied with the pace of progress. Organized labor complained of an antilabor sentiment among the Republicans, who controlled both chambers of the legislature, while progressives thought legislators were too closely connected with the city bosses and county courthouse groups.

As in most other states, populists were joined first by socialists, then by diverse intellectual "good government" interests; in 1912 the Democratic and Progressive parties lent their support. As agitation for an initiative and a referendum grew, so did the call for a popularly elected constitutional convention. Such a convention was elected in 1917 and spent forty-five days on the initiative and the referendum, bitterly dividing the 320 delegates.[28]

Proponents claimed these direct democracy devices would diminish the impact of corrupt influences on the legislature, undermine bossism, and induce legislators to be more attentive to public opinion and the broader public interest. With direct democracy devices, they added, better people would want to serve in the legislature, and it would be possible to reduce the sizes of the two chambers. In the Jeffersonian tradition, Democratic governor David I. Walsh and other champions of these changes asserted voters were informed and capable enough to cast prudent votes on ballot issues; if voters were fit to sit on juries, they could also develop an informed view on public issues.

Republican opponents believed the people would be misled by demagogues, lied to and manipulated by leaders of narrow interest groups, and compromised and overwhelmed by highly technical questions. They rejected the charge that Massachusetts legislators were unduly influenced by bosses or lobbies and reminded reformers that one of the great virtues of representative government was its capacity to maintain and protect the rights of minorities and individuals against tyranny by majorities. Finally, they noted that the American solution to the problem of reconciling government with liberty consisted in the acceptance of several fundamental ideas, of which representative government and division of public powers were key features. Nevertheless, the convention proposed a constitutional amendment permitting a modified, indirect form of the initiative, which was narrowly ratified in 1918.

The Defects of State Legislatures, 1890–1912

Public mistrust of state legislatures was considerable in the 1890s and at the turn of the century. Legislatures have always been the scapegoat and the punching bag for those who are politically disenchanted or ignored or who have suffered economic or social misfortune. Direct democracy reformers sought to improve the situation. Thus a major premise underlying their campaign for the initiative and referendum was that representative government had failed to live up to expectations. According to Woodrow Wilson, if there had been genuinely representative government in the state legislatures, no one would have pressed for the adoption of the initiative and referendum. The reformers, he said, were not bent upon any radical alteration: they had no intention of undermining legislative or representative processes, but rather of redeeming them. "It must be remembered that we are contrasting the operation of the initiative and referendum, not with the representative government which we possess in theory and which we have long persuaded ourselves that we possessed in fact, but with the actual state of affairs, with legislative processes which are carried on in secret, responding to the impulse of subsidized machines and carried through by men whose unhappiness it is to realize that they are not their own masters, but puppets in a game."[29]

Citizens were increasingly convinced that powerful, organized, self-seeking interests shaped legislative outcomes at the expense of the public interest. They believed that for one reason or another—bossism, bribery, or sheer inefficiency—the legislatures prevented the will of the people from finding adequate expression. The integrity of representative government was in doubt.

Muckrakers such as Lincoln Steffens, seeking out evidence of political deals and hidden cesspools, discovered them under every city hall and nearly every state capitol: a business or a party boss controlled government, and often the two played hand in hand.

Some observers claimed this situation had arisen because "good men" no longer cared enough to serve as state legislators. In many states the capitals were small, out-of-the-way cities where leading lawyers and businessmen were less inclined to want to spend time. Most issues coming before the legislatures, though important, were routine, and seldom stirred the imagination of talented and entrepreneurial professionals.[30] Edwin L. Godkin, editor of *The Nation*, predicted in 1898 that the existing system of democracy was about to collapse because of the inferior quality of representatives. "The withdrawal of the more intelligent class from legislative duties is more and more lamented," wrote Godkin. "It is increasingly difficult today to get a man of serious knowledge on any subject to go to Congress, if he has other pursuits and other sources of income. To get him to go to the state legislature, in any of the populous and busy states, is well-nigh impossible."[31]

Into this vacuum stepped the party bosses. The bosses recruited inferior candidates, bribed them, and controlled them, making the system even worse and further discouraging talented individuals from participation. Godkin speculated that perhaps we were getting tired of the representative system.[32]

It is more likely, however, that representative institutions were severely tested in the 1890s because while our economic system was being transformed so also were the prizes and stakes involved in lawmaking and state policymaking. Legislatures had to make important decisions about the vital rights of railroads, lumber and mining interests, banks, and land speculators, not to mention decisions about the fate of social and welfare legislation. Not surprisingly, these vested interests sought the favorable verdict of state legislative officials and generally had resources with which to lobby the legislators. "Special interests which would be powerless in a general election may be all-powerful in a legislature if they enlist the services of a few skilled tacticians," observed Theodore Roosevelt, himself a former legislator and governor. He added that the result was the same "whether these tacticians are unscrupulous and are hired by the special interests, or whether they are sincere men who honestly believe that the people desire what is wrong and should not be allowed to have it."[33]

As the progressive movement took hold after the turn of the century, its members promoted the direct democracy devices earlier espoused by the populists, in the hope of neutralizing the power of flagrant special interests. Progressives found fault with representative government for several reasons. They believed private interests and narrow-minded party bosses could too easily exploit the natural resources and treasuries of the state for their own purposes. Progressives were also concerned that state legislatures were not functioning as they should. Their proceedings involved too much secrecy, too little discussion, too much automatic passage of what legislative committees proposed. Too often, in the short biennial sessions (except in a few larger states) crucial measures were rushed through at the last minute. Temptations for corruption were pervasive. Moreover, many legislators, rather than representing their constituents, seemed to represent the interests of party bosses and to be accountable only to them. Indeed, the power to nominate, exercised by the boss, was also the power to appoint and remove. Thus voters seemed to have only a narrow choice between the appointees of one boss or those of another. (In fact some bosses performed useful services: some provided welfare services and assistance for the truly needy; others helped educate new citizens about voting, getting jobs, and other opportunities.) Finally, the activities of sophisticated lobbying groups especially troubled progressive activists. Because of threats to financial livelihood, appointments to Washington jobs, bribes of money and women, and even getting legislators drunk before a critical vote, certain legislators seemed powerless to resist the overtures of vested interests. "It was a pathetic and tragic thing," said Wisconsin progressive Robert La Follette, "to see honest men falling before these insidious forces."[34]

Reformers, holdover populists, and the now more prominent progressives sought to open up the system of government and restore more power to the people. Unless the machine and its bosses could be broken, unless the corrupt alliance between greedy corporate interests and the machines could be smashed, it seemed that no lasting improvement could be achieved. Yet it was not, they said, to be a revolution, merely a restoration. The remedy would be the initiative, referendum, and recall. These were not by any means the "panacea for all our ills," said California governor Hiram Johnson, "yet they do give to the electorate the power of action when desired, and they do place in the hands of the people the means by which they may protect themselves."[35]

Their dream was to liberate the legislative process from the temptations of corrupt influences, and to allow the expression of popular sentiment to be accurately reflected in policymaking processes. Unbeholden to the special interests or bosses, this new ideal or "textbook citizen" would study the issues and think them through on impartial terms.

These progressive aspirations have been criticized by scholars. Some merely say it is ironic that progressives sought to neutralize the power of special interests when they themselves obviously wished to maximize particular values and interests. Moreover, direct democracy measures won adoption precisely because a whole host of interests, including many with a narrow focus, banded together to press for these institutional changes.

Second, critics say the search for "men of good will" was largely a delusion. It was a nostalgic quest for a golden age that really had never existed. Moreover, it was a simpleminded if earnest effort to ignore the new economic realities of a modern era. In his revisionist treatise, historian Richard Hofstadter looked back at this reform zealousness and found it naive and misguided; the movement for direct democracy was "an attempt to realize Yankee-Protestant ideals of personal responsibility, and the Progressive notion of good citizenship was the culmination of the Yankee-Mugwump ethos of political participation without self-interest." But, warned Hofstadter, "while this ethos undoubtedly has its distinct points of superiority to the boss-machine ethos of hierarchy, discipline, personal loyalty, and personal favors, it was less adaptive to the realities of the highly organized society of the late nineteenth and the twentieth century."[36]

Other scholars have insisted that the defects of legislatures were exaggerated. "The tendency to exaggerate the defects of representative assemblies," wrote A. Lawrence Lowell, "is due in part to the inclination of men not in active public life to assume that their views are shared by the community and improperly slighted by politicians." Lowell also suggested it was hard to formulate public opinion in such a way that it could be easily and accurately mirrored in legislative assemblies. "We need to learn on what subjects a real public opinion can be formed, how far it can extend to particular measures, and how far it is of necessity confined to general principles."[37]

Finally, contemporary critics of the populist-progressive direct democracy movement said the way to remedy defects in the legislative process was to strengthen the legislatures and not to bypass them. Get better people to run for office. Improve the staffs. Lengthen the sessions. Increase the resources, the status, and the incentives for doing a responsible job. These recommendations persist nearly a century later.

Reactionaries dismissed both the populist impulse and the virtues of legislatures. They viewed the judicial and executive branches as the superior representatives of the people. Thus in his tract *True and False Democracy* Columbia University president Nicholas Murray Butler wrote that the executive, not the legislative, branch was the most efficient representative and spokesman of the popular will. Butler concluded: "True democracy, therefore, while seeking by all possible means to improve the quality of its legislatures and to make them representative of principles and ideas rather than of special and local interest, will strengthen the executive arm and protect it from the legislative invasion in matters purely administrative."[38] In short, according to this reasoning, Americans might be suffering from overlegislation and from an overemphasis on the legislatures. Legislatures were but one aspect and perhaps a relatively less important aspect of representative government.

These criticisms of the populist and progressive movements raise some valid points; yet several exaggerate the naive or irrational tendencies in these protest efforts. Many populists had real grievances and few or no opportunities to express them through the two dominant parties. Moreover, "Populists were far from adopting a retrogressively utopian view towards society; many of them accepted the fact of industrialization and sought to democratize its impact through highly specific measures."[39] The animating spirit behind the on-again, off-again populist impulse in America has been experimentation, pragmatism, and, in general, a groping attempt to maximize opportunities for those who have felt left out by the political arrangements of the moment.

Those who favored direct democracy in the states did have political, economic, and social interests of their own. They might claim to be neutralizing the powers of the special interests, but they favored direct democracy devices because they favored alternative policy outcomes—such as the single tax, prohibition, women's suffrage, prolabor legislation, and the graduated income tax. Undoubtedly, authentic egalitarian sentiments were often at the root of these movements and campaigns, yet self-interest, broadly construed, was invariably also present.

The crowning paradox of the direct democracy crusade is that even though its most fervent champions often intended less to strengthen representative democracy than to bypass or punish it, it simultaneously helped remedy the defects of representative political institutions. Born of impatience and frustration with traditional face-to-face and semielitist deliberative assemblies, direct democracy procedures nevertheless did not become viable substitutes for the legislative process. They provided an occasional safety valve for interests that failed to get a fair hearing in the legislatures, and they sometimes served to keep elected officials at least moderately attentive to grassroots moods and aspirations; but representative processes, and especially the election of legislators, continued to be the primary, indeed the overwhelmingly predominant and practical, means of enabling the views and interests of the American citizen to be regularly represented in state capitols. Elected officials, not the voters at the ballot box, still enacted the vast bulk of laws.

Some of the defects of representative processes are the defects of democracy, no matter how well designed, and many turn-of-the-century defects associated with American political institutions had more to do with massive transformations in the economy than with the procedures and unresponsiveness of legislatures. Yet voters had justifiable reasons to complain, protest, and join in coalitions to invent or at least experiment with new procedures aimed at improving their governance processes. These same arrangements were also the source of movements to bring about the direct election of U.S. senators, the direct primary in nominating processes, the right of women to vote, reapportionment, and one-person, one-vote court rulings. More recently, the same impulses encouraged financial disclosure and conflict-of-interest laws as well as efforts to finance general elections publicly. Collectively, these changes have enhanced the responsiveness of the political decision-making process.

Direct democracy reform was a typically American response. If one of our oldest sayings in American folklore holds that "If it ain't broke, don't fix it," it is at least equally true that we believe we should surely try to renew, reform, or improve a process that *has* broken down. The direct democracy movement's efforts did create change and did have consequences—some good and some less desirable.

▼

CHAPTER 4

The Question of Voter Competence

▼

The voice of the people has been said to be the voice of God: and however generally this maxim has been quoted and believed, it is not true in fact. The people are turbulent and changing; they seldom judge or determine right.

—Alexander Hamilton, 1787

If Americans sometimes seem unfit to legislate, it may be because they have for so long been passive observers of government. The remedy is not to continue to exclude them from governing, but to provide practical and active forms of civic education that will make them more fit than they were. Initiative and referendum processes are ideal instruments of civic education.

—Benjamin R. Barber, 1977

HOW well do citizens perform their part in direct democracy processes? Do they know what they are signing when petitions are circulated? Do they vote consistently with their own interests? Do they understand the issues on the ballot? How do they make up their minds? In short, are voters reasonably competent to vote on public policy and constitutional matters?

Populist and progressive leaders claimed people were sufficiently intelligent and discerning to govern themselves. And issue voting, they said, would enhance civic education. Direct democracy practices might even help recapture the more desirable qualities of town meeting democracy. Typical was this 1902 view: "With the exercise of the Referendum, American citizenship will appreciate in value; it will impress the voter with the solemn obligation he is assuming, as he becomes conscious of the fact that his vote might determine the fate of an important public measure. While some will always remain indifferent and ignorant, there is hardly a community in this land, large or small, the majority of which is not well disposed and either well informed or willing to learn."[1]

A century later supporters and critics of direct democracy continue their debate. Advocates say that if people are intelligent enough to vote on a candidate, they are just as competent to vote on most major issues. "It is far easier for people to make wise decisions on issues than on the shifting personalities and promises of individuals."[2] League of Women Voters spokesperson Carol Carlton adds, "If we accept the premise that people can choose between good and bad leaders, we must accept the premise that people can choose between good and bad laws."[3] The late Howard Jarvis, who spearheaded the Proposition 13 campaign in California, put it bluntly: "The people in these states are not going to buy a phony petition, they are not going to buy it, they are a lot smarter than we think."[4]

But critics of direct democracy say the people are not informed or caring enough to vote on complicated public policy issues. Too many would not understand technical issues. Too many would simply be confused, and not enough would actually vote. The quality of our laws and constitutions would suffer. Political scientist Harold Gosnell in the late 1940s concluded: "The fact remains that the body of voters is not at all equipped to understand even ordinary bills, and one of the chief failings of the referendum has been the inability of the voters to use it intelligently."[5]

Political scientists have been divided on this question since the earliest discussions of direct democracy. Those with activist and more distinctive ideological policy preferences usually support direct legislation and the recall. But most political scientists are skeptical; some are actively hostile to these populist practices. Political historian Richard Hofstadter's prizewinning 1955 study, *The Age of Reform*, portrayed turn-of-the-century populists as naive, emotional, and often ill-informed about the effects of their proposals, and his book influenced a generation of political and social scientists. Moreover, many analysts who study populist democracy practices develop considerable reservations about them after finding that citizens and voters often do *not* fully understand the process, frequently vote with limited information, and sometimes vote contrary to their own policy preferences. They worry, too, about the influence of money and the way single-interest groups sometimes seize on the initiative or recall to press for issue positions they would never be able to get approved in their state legislatures. Research on voter understanding and the role of money in direct democracy processes raises a series of compelling questions as to whether voters are asked to pass judgments on matters that strain their information and interest.

Gathering Initiative Petition Signatures

It takes substantial money or a dedicated army of workers to qualify an initiative for the ballot. Proponents must obtain a relatively large number of signatures; although the number varies from state to state and from jurisdiction to jurisdiction, states typically require signatures from about 8 percent of those who voted for governor in the previous election.

In the early days of direct democracy, signatures were mainly collected by volunteer or civic and professional organizations. Thus, the temperance leagues would circulate petitions among their members and to favorably disposed churches, and unions, farm organizations, and teacher associations would put their members to work collecting signatures in their neighborhoods and among their relatives. Today, however, most signatures must be gathered within 90 to 150 days, depending on the jurisdiction; the emphasis is on efficiency rather than on disseminating information. In the ideal world, citizens would carefully read a proposed petition, reflect on it, and discuss it with family, friends, and informed neighbors. This ideal process may have been rare even in the early days of the initiative process, but it seldom characterizes the signature stage these days.

Today, not only do petition circulators actively working for their issue concentrate on obtaining as many signatures as fast as possible, but several states even permit paid petition circulators. For instance, Robert McCarney, an auto dealer in Bismarck, North Dakota, helped place more than a dozen state initiatives on the North Dakota ballots, spending over $270,000 between 1963 and 1980. "I just hire people from town to town," said McCarney. "I have a general supervisor who gets about $2,000, and then it is about 30 cents a signature. Every day they count them up and keep tabs on it."[6]

Questionable methods of obtaining signatures have been used in nearly every state that permits the initiative. For example, citizens are often purposely approached at inconvenient times, when they will often sign the petition just to get on with their business. Circulators often also misrepresent the substance of the measure, fictitious names are sometimes added to petitions, and names of legal voters are sometimes transferred from one sheet to another. In the passion of the moment, an occasional group has even forged names from the area telephone book.[7]

Even when a group plays by the rules, an incentive exists to get as many people to sign as fast as possible. The circulation of petitions seldom educates voters; rather, it is a marathon of endurance. Various ruses have been used to obtain signatures. No law says the petition gatherer must read and explain the proposed initiative to the signer, and most people take the solicitor's word for what an initiative would do. Most petition collectors therefore rely on slogans and a certain amount of "hoopla." The late Ed Koupal, a leader of California's neopopulist People's Lobby, candidly summed up his technique:

> Generally, people who are getting our signatures are too god-damned interested in their ideology to get the required number in the required time. We use the hoopla process.
>
> First, you set up a table with six petitions taped to it, and a sign in front that says, SIGN HERE. One person sits at the table. Another person stands in front. That's all you need—two people.
>
> While one person sits at the table, the other walks up to people and asks two questions. We operate on the old selling maxim that two yeses make a sale. First, we ask them if they are a registered voter. If they say yes to that, we ask if they are registered in that county. If they say yes to that, we immediately push them up to the table where the person sitting points to a petition and says, "Sign this." By this time, the person feels, "Oh goodie, I get to play," and signs it. If the table doesn't get 80 signatures an hour using this method, it's moved the next day.[8]

Do citizens know what they are signing? Most of the time people do not ask to read the petition. Petition circulators seldom offer to read it. As Koupal put it, "Why try to educate the world when you're trying to get signatures?"[9]

Those who ask to read the petition are given the chance to do so—but are usually asked to step aside and read it so as not to slow up the 50 to 70 percent who simply sign after hearing a catchy slogan such as "Do you want taxes cut?" "Are you against corruption and conflict of interest in government?" "Are you against nuclear waste and more Three Mile Islands?" or "Are you against abortion and pornography?"

Perhaps a quarter to a third, by best estimates, take the time to read a petition and talk to the circulators about whether or not to sign. And many signature collectors do indeed try to answer honestly all questions and are open and fair-minded about the process. Still, a Denver-based pollster said he believes he could go out in the street and readily get people to sign a petition that was randomly worded or made up of nonsense sentences. If you are skilled enough in the art of manipulation you can talk many people into signing almost anything. People either do not read the petition at all or do not read it carefully.

A certain proportion—perhaps up to a third of those signing—of the public sign petitions merely because they are persuaded that the *fair thing* to do is let the measure in question be placed before the voters. Signature crews can use this rationale if someone hesitates or is "not entirely sure about the petition." "Well," says the person at the table, "won't you help us to get it on the ballot so it can get a full public debate and so it can be put on the ballot in November?"

Thus perhaps half of those who sign petitions have only a vague idea of what they are signing. Some people who either cannot resist the pressure to sign or are persuaded by the argument that this group deserves the right to present the issue to the voters sign the petition even though they are opposed to the measure.

Direct-mail consulting firms transformed initiative petition collecting in California in the late 1970s and 1980s by shifting signature collection from the traditional card table in front of the shopping center to the mail. Direct-mail consulting companies contracted by petition-drive leaders design mail-solicitation campaigns employing sophisticated computer letters that often look like official mail. Sometimes they are written on the stationery of a state legislative leader or of a senior political party official. One 1980 letter to California voters from police and fire fighters stated on the envelope that this letter was "in reference to police matter at [a computer-printed household address]." Elsewhere the cover letter said the matter was referred by Sergeant Mike Tracy. The word URGENT appeared three times on the envelope, and the letter closed with "Urgently yours." Many of these mail-order companies have been highly effective, bringing in both ample signatures and funds. Usually there is a box requesting funds, to be mailed back along with the signatures of family, friends, and neighbors.

These mailed-to-the-home petitions have at least one positive feature: they allow for a more careful reading of the petition. The typical recipient surely has more time to seek information about it before signing and is not subjected to face-to-face selling pressure. Indeed the arrival of the letter and petition may even prompt a thoughtful discussion over the merits of the initiated proposal.

Direct-mail efforts, their defenders insist, are still grass-roots politics. And it is true, too, that direct-mail campaigns often engage in no more or less hyperbole or emotion than do political rallies, central committee instructions to party regulars in the big cities, or the typical political newsletter published by a union or trade association.

However, computerized mail-order initiatives are expensive and raise new concerns about the high costs of obtaining signatures. They also rekindle the view that only the already well organized and well financed can readily use the process—surely contrary to the early intentions of direct democracy advocates. Further, the mailings' use of propaganda, scare tactics, and questionable "endorsement" techniques has heightened the emotional and irrational aspects of the process.[10]

How do for-profit "petition pushers" operate? First they poll voters to determine how they view an issue and what words or slogans might have the best impact in a given campaign. Then they mount a major advertising and public relations promotion campaign. Next they prepare newspaper and magazine ads. They explore every possible use of free television and radio time. Sometimes these petition pushers produce and distribute television spots in their efforts to raise signatures and funds and to convert as many voters as possible to support a particular proposition.

As these public relations, campaign consulting, and computer mailing firms gain experience, they are able to develop lists of persons they know sign certain kinds of petitions. They even have some lists of voters who will sign and return virtually any petition sent to them. Other lists are of voters who can regularly be expected to send in funds as well as signatures. The more sophisticated this targeting becomes, especially with the help of party, trade association, "moral majority," or Sierra Club kinds of lists, the more single-interest or narrow partisan issues are put on the ballot.

Not all petition drives have the money to hire these petition-pushing companies. And a few states (including Colorado and Washington) prohibit paid petition gatherers. Some petition drives are truly up-from-the-grass-roots happenings. And, according to various estimates, at least two-thirds of initiated propositions in recent years were placed on state ballots as the result of volunteer signature collections. Still, the process in many states involves several questionable, if not outright undesirable, practices. The growth of the so-called initiative industry and of crafty and devious initiative consultant practices poses important new questions that cry out for new safeguards and procedural reforms.

Voting and Nonvoting in Direct Legislation Elections

Some people vote in every election and on all the options: candidates, initiatives, amendment issues, and recalls. Other people vote more selectively, depending on what kind of election it is, what issues concern them, and so on. It is well established, for example, that presidential elections bring out more voters than do off-year elections, and that primary elections ordinarily bring fewer people to the polls than do general elections. Special elections (that is, elections involving just a single issue or perhaps one vacancy to be filled on a local council or school board) generally have the lowest voter turnout. As a rule, national elections bring out more voters than do state elections, and state elections more voters than local elections.

Voting is never without some cost to the voters. *Time* is a principal cost of voting: time to register, to discover who is running, to deliberate over issues and seek out information, to go to the polls, to wait in polling lines, and to vote. Since time is a scarce resource, there are what economists call "opportunity costs" involved in the act of voting; one could spend the time watching television, reading a book, bowling, and so forth. The less-educated and lower-income groups have a harder time bearing these voting "costs" than better-educated and financially well-off persons.

The costs of voting are reduced by certain factors—most notably education and age. The more educated people are, the more skills they have that make learning about candidates and issues easier and possibly more gratifying.[11] Similarly, an older person's "life experience" imparts political skills and lessons that younger people generally lack as they turn voting age.

People who are fatalistic vote less regularly than those who believe in planning and believe they are in control of their lives; those who are beneficiaries of the economic and political system are more likely to believe in the efficiency and desirability of voting.[12] People who believe that casting even one vote can make a difference are of course more likely to vote. That kind of belief or civic faith "is more widespread among groups that have been well served by our economic and political institutions in the past, and much less widely shared by groups and individuals who feel they have been denied, for whatever reason, the full benefits of American life."[13]

If the less educated, the less well-off, the young, and minorities are less likely to vote in elections of all kinds, then plainly they are also less likely to vote in ballot issue elections, in which what economists call "information costs" (the costs of learning about the various aspects of the issue) are generally even higher than in candidate elections. Legal and technical language on ballot issues sometimes causes confusion, and the absence of party labels usually attached to candidates denies a majority of these voters of a familiar cue. Proponents of direct democracy do not mind this absence of party label. For them, there is no inherent value in "party cues" other than the "value" of promoting the agenda of the elitists who govern both parties.

In the end, a 5 to 15 percent drop-off or falloff of voter participation is common in state issue elections. Technically, drop-off is the percentage of voters who come to the polls but fail to vote on candidates or proposals found lower on the ballot. In presidential or statewide elections in which a governor or U.S. senator is running, these candidates will usually receive 95 percent or more of the vote. In recent presidential elections, state-initiated issues averaged between 90 and 95 percent of the vote given to the highest statewide official on the ballot (usually the governor). On the basis of this information, one analyst claims voter understanding about initiatives is at least 90 percent as high, on the average, as voter awareness of candidate campaigns for top state and national offices, even in presidential election years.[14] Given higher information costs involved in understanding and making decisions on issues on the ballot, this appears to be a reasonably high level of participation.

Ballot issues sometimes, however, stir up interest in an election. Although voter falloff is typical, voter "turnon" occurs when controversial and highly visible issues are placed on the ballot. In 1986, for example, Idaho voters paid more attention to a controversial "right-to-work" referendum than to the hotly fought U.S. Senate and gubernatorial races. In Oregon in recent years, certain ballot measures have captured more votes than have any other statewide races. One student of voter turnout and voter awareness of ballot issues in the Colorado 1976 elections found that the initiative process interested, motivated, and sometimes even "galvanized" voters. More people voted on the ballot measures than voted in state legislative races. "The vote for Congress statewide was also less than for any of the six initiatives on the ballot."[15] In several counties with a large proportion of voters of higher socioeconomic status, more people voted on a particular initiative than voted for the president. Interviews of a sample of voters revealed that, except for the presidential race, "there was generally much greater voter awareness on the initiative than on the candidate races."[16] Most people who were interviewed had little or no awareness of candidates running for the state legislature, and few indicated they knew which party controlled majorities in the state general assembly. In short, this study found citizens interested in and reasonably well informed on the initiative process.

On the other hand, voter understanding of candidates' positions in legislative races is usually unimpressive. Analysis of the 1978 House elections suggests that 58 percent of adults could not answer the question as to whether or not they agreed with their representative's voting record in Congress. Only 10 percent could even remember a particular bill on which their representative had voted.[17]

Ballot Position and Voter Participation

Political scientists have long been fascinated by the phenomenon called "ballot fatigue," "voter falloff," or "voter rolloff." Early studies showed a gradual decline in voter participation as the number of issues and/or candidates on a ballot increased. A generation ago, political scientist James Pollock found that whereas approximately 88 percent of Michigan voters participated on issues located first on the ballot, only 73 percent voted on the issue in the eighth position.[18] More recently, two researchers concluded the more issues there were on a ballot, the more likely voters would vote favorably on the first few and then rather blindly vote "no" thereafter.[19]

What does this mean? Too many choices, especially on issues, appeared to overburden the average voter. Some analysts concluded that proponents of populist democracy practices had overestimated the typical voters' interest in and willingness to exercise their additional political rights to the fullest. Supporters could only retort that strengthening the civic habits of a more vital democracy required more time, more experience, and more education than voters' pamphlets and the imaginative use of the media could supply.

Other evidence, however, suggests that voters pick and choose among the ballot issues and do not routinely cast the greatest number of votes for the first few ballot items and the lowest number of votes for the last ballot items. The phenomenon of ballot fatigue is exaggerated. A student of North Dakota initiatives and referenda concluded, "ballot position has very little influence, if any, upon a measure's chance for success";[20] indeed, he found seventh place the most desirable spot in terms of voter acceptance. North Dakota results also suggest a pattern that has been confirmed in other states more recently, namely that heavier voting takes place on measures arising from citizen-petition processes than on those referred to the ballot by the legislature. "Fatigue is a minor consideration when an indignant voter wants to cast his ballot against a liquor bill, gambling proposal, sales tax, cigarette tax, or pension plan," according to a study of Oregon direct democracy. "It seems not unreasonable to assume that the votes for or against those measures which have created the greatest amount of public discussion and controversy will reflect the greatest popular participation regardless of ballot position."[21]

Controversial initiatives such as the death penalty, property tax relief, banning bottles, and a severance tax often draw voters' attention to the direct legislation section of the ballot. In addition, advertising campaigns alert voters to the most controversial proposals. Most states place initiated measures after the legislature's referred measures, and initiated statutory issues right at the end of the statewide ballot. Since initiated statutory measures are commonly the most controversial ballot propositions, their presence on the ballot encourages voters to skip around and perhaps vote on the controversial items first. Controversy and ballot position are not correlated; hence voter participation and voter approval are unrelated to ballot position. "There is no evidence that a particular position on the ballot assures the success of the measure," according to one scholar; the data "indicate that the voter is willing to look over the ballot rather carefully."[22] An Arizona researcher and a student of Washington State politics report similar findings.[23]

As these reports suggest, differences in voter participation on ballot issues are neither random nor the result of ballot fatigue, but matters of voter interest and motivation. Differences in voter participation on ballot issues do not primarily reflect the location of an issue on the ballot, but rather the importance of the issue and the intensity of the campaign mounted to pass or defeat it.

The only real voter falloff or fatigue that occurs, then, is that between the number who vote for partisan candidates and those who vote on issues in general. Candidate races come first on the ballot, but other motivational factors generally explain higher voter participation in these. Thus the political party loyalty based upon party groupings that motivates many voters to vote in candidate elections is almost always absent in direct democracy campaigns. Proponents and opponents of most ballot measures do not have access to the resources of party organizations to aid them in campaigning. Moreover, candidate personalities and candidate debates (now often televised) provide a basis for choice for many voters in partisan elections for public office, whereas proposition campaigns are almost always more impersonal in character.

On balance, then, there is little evidence that position on the ballot influences either the amount of participation on ballot measures or their success or failure. Most studies suggest also that direct legislation campaigns seem to take on a life of their own, and that neither ballot position nor the presence or absence of a presidential race or a hotly contested Senate or gubernatorial race affects voter interest or the quality of ballot issue voting. To be sure, low-profile ballot issues will attract fewer voters, but the opposite is also regularly true. Referendum voters generally pick and act according to their interest in ballot measures.

Voters' Understanding of Ballot Issues

Critics of direct democracy question whether the people are informed enough to exercise good judgment on complicated policy questions. Some contend the average voter is ignorant and largely apathetic about issues appearing on the ballot. Supporters maintain that the common sense of the common citizen should not be underestimated, that a significant proportion of voters know what the issues are and how they want to vote on them. In fact, not surprisingly, voters are inadequately informed on some issues and well informed on many others. Surveys taken several weeks before an election generally indicate considerable voter confusion. However, they also show voters tend to postpone their decision on ballot issues until just before the election, *after* they have decided on how they will vote on candidates.

In two pre-election surveys conducted about seven weeks apart in 1980, Colorado voters were asked: "When you vote on the ballot issues, in general, do you feel very informed, somewhat informed, not too informed, or not at all informed about the specific issues?" Table 4.1 indicates a marked increase in voter awareness as the election neared. Seventy-eight percent of those who said they were most likely to vote felt informed about the ballot issues they would confront on the usually copious and often complex Colorado ballot. Awareness of ballot issues correlated with higher levels of education and with being older (over thirty-five), white, and Republican.

Similarly, in a 1976 exit poll of 1,500 Massachusetts voters, 79 percent considered themselves informed on "almost all of the questions," 20 percent felt informed on "some" of the questions, and only 1 percent did not feel informed on any of the questions. This same survey found voters understood best the nontechnical issues, such as proposals to have a mandatory deposit on bottles or cans, absentee voting, the Equal Rights Amendment, and handgun regulation. More technical and complicated issues, such as an oil-refining measure, a measure to create a Massachusetts Power Authority, and another

Table 4.1. Citizen awareness of ballot issues, Colorado, 1980 (%)

	"When you vote on the ballot issues, in general, do you feel very informed, somewhat informed, not too informed, or not at all informed about the specific issues?"		
	Sept. survey (N = 494)	**Late Oct. survey** (N = 1119)	**Late Oct. survey: most likely voters**[a]
Informed (very informed, somewhat informed)	57	70	78
Not informed (not too informed, not at all informed)	41	30	22

Source: Questions asked for Thomas E. Cronin by Research Services, Inc., Denver, September–October 1980.

a. Subgroup of sample of 1119.

measure "to regulate electric utility charges and permit peak load pricing," were less well understood.[24]

Political scientist James A. Meader examined voter competence and issue voting behavior in yet another way in the 1980 South Dakota elections. A variation of California's Proposition 13 property tax cut had been placed on the ballot by the initiative process. And South Dakota voters were in a conservative mood. They readily elected Ronald Reagan and handily rejected their liberal incumbent senator, George McGovern. They told survey interviewers they thought taxes were too high, and nearly half of those interviewed believed local government was inefficient and wasteful. Voters also clearly understood what "the Dakota Proposition," as it was called, would do in terms of reduced local services and diminished quality of public education. Most voters, Meader found, realized some new tax would have to replace any loss of revenue caused by adoption of this property tax cut. His analysis of both survey data and the election results led him to conclude:

> the voters are capable of taking a long-range outlook when they consider initiatives on the ballot. Rather than opt for a short-range financial benefit, the voters showed a stronger concern for maintaining those aspects of the public sector which will enhance the quality of life in South Dakota into the future.
>
> The voters evidenced a fairly high degree of sophistication and an ability to differentiate the issue on the ballot. South Dakotans voted down a tax cut despite the fact that the 1980 election in South Dakota could be characterized by a conservative landslide.[25]

Hence, Meader contends, South Dakotans exercised informed judgment and rational choices. And he is undoubtedly correct, because taxes were already relatively low in South Dakota at the time. Yet what is "rational"? Is it a vote cast in the overall public interest or in one's self-interest? The only practical conclusion is that this is a value judgment: "legislators, interest group leaders, and the informed voters might answer differently on a given measure."[26]

In 1980 a New York state senate committee wrestled with the question of voter rationality in issue elections in many different states and concluded voters have shown surprising sophistication at the polls on ballot questions. According to the committee's majority report, voters were able to look beyond self-interest and take into account what was good for the state, its government, and society. Though acknowledging that it is sometimes difficult to judge whether voters made the "right" or "wrong" decision, the committee nevertheless maintained that

in none of the 52 initiatives on the ballot in 1978 did voters approve what might be termed a "disaster" for state and society. Two of those approved might be questionable to many . . . Almost overwhelmingly, however, the voters rejected those measures which might have caused problems (including a California initiative that allowed the firing of a teacher for homosexual "conduct"—a rather loosely defined term—and an Oregon initiative repealing land use planning goals). Similarly, the voters approved the vast majority of "good" initiatives (including a North Dakota sunshine law and a restriction of parole for violent convicted felons in Michigan).

The committee also reported, however, that voters in 1978 rejected a few initiatives which many observers would have judged to be beneficial (including certain state spending increase limitations and changes in the financing of public education), as well as others which, although controversial, are thought of as "good government" issues (including bottle bills in several states and a right to work law in Missouri). Turning down "good" initiatives is a result of many factors, the two major ones are: lack of voter familiarity with the issue (when in doubt, the tendency is to vote no) and reluctance by the electorate to change the status-quo. These cases were a small minority of the 52 initiatives on the ballot that year, however, and do not represent a trend.[27]

In effect, the report found that voters can discriminate when voting on ballot measures and, more particularly, on initiatives. From a voter's perspective, most initiatives cannot be relegated neatly to a "should be passed" or "should not be passed" category. These measures are sometimes passed and sometimes defeated. Voters appreciate having the chance to express their opinion on issues. Those initiatives that most agree would be best defeated almost invariably are. Those that deserve to be passed by a discerning electorate usually become law.

However, various surveys of California voters suggest that between 10 and 30 percent of the voters are sometimes confused about their stands and often display inconsistent attitudes about their views and how they voted. Thus one analysis of voter understanding of a 1976 nuclear power plant measure found that 14 percent of the sample interviewed voted contrary to their stated intentions.[28]

Voters' confusion increases sharply when they are required to "vote no if you mean yes" or "vote yes if you mean no." Thus, in a June 1980 California election on a proposition to restrict locally passed rent control ordinances, voters wishing to keep rent control laws had to vote against the measure. A majority of those who wanted to abolish rent control voted contrary to their policy preferences, although rent control supporters were much less confused.[29]

A 1976 mail survey of registered voters who voted on ballot propositions in four western states—Arizona, Colorado, Oregon, and Washington—asked about voter levels of understanding the issues. The results suggest that most voters are at least somewhat confused when deciding about complex policy matters (see Table 4.2). For instance, all four states presented initiatives that would have restricted the development of nuclear power plants, and approximately a quarter of those who voted on them admitted they were sometimes confused

Table 4.2. Voter perceptions of ballot issue complexity in four western states, 1976 (%)

	"The initiative and referendum measures on the ballot are usually so complicated that one can't understand what is going on."				
State	Strongly agree	Somewhat agree	Neither agree nor disagree	Somewhat disagree	Strongly disagree
Arizona (N = 322)	41	33	8	13	5
Colorado (N = 333)	23	36	8	22	10
Oregon (N = 359)	20	40	6	23	12
Washington (N = 386)	18	34	8	26	14

Source: Robert C. Benedict and Lauren H. Holland, "Initiatives and Referenda in the Western United States, 1976–1980: Some Implications for a National Initiative?" (Paper presented at the American Political Science Association annual meeting, Washington, D.C., August 1980), p. 40.

by the technical arguments for and against such facilities (see Table 4.3). However, the voters expressed less confusion when they were asked about a specific ballot measure than about the process in general.

These findings led the political analysts working with these data to conclude that "people readily acknowledge the complexity of ballot propositions."[30] But this did not, the authors claim, imply voter apathy or inaction. Even on the difficult issue of nuclear power plant regulation, a high proportion of the voters cast a ballot, and nearly 95 percent voted accurately for their policy preferences. But these same data can be used, I think, to suggest that many voters are also confused and somewhat overwhelmed by the complexity of voting on highly technical policy measures. Plainly, direct legislation requires voters who are informed and who can digest and evaluate sophisticated information.

Because of this required sophistication, ballot-measure democracy sometimes works to *disfranchise* certain kinds of voters. No doubt some would-be voters are so intimidated that they stay away from the ballot box altogether. Others come and vote for candidates and for only the most publicized issues. Still others, who may vote out of

Table 4.3. **Voter perceptions of nuclear power ballot issues in four western states, 1976 (%)**

| State | "The statements made by proponents and opponents of the Nuclear Power Plant measure were so technical and confusing that I found it difficult to decide which way to vote." | | | | |
	Strongly agree	Somewhat agree	Neither agree nor disagree	Somewhat disagree	Strongly disagree
Arizona (N = 322)	6	21	15	31	29
Colorado (N = 333)	3	17	16	26	39
Oregon (N = 353)	10	23	12	33	22
Washington (N = 381)	5	19	15	35	26

Source: Robert C. Benedict and Lauren H. Holland, "Initiatives and Referenda in the Western United States, 1976–1980: Some Implications for a National Initiative?" (Paper presented at the American Political Science Association annual meeting, Washington, D.C., August 1980), p. 40.

a sense of civic duty, vote on initiatives and other measures in an unsystematic or almost random manner. A University of Michigan team offered convincing evidence on this point in a nationwide survey after the 1968 elections that treated initiatives as well as legislatively referred measures (see Table 4.4). A 1976 survey of 600 Massachusetts

Table 4.4. Referendum and nonreferendum voters characteristics, 1968 (%)

	Nonvoters	Voted for elected officials only	Voted on ballot issues
Race			
White	85	87	92
Black	13	12	7
Other	2	1	1
	(N = 286)	(N = 409)	(N = 469)
Education			
Eight grades or less	37	23	13
High school	44	51	52
Some college or more	19	27	35
	(N = 285)	(N = 409)	(N = 469)
Social class self-identification			
Working class	67	55	48
Middle class	28	36	36
Upper middle class	5	9	16
	(N = 778)	(N = 400)	(N = 449)
Read pertinent newspaper articles			
Regularly	21	35	52
Often	7	16	12
Periodically	14	22	17
Seldom	30	7	5
Did not read	48	20	14
	(N = 280)	(N = 399)	(N = 469)
Follow public affairs			
Most of the time	19	29	47
Some of the time	24	34	32
Only now and then	23	21	14
Rarely	34	16	7
	(N = 285)	(N = 408)	(N = 469)

Source: Adapted from Jerome M. Clubb and Michael W. Traugott, "National Patterns of Referenda Voting: The 1968 Election, in *People and Politics in Urban Society*, ed. Harlan Hahn (Newbury Park, Calif.: Sage Publications, 1972), pp. 137–169.

voters conducted for the *Boston Globe* reported similar findings: people with higher incomes, Republicans, liberals, and males were more likely than others to vote on ballot propositions. Lower-income voters often implied they refrained from voting when the wording of ballot issues got complicated.

As income increases, so does voting, concludes one analyst. "On the economic issues [on the Massachusetts ballot in 1976] of graduated income tax and flat-rate electricity, 32–36 percent of the low-income respondents simply did not participate. In sharp contrast, only 6 percent of those with high incomes reported that they would skip voting on these propositions."[31]

It comes as little surprise that the less well-off are underrepresented in issue elections. "For these citizens at least, voting on propositions does not lead to a more accurate representation of the popular will than [do] the traditional candidate elections."[32]

The Consequences of Who Votes on Ballot Measures

It may well be that although ballot issue voters are *somewhat less representative* of the general population, they act with considerable prudence and what might be called rationality. Further, although they may be less representative of the general population and even less representative of those who vote for partisan elected officers, they are surely more representative, in a variety of ways, than the members of state legislatures.

As we have seen, ample evidence exists to suggest that referendum voters are not only better educated but also read more, follow public affairs more, and feel more informed about voting on issues. They understand ballot issues better than do those who abstain from ballot-issue voting. Hence, we can say that those who do participate are citizens who exercise more reason in their decision to vote yes or no on measures put before them. (This is not to suggest that only those who participate in issue voting are rational citizens. The decision of some citizens not to cast votes on issue measures may also be a rational act.) In a sense, those who decide not to vote on these initiatives and referenda delegate this small aspect of policy and lawmaking to those who are better informed and to those who have a more intense interest in the outcome.

Because referendum voters are not truly representative of the general public, some analysts conclude public opinion gets misrepresented in direct democracy elections. And although it is often true that a more representative sample of the public does vote in elections for state governors (and sometimes for state legislators), it can also be argued that legislatures may misrepresent public opinion to an even greater degree than do voters in referendum elections. This is the case in part because legislators—and the activists, lobbyists, and staffs to whom they listen—have an educational and information status that is decidedly middle or even upper-middle class:

> Since higher status voters seem disproportionately liberal on economic issues, legislatures may therefore be more liberal than referendum voters on these issues. The idea that legislators may be more liberal on many noneconomic issues as well is supported by the impression . . . that a disproportionate number of the apparently few conservative proposals on the ballot . . . were put there by citizen initiative rather than through legislative action . . . So while referendum voters may sometimes over-represent certain opinions more than the partisan electorate, the imperfection of the linkages between the electorate and those elected may mean that, nonetheless, the policies made by referenda better reflect public opinion than those that result from partisan election.[33]

The costs of obtaining information are sufficiently burdensome on certain people to preclude their participation. Nearly a quarter of voters and even more nonvoters in some studies report that voting wisely on initiatives is very difficult for them.[34]

This does not mean, however, that citizens would willingly abdicate this opportunity or responsibility. On the contrary, 86 percent of a Seattle sample disagreed with the idea that all state issues should be decided by the state legislature. Most people also said that voting on issues was important to them. Moreover, voters said by a two-to-one margin that voting on initiatives was as important as or more important than voting for candidates for governor and other statewide offices (see Table 4.5). A study in Toledo, Ohio, found similar support for direct legislation election: 80 percent of those surveyed disagreed with the assertion that "the City Council should decide all local issues instead of having elections on issues,"[35] even though a majority acknowledged they needed more information in order to vote wisely on a fair housing measure.

Americans repeatedly tell pollsters in state surveys that they would

Table 4.5. Citizen support for initiative process, Seattle, 1973 (%) (N = 399)

Issue	Agree	Disagree	No answer
The state legislature should decide all state issues instead of having initiative elections on issues.	9	86	5
Voting on state candidates (i.e., governor, attorney general, etc.) is generally more important to me than voting for initiatives.	28	59	13
Initiatives that are passed can have a great effect on how I live my life.	73	19	9

Source: Robert C. Benedict, "Some Aspects of the Direct Legislation Process in Washington State: Theory and Practice, 1914–1973" (Ph.D. diss., University of Washington, 1975), p. 193.

be more inclined to vote and more likely to be interested and participate in elections if they had the opportunity to vote on occasional proposed laws. This does not necessarily mean they do so when they get the chance; yet two-thirds of 989 registered voters in a 1982 California survey agreed with the statement: "Citizens ought to be able to vote on important issues and policies instead of having their representatives voting for them."[36] Similarly, two-thirds of a national sample of 1,009 Americans in a 1987 Gallup Organization survey agreed that citizens should be able to vote directly on some state and local laws "if enough people signed a petition to put an issue on the ballot."[37] An impressive 76 percent of the same survey disagreed with the assertion that the people would not be able to cast an informed vote in direct democracy elections at the state and local levels and thus should trust elected officials to make public decisions on all the issues. Only 18 percent agreed with that assertion; the vast majority favored voters' having a direct say in making laws on certain issues (see Table 4.6).

Where and How Voters Get Their Information

Crucial to the theory of direct democracy is the notion that it would encourage most voters to become informed about ballot propositions and to know some arguments both for and against measures

Table 4.6. Citizen confidence in direct democracy elections, 1987 (%)
(N = 1009)

"Opponents of referendums and recall elections say people won't be able to cast informed votes and we should trust our elected representatives to make public decisions. Supporters of referendums and recall elections say people are able to cast informed votes and deserve more of a say in government. What is your opinion—should we trust our elected officials to make public decisions on all issues, or should the voters have a direct say on some issues?"

Voters should have a direct say	76
Trust public officials to make laws	18
Don't know	6

Source: Gallup Organization, "The Gallup Study of Public Opinion regarding Direct Democracy Devices," conducted for Thomas E. Cronin (Princeton, N.J., September 1987).

on the ballot. Ideally, the voter would also know who the measure's principal supporters and opponents were.

This ideal situation still eludes us. Well-educated citizens—including political science professors, journalists, and even state officials—often are unsure how they should vote on certain issues, even though ample information is available. The remaining problem is that it requires time to gather as well as digest that information. And in certain circumstances it is just too difficult to predict the exact consequences and side effects of a ballot proposition. Even a state official who prepares Colorado's election-year pamphlet on initiatives has confessed to some confusion: "I write the pros and cons that go into the official state booklet [that goes out to officials and the media], and I also work for the state legislature [deputy director, Legislative Counsel's office], but, in all honesty, I sometimes don't know what's the guts of an issue; that is, what the consequences of it would be if the voters passed it."[38]

Some states prepare a voter information pamphlet that is sent to all households and gives the content of ballot issues as well as arguments for and against them. Where these pamphlets are available (California, Massachusetts, Montana, Oregon, and Washington), estimates are that between 30 and 60 percent of those who go to the polls read them and rely on them as an important source of information.

Officials in the secretary of state's offices praise these voter pamphlets and claim they are a major reason for good turnout and participation rates in their states. A Montana elections official, for example, said the pamphlet "gets great praise in our state. People take it with them to the polls and have already decided how they will vote and have marked it on their voter pamphlet. It definitely increases voter interest. I think we had the fourth highest turnout rate in the nation last year."[39]

Oregon's voter pamphlet probably provides the most extensive information on the pros and cons of all ballot issues as well as on state and local candidates. In a survey of 1,204 Oregon citizens in 1970, 45 percent said they had read "all or most" of the pamphlet; 69 percent rated the quality of the information it contained "excellent" or "pretty good."[40] (See also Table 4.7.)

Studies in Massachusetts and Seattle also indicate that where voter pamphlets are available, voters claim to read some or all of them and consider them a valuable resource in helping them decide how they will vote. In Seattle, for example, most voters have repeatedly told interviewers that they rely on the state's voter pamphlet as their chief source of information on propositions. A respected political scientist concluded: "it seems obvious that a clear, high-quality official voter pamphlet is essential if wise policy outcomes are to be derived from the use of direct legislation and from judgments on the increasing number of legislatively referred statutes and constitutional amendments."[41] As Table 4.8 shows, 75 percent of Massachusetts voters coming to the polls in 81 precincts in 1976 said they had made some or a lot of use of the state's voter information booklet.

Despite these data, critics have found fault with voter pamphlets.

Table 4.7. **Perceived usefulness of voter pamphlet, Oregon, 1970 (%)** (N = 1204)

"How useful is the voters' pamphlet in helping voters decide how to vote?"				
Type of election	Very	Somewhat	Little or no	Not sure
Ballot measures	41	38	19	2
Statewide and congressional races	16	43	37	4
Legislative and county races	19	48	30	4

Source: Donald G. Balmer, *State Election Services in Oregon,* 1972 (Princeton, N.J.: Citizens' Research Foundation, 1972), p. 42.

Table 4.8. Information sources for ballot issue voting, Massachusetts, 1976 (%) (N = 1546)

"There are a lot of different ways that people get their information. I have a list of several sources of information on the ballot questions. As I read them off, I would like you to tell me whether you used them in deciding how to vote today . . . Would you say you made a lot of use, some use, little use, or you didn't use [the source] at all?"

| Information source | Level of use | | | |
	A lot	Some	A little	Did not use
Mass. *Information for Voters* pamphlet	59	16	6	19
Newspaper reports	39	34	13	14
Television news reports	32	32	17	19
Radio news or talk shows	21	34	19	26
Paid advertising on ballot questions	10	22	21	46
Advice of friends	7	21	23	49
Information from employers	3	6	9	82

Source: Secretary of state's exit poll survey in 81 precincts across Massachusetts, November 2, 1976 (Mimeograph).

One political scientist decried the California booklet as full of "impenetrable prose" and doubted it really helped people to vote more intelligently. Others claim these booklets usually "just put people to sleep."[42] A recent analysis of California surveys finds evidence that the voter handbooks are not widely read: "In highly contested proposition elections, the pamphlet ranks well behind television, newspapers, and often the radio as a source of information. Even on the less contested propositions, no more than a third of the voters report using the pamphlet as a source of information." Thus, it concludes, "survey evidence indicates that most voters do not read the pamphlet or use it as a source of information for decisions on propositions."[43]

To be sure, there is a class or "educational status" bias in who reads the pamphlets. Current literacy campaigns imply that from 15 to 20 percent of American adults either cannot read or have very low reading ability. No voter pamphlets can solve this more fundamental problem. Yet the commonsense verdict has to be that, better designed and prepared, they could be valuable and should be encouraged for those who can read. The challenge is how to make them attractive, readable, accessible, and relevant as a voter resource.

Other main sources of information on ballot measures are newspapers, television, advertisements, family, and friends. In states not having a voter pamphlet, television and radio obviously take on greater importance. Put another way, the fewer the sources of information, the more influential are the media and paid advertisements. In Colorado, for instance, there is evidence to suggest that some voters are influenced by clever, simpleminded, and often deceptive television advertisements: they often repeat to survey interviewers those advertisements' precise arguments and slogans as their reasons for voting one way or another.[44]

In the absence of party cues and (in most states) voter pamphlets, the typical voter is pretty much forced to rely on newspapers and television. The well educated typically get more of their information from reading than from television; the average working-class voters, on the other hand, usually depend on television ads and thus are more subject to manipulated "information."

On balance, a variety of sources are usually available to those who seek information before voting on ballot measures. However, some busy voters may go to the polls without any knowledge of the proposals to be voted upon. The quality of information varies from state to state and depends very much on the availability of a state-prepared voter pamphlet and on coverage of the issues by newspapers and television stations within the state. My own experience with ballot issue campaigns suggests that media coverage, even in good state newspapers, is typically thin and late. Clearly, the number and kinds of issues on the ballot affect the amount and quality of information generally available. The size of the state is yet another factor. In a small state such as North Dakota, "People learn by word of mouth if it is on a pocketbook issue."[45] In larger states such as Massachusetts, California, or Colorado, information dispersion can become a problem. Good television access or advertisements in newspapers and major media markets are expensive, and thus serve as resources only to those who have money. Money does not necessarily always buy the desired outcome, but large sums of money can often be a major factor, if not *the* major factor, in influencing voter attitudes (as will be discussed in Chapter 5).

The quality of information available to today's average voter is not as good as the early proponents of direct legislation had intended.

The system is far from perfect. However, voters do not get extensive or reliable information on candidates either. Improvements are needed in both areas (as will be discussed in Chapter 9).

How Voters Make Up Their Minds

Most voters spend little time thinking about initiatives and referenda until election day nears, although they often tell pollsters weeks in advance of an election that they like an idea contained in a proposed initiative. Initial favorable reaction, especially to nice-sounding "improvements," "reforms," "relief," or "consumer protection," is not uncommon. Organizations that have initiated ballot measures usually go to some length to come up with an appealing title and a catchy acronym to attract attention to their efforts for change. But it is seldom until a week or so before election time that citizens adopt a fixed view on a new proposal. California public opinion expert Mervin Field explains the dynamic aspects of the process:

> An initiative ballot proposition as it is first presented to voters in summary form appears to fill a need or correct a situation in which a large segment of the public is in sympathy. Initially, while not many people fully grasp all the details and ramifications, their instinctive reaction is generally favorable. Then the issue is joined by the opposition, usually well after the initiative qualifies and is placed on the ballot. Typically, the public only becomes fully aware of the opposition to the measure relatively late in the campaign, sometimes only a few weeks before election day. Then, if the force and extent of opposition to the proposal are considerable, public awareness of the measure increases dramatically. And more times than not the original instinctive support of the idea is replaced by a negative view.[46]

In ballot issue contests voters change their minds more than in partisan candidate elections. A variety of factors can influence such change: *intense interest group organization work* (by, say, the AFL-CIO, Common Cause, taxpayers associations); *prominent endorsement from opinion leaders* (such as a governor or recently retired public officials); *clever paid television or billboard advertisements* (such as advertisements opposed to severance taxes, graduated income taxes, smoking in public places); and *large sums of money used in other ways* (for example, on radio, subsidizing community organizations, and mass mailings). "It seems easier," writes John S. Shockley, "to sow seeds of confusion about initiatives (which will lead people to vote against them) than to get voters to support measures positively."[47]

According to the conventional wisdom, ballot issue voters are cautious and will vote against proposed changes unless they can clearly perceive some tangible personal or public benefit. Early opponents of direct democracy speculated that direct legislation processes would beget a torrent of unsound and radical legislation, but this has happened infrequently. Students of the initiative in some states claim that conservatives have often used the initiative and referendum to thwart progressive legislation.[48] Yet the expected threat of demagoguery has not materialized. Liberal and conservative measures appear to win with about equal frequency, apparently depending on shifts in the voters' mood and the degree of change involved. Voters appear to exercise caution in the case of extremist or radical measures, left and right. Support for the "cautious voter" theory is provided by findings that about two-thirds of the citizen-initiated measures appearing on statewide ballots have been rejected. "When in doubt, vote no" is the general attitude. In fact, organized "Vote no on all the issues" campaigns are frequent, usually because opponents know that negative responses are easy to secure. A slogan such as "No-No-No" is often effective.

An excellent example is a "no" campaign that took place during a 1939 North Dakota special election. Four measures were on the ballot, three of which involved controversial pension plans for the aged. A coalition organized to counter these three measures promoted an all-out "Vote no" effort and decisively defeated all four measures by a four-to-one margin. In the process, however, an unrelated and innocent measure abolishing the office of grain commissioner was also rejected. This measure had passed by a unanimous vote in both houses of the state legislature after the duties of the commissioner had been clearly shown to be nonexistent, and thus the position absolutely unnecessary. "Had the people voted intelligently, they would have overwhelmingly sustained the law."[49]

A major "Vote no" campaign was mounted by industry, unions, and public officials to defeat Proposition 4 in Colorado's 1986 election. A citizen-initiated measure, Proposition 4 would have placed extensive restrictions on public bodies to raise new taxes. Sponsored by antitax or "tax revolt" groups, it enjoyed impressive three-to-one support in the initial polls. The "Vote no" campaign, aiming to raise strong doubts about its possible negative side effects, stressed that voters should read the "fine print" about this initiative—implying that it would undermine responsible local government efforts to deal with the effects of floods and other natural disasters such as rebuilding schools that had caught fire. Virtually the entire opposition media campaign sought to alarm voters about the damage that might be caused by this "wrongheaded" measure. The proposition was resoundingly defeated.

Voters will support the status quo unless they are given clear arguments for changing it, especially if each side of a proposition presents a plausible case and challenges the veracity of the other side. Such was the case when tax reform measures passed in Oregon, but failed in Massachusetts. In the Oregon "tax substitution referendum," tax rates and the base of a sales tax proposed as an alternative to a property tax were specified on the ballot. Voters understood the impact on themselves and voted to maximize their narrowly defined economic self-interest.[50] In Massachusetts, however, proponents of a proposed graduated income tax failed to state the most likely base and tax rate structure that would be enacted if their initiative passed. The result: voters rejected the measure—even though in many cases to vote against it was contrary to maximizing their economic self-interest. These examples suggest that *ambiguity* is generally an asset to opponents.

A further example of how doubts and confusion can help thwart the adoption of an initiative occurred in the 1978 California campaign to stop Proposition 5. Proposition 5, which would have prohibited smoking in most public places and would also have required non-smoking sections, enjoyed a 58 to 38 percent level of support in the September polls. But it was handily rejected in the November election and again in 1980. One of the effective tactics in the anti–Proposition 5 arsenal was ridicule. "Radio commercials against the initiative portray confused policemen and citizens trying to sort out the differences between jazz concerts and amateur boxing matches, where smoking would be illegal, and rock concerts and professional fights, where smoking would be allowed."[51] Opponents had sheriffs saying that this kind of law would be nearly impossible to administer and enforce. The opposition also put up billboards suggesting that if big brother (the government) was now going to be able to tell you where you could and could not smoke, what would be regulated next? How next, in other words, would government intrude on our privacy? This campaign, financed in large part by the tobacco industry, bred confusion, doubt, and even fear and helped reverse the tide of popular opinion on this measure.

Critics sometimes point to the June 1978 passage of California's controversial Proposition 13 property tax relief measure as a case in which the people were somehow manipulated or duped. But voters knew what they were doing: information levels were high; opponents had their say. "In simple terms," wrote Mervin Field, "hesitant voters heard the opposition arguments and were not persuaded."[52] Voters understood the trade-off; fewer government services in exchange for tax relief. The two-thirds who voted yes wanted to send a message as well as secure economic benefits for themselves. That message was at least twofold: give us back some of the revenue surplus the state government is sitting on, and cut out waste and needless bureaucratic programs. Massachusetts voters acted along the same line. Proposition 2½, a 1980 property tax cut measure, was a major jolt to local governments. But it was a jolt Massachusetts voters intended. They wanted their city councils and administrators to squirm. They wanted reductions in bureaucracies as well as tax relief. Voters knew what they wanted to do, and subsequent studies suggest that these tax cuts did not hamper economic development or severely impair city services.

Conclusion

How competent, informed, and rational are ballot issue voters? Not as competent as we would like them to be, yet not as ill informed or irrational as critics often insist.

Critics of direct legislation frequently have a view of state legislators that borders on the mythical: highly intelligent; extremely well informed; as rational as a virtuous, wise, and deliberative statesman; and as competent as corporate presidents and university professors. These same critics tend to view the people as a "mob," unworthy of being trusted. Yet the people, or so-called mob, are the same persons who elect legislators. How is it that they can choose between good and bad candidates but cannot choose between good and bad laws?

Experience in the states suggests that on most issues, especially well-publicized ones, voters do grasp the meaning of the issue on which they are asked to vote, and that they act competently. Political scientist Betty Zisk's research on direct ballot voting provides evidence contradicting the once-conventional pessimistic verdicts about voter confusion and negative voting: "Long ballots do *not* seem to cause consistent patterns of either negative voting or a drop in participation at the end of the ballot. Nor do 'difficult' propositions (in substance or in wording) invariably evoke negative reactions."[53]

Early in an initiative campaign there is a tendency for voters to polarize, perhaps jumping to premature conclusions on an issue. Yet, after initial advertisements and when information begins to become available, a majority of those who are likely to vote begin to think about the issue. Most voters, when election day nears, seek out additional information and are willing to think seriously about ballot measures and to change their views. Manipulation by direct mail or media blitzes still occurs, yet with proper regulations and multiple sources of information, educated voters should be increasingly able to cast informed votes on ballot measures.

There are, to be sure, notable deficiencies in the popular democracy procedures. Advocates of the initiative and referendum overemphasize the average citizen's current interest in and willingness to work at becoming more informed; less well educated, younger, and some minority voters often remain unmotivated to study the issues appearing on their ballots. Although this situation may change in the years ahead, information costs remain high for the average citizen. Complex ballot issues often require more homework than a third or more of the electorate are willing to do. Too few states have made the effort to regulate the process to the point where information and clarifying evidence are sufficiently available to their voters.

Voter pamphlets—even if made available in more states—cannot, alone, provide a solution. These pamphlets, or comparable advertisements in the newspapers or public service spots on the electronic media, should aim at helping the average voter grasp the basic issues. Considerable ingenuity will be needed to make these both interesting and informative, yet nothing less than that should be the goal of states that want to rely on these populist voting devices. As several students of direct democracy have suggested, a variety of state-sponsored advertisements in major newspapers also should be tried as an alternative or supplement to voter pamphlets. To be sure, only about a third of the public carefully reads daily newspapers, yet these are the same citizens who regularly vote. And they are also the people who influence or trigger word-of-mouth communications in most communities. We have not really begun to prepare voters for the challenge of citizenship in a strong democracy. Just putting initiatives on the ballot has not automatically triggered heightened civic education and participation, as some reformers implied would result.

Voters who do vote on ballot measures do so more responsibly and intelligently than we have any right to expect. Voters can make rational decisions at the voting booth; they can discern costs and benefits and the various trade-offs often involved in ballot issues. Further regulation would improve the process (see Chapter 9). But what two analysts concluded about the competence of Oregon voters in the 1950s still applies to voters elsewhere:

> Over the long period, the electorate is not likely to do anything more foolish than the legislature is likely to do. The legislature emerges from the people and clearly cannot differ too radically from it . . . both the legislature and the electorate have had and will have their periods of legislative "sagacity" . . . both of them have "erred" and will "err." Whatever weakness may exist in this situation is not inherent in the direct legislation process. That the people, acting for themselves or through representatives, may someday enact a proposal that proves to be politically, economically, or socially catastrophic must be conceded. That risk is not great.[54]

Legislators, political analysts, and others whom I have interviewed around the country concur in this verdict. All say they would prefer to see stronger legislatures, stronger and more responsible parties, and higher voter turnout, but few could cite any negative results of popular democratic procedures. These same respondents often acknowledge that the legislative processes in their states leave much to be desired and acknowledge that even with staffs, hearings, bicameralism, and the other features of representative democracy, mistakes are made and defective bills are enacted into law by the legislature. Moreover, the Supreme Court has overturned at least 1,000 laws passed by state and local legislatures on the grounds that they were unconstitutional— additional evidence that state legislators do not have a monopoly on wisdom, rationality, or virtue.

Closely examined, the competence of both the ballot issue voter and the legislature can be questioned. As a practical matter, the competence and rationality levels of both can stand improvement. The charge, however, that voters are not competent enough to decide on occasional issues put before them is usually exaggerated.

▼

CHAPTER 5

Minority Rights, Money, and the Media

▼

The big problem with ballot proposals is that the outcome is subject to being swayed by big money, especially through TV blitzes.

—Kenneth T. Walsh, 1980

As long as wealth is as unequally distributed as it is in American society, and political interest groups are organized around private rather than public rewards, ballot proposition campaigns, like American politics generally, will reflect the power of the best organized and wealthiest groups in society.

—John S. Shockley, 1985

THREE additional major concerns about the use of direct democracy devices are that tyranny by the majority will, through such devices, help to diminish the rights and liberties of the politically powerless; that large sums of money can be used to shape and confuse voters' attitudes on specific ballot measures; and that those who can afford access to the mass media can unduly influence the outcome of direct ballot lawmaking.

Direct Democracy and Minorities

Fear of tyranny by the majority has haunted Americans since the nation's founding. John Adams and Alexander Hamilton were especially concerned. Adams said the people, even in representative assemblies, were not the best keepers of the people's liberties. "At least the majority of them would invade the liberties of the minority, sooner and oftener than any absolute monarch."[1] Hamilton likewise warned:

It is of great importance in a republic, not only to guard the society against the oppression of its rulers; but to guard one part of the society against the injustice of the other part. Different interests necessarily exist in different classes of citizens. If a majority be united by a common interest, the rights of the minority will be insecure . . . Justice is the end of government. It is the end of civil society . . . In a society under the forms of which the stronger faction can readily unite and oppress the weaker, anarchy may as truly be said to reign as in a state of nature where the weaker individual is not secured against the violence of the stronger.[2]

The framers of the Constitution sought to resolve this conflict by instituting an indirect or qualified democracy, a representative form of government with an extensive system of checks and balances. Representative government was to be an essential means of protecting the civil liberties and civil rights of the powerless. It was assumed that the legislatures would attract prudent, wise, and conscientious men, a natural aristocracy that would rise above mindless emotionalism and would protect citizens' rights. The ordinary citizen, without the time or inclination for reflection and thus more given to local, religious, racial, or ethnic prejudice, would be less able than a legislator to handle the intricacies of minority rights and less able to provide fair-minded political judgment on complicated issues.

But the record of representative government is an imperfect one. Sometimes state legislatures have materially impaired civil liberties. Historian Henry Steele Commager cites examples:

A cumulative list of these might well dishearten even the most optimistic Jeffersonian. Censorship laws, anti-evolution laws, flag-salute laws, red-flag laws, anti-syndicalists, anti-socialist, anti-communist laws, sedition and criminal-anarchy laws, anti-contraceptive information laws—these and others come all too readily to mind. The New York legislature purged itself of socialists; the Massachusetts legislature imposed loyalty oaths on teachers; the Oregon legislature outlawed private schools and the Nebraska legislature forbade the teaching of German in public schools; the Tennessee legislature prohibited the teaching

of evolution; the Pennsylvania legislature authorized the requirement of a flag-salute from school children; the Louisiana
legislature imposed a discriminatory tax upon newspapers . . .
The list could be extended indefinitely.[3]

Legislatures and courts also committed widespread injustices against
Americans of Japanese descent during the 1940s. At least 120,000
people, most of them U.S. citizens, were ordered out of the West Coast
states where they lived and placed in "relocation" or detention camps
for the duration of World War II, despite the fact that no Japanese-
American was ever charged with, much less convicted of, domestic
espionage or sabotage.

To be sure, elected leaders and court officials more often have
protected Americans' liberties and often have even extended their
rights. But mistakes have been made. And, on occasion, legislatures
have capitulated to the prejudices of the larger population.

Proposals to adopt direct democracy procedures have always
prompted fears that the system of checks and balances and the filtering
effects of the legislative process would be bypassed, opening up even
greater possibilities for abuses of minority rights and civil liberties.
Yet the initiative and referendum record suggests that those direct
democracy devices can only rarely be faulted for impairing the rights
of the powerless. Even a general comparison of the results of ballot
measures with those of legislatures reveals that although both direct
and representative lawmaking have occasionally diminished the liberties of the politically powerless, neither can be singled out as more
prone to this tendency.

Since 1900, when various direct democracy procedures were enacted in several states and countless local governments, few measures
that would have the effect of narrowing civil rights and civil liberties
have been put before the voters, and most of those have been defeated.
On those occasions when limiting or narrowing measures have been
approved, there is little evidence state legislatures would have acted
differently, and some evidence state legislators or legislatures actually
encouraged the result.

The most notable cases of majority disregard for minorities' rights
have related to racial discrimination. Oklahomans initiated a "grand-
father clause" amendment to their state constitution, establishing an
educational requirement for voting, but in effect applied it to blacks
while exempting poorly educated whites. The initiative, signed by

43,400 citizens in thirty-three days, was approved in 1910 by a vote of 135,443 to 106,222. Democratic legislators and party leaders championed the measure. Lee Cruce, the Democratic nominee for governor that year, was strongly in favor of it, saying that "if we place the franchise in the hands of the ignorant Negro it will make Oklahoma a dumping ground for those of the whole United States."[4] But this initiative had been approved in both chambers of the state legislature and had actually been drafted and introduced by state legislators. The public and the legislature were equally at fault. In 1915 the measure was invalidated by the U.S. Supreme Court. The next year, Democratic legislators again attempted to disfranchise black voters, passing a new measure that avoided the wording struck down by the Court. Again they readily obtained the required signatures. However, this time the voters roundly rejected this blatantly antiblack measure.

California voters similarly expressed their cultural prejudices in 1920 by approving an anti-Japanese initiative that amended the state's alien land law. Again the measure began in the legislature, which then delayed action because of certain foreign policy ramifications and because the U.S. secretary of state cabled from an international peace conference that California action on this measure might jeopardize the results of the conference. But after the legislature had adjourned the measure was introduced as an initiative and approved by the voters by a three-to-one margin. The act prohibited ownership of land by corporations controlled by persons ineligible for naturalization; prohibited such persons from acquiring control of land through appointment of their minor children of American birth as guardians; and abrogated for three years the right to lease land, a privilege that had existed under a 1913 alien land law. The demand for this legislation had come from farmers and farm laborers who felt adversely affected by expanding Japanese agricultural communities; yet it was also favored by a variety of legislative and political leaders throughout the state, including the governor and the owner of the *Sacramento Bee*.[5]

Earlier this century voters in Arizona approved an initiative requiring at least 80 percent of the employees of any person or company employing six or more individuals to be U.S. citizens. Initiatives in Colorado, Washington, and California have either forbidden or in some way restricted busing to achieve racial balance in the schools. Most Americans clearly dislike such "forced busing." Survey data also indicate that minority precincts often support some of these busing curbs. Washington's 1976 antibusing measure was ruled unconstitutional by the courts. Judges held racial discrimination as a factor in the success of the measure.

There have been rare but clear-cut cases in which voters at large were decidedly less caring about minority rights than were legislators. In the early 1960s the California legislature had passed a law prohibiting racial discrimination by realtors and owners of apartment houses and homes built with public assistance. California's real estate interests, which had opposed the legislation, sought to repeal the law with a 1964 initiative. In an emotional and heavily financed campaign the realtors won a two-to-one victory, with almost 96 percent of Californians voting on this measure.

At the local level there is evidence that direct legislation devices have impaired racial equality. According to law professor Derrick A. Bell, Jr., the referendum has been a most effective facilitator of the bias, discrimination, and prejudice that have marred American democracy from its beginning. In his view, the emotionally charged atmosphere often surrounding direct legislative campaigns can easily reduce voter tolerance in deciding measures. A survey of several zoning and low-income housing referendum campaigns led him to conclude that the record of ballot legislation "reflects all too accurately the conservative, even intolerant, attitudes citizens display when given the chance to vote their fears and prejudices, especially when exposed to expensive media campaigns. The security of minority rights and the value of racial equality which those rights affirm are endangered by the possibility of popular repeals."[6] Between 1963 and 1968, for example, ten cities and the state of California conducted open-housing referenda, all of them initiated by opponents of fair-housing measures. Those opponents were successful in all but one case.

The one difficulty with Bell's analysis is that votes on low-income housing proposals involve factors other than racial prejudice. Low-income housing projects affect appreciation and resale values of existing homes in their area and raise questions of population density, traffic flow, and so forth. Nor did Bell compare the local referenda with the proceedings of city councils; so there is no way of knowing whether people in those localities were less tolerant than their representatives.

The issue of gay rights provides yet another example of majorities' occasional disregard for the rights of minorities. Usually the issue arises at the city or county level when a local legislature approves some form of ordinance that bans discrimination against homosexuals in terms of employment or housing. Perhaps Dade County (Miami area), Florida, is the most famous case; but Boulder, Colorado; St. Paul, Minnesota; Eugene, Oregon; and San Jose, California, are among other communities that have witnessed popular repeal by initiative or referendum of similar gay rights ordinances. In San Jose in 1980 local "moral majority" groups raised ample signatures to force a referendum on ordinances passed earlier that year by the city council and the Santa Clara County Board of Supervisors. "Our whole theme was, 'Don't Let It Spread,'" said San Jose's anti–gay rights referendum leader. The emotional level of this campaign was captured in the following postelection newspaper account:

> During the campaign, religious leaders fought the ordinances on moral grounds, pointing to nearby San Francisco, where a large population of homosexuals is much in evidence and exercises substantial political power.
>
> Televised advertisements showed a girl crying in a park, surrounded by homosexuals and lesbians. Widely distributed brochures contained photos of homosexuals embracing, partly nude or dressed in drag. Public "demands" by homosexual activists—including "gay quotas" for colleges—were circulated as evidence of gay militancy.
>
> Supporters of the ordinances accused opponents of lies and distortions, contending the issue was civil rights, not morals. In the last few days before the election, scores of posters opposing the ordinances disappeared almost as fast as they were put up.
>
> Voters rejected the county ordinance 244,095 to 103,479. The city ordinance was defeated 109,238 to 35,957.[7]

In Boulder, Colorado, a city councilman was recalled because of his favorable vote on a pro–gay rights city ordinance. Boulder's mayor at the time just barely escaped recall in the same case.

This pattern of defeat for gay rights ordinances suggests majority disapproval for homosexual relations. Public intolerance on this subject remains high throughout the country except in communities such as San Francisco, where because of their numbers gays have gained significant political and economic influence. Only a few dozen cities have passed progay ordinances; and it is in those communities that repeal by direct vote has occurred. Plainly, those local elected officials have been more willing than the general public to protect gay rights and liberties.

Californians, however, rejected a 1978 statewide initiative restricting gay rights. Led by California state representative John Briggs, Proposition 6 placed on the ballot a measure that would have severely limited the rights of homosexual public school teachers, permitting school boards to fire any teacher who advocated, solicited, encouraged, or promoted public or private homosexual activity. Initial public surveys indicated that California's voters would approve the measure by a two-to-one majority, but extensive public debate and media coverage of the issue helped to change public attitudes. An impressive number of political officials opposed the measure, including Ronald Reagan, the then-retired two-term governor of the state. Reagan's public opposition apparently helped to change the attitude on this issue, especially among conservative Republicans.[8] The proposition lost.

Such was also the fate of a 1986 California initiative—sponsored by followers of fringe political activist Lyndon LaRouche—which sought to add AIDS to the state's list of communicable diseases and would have empowered state health authorities to quarantine AIDS victims. "Despite grave statewide concern about the growing problem of AIDS, California voters universally repudiated the efforts of the LaRouche organization by a margin of 29 to 71 percent."[9]

Californians did, however, approve in 1986 a measure making English the official language of that state. The measure was primarily a formal declaration that English was California's "official language" and that the state's legislature would take care to ensure that this goal was achieved and not undermined. A Republican state legislator who served as cochair of this "Yes on 63" initiative made clear during the campaign that he would work in the next session of the legislature to clarify legislation requiring essential services such as police, fire, and paramedic units to retain multilingual capabilities. His clarifying efforts apparently allayed the fears of some of the measure's opponents.[10]

A former Republican U.S. senator, S. I. Hayakawa, heads a California group that sought passage of this and similar initiatives in other states. Hayakawa argued that the language measure should be passed to express symbolic disapproval of increasing acceptance of "ethnic separation," "linguistic pluralism," and the erosion of English as Americans' common bond. Not surprisingly, many Hispanic and Asian organizations viewed this California proposition as racist and a setback for multilingual education programs. They feared, too, that it would increase discrimination against many immigrants.

This and other language issues will undoubtedly be debated in future referendum campaigns, just as they are the subject of debate and hearings in legislative and judicial processes throughout the nation.

Another civil rights issue that has appeared on the ballot over the years involves women: first female suffrage and, more recently, the proposed Equal Rights Amendment (ERA) to the Constitution. Several states placed the question of female suffrage on the ballot before 1920. Missouri, Nebraska, Ohio, Oregon, and Colorado all voted against the measures. However, after several failed attempts, initiative petition in Colorado and Oregon granted the vote to women. Voters in Wyoming (in adopting its constitution) and in Arizona (by initiative petition) also granted women the vote years before the U.S. Constitution was finally amended to permit women's suffrage.

Equal protection for women has been a ballot issue in over half the states. By one count it has been approved on eighteen occasions and defeated on nine, including negative votes in Maine in 1984 and Vermont in 1986.[11] The list of victories includes one Colorado referendum in which voters rejected an initiative that would have repealed an earlier endorsement of various forms of an equal rights amendment at the state level.

Historically, women's rights and equal rights initiatives have fared well at the polls. However, since 1973, when the national ERA measure had been approved by two-thirds of both houses of Congress and appeared to be quickly moving toward ratification, opponents of ERA have defeated statewide initiatives in such normally progressive states as Wisconsin, New Jersey, New York, and Maine. When national polls consistently suggest public support for the ERA concept, why then have these measures failed?

One analyst, Patrick B. McGuigan, has studied the statewide initiatives on these matters and believes the national polls underestimate the intensity of voter opposition. He also believes that the anti-ERA forces, especially Phyllis Schlafly's STOP ERA organization and, to a lesser extent, certain Catholic church leaders, have achieved a degree of success by building on the latent negative voting tendency. McGuigan, the editor of *Initiative and Referendum Report*, also claims that profamily arguments against state ERAs were effective in creating doubts about the ERA. "For the most part," he contends, "these arguments focus on what the courts *might* do with an ERA. So long as the ERA can be plausibly described as requiring massive changes in (a) the legal, social and cultural status of women (including their entry into combat), (b) the legal treatment of homosexuality, (c) taxpayer funding of abortions and (d) assorted other legal, moral and social questions, significant numbers of potential supporters will pass ultimately negative judgments on the ERA."[12]

McGuigan's assessment is that of an archconservative, but the reasons he cites for the defeat of several ERA measures appear to be valid. The Republican party and Ronald Reagan adopted a similar rationale for opposing these same equal rights initiatives.

Are direct democracy devices being exploited by those who seek to narrow the range of minority rights? Do these measures appeal to the emotions and frustrations of majorities, becoming merely thinly veiled attempts to trivialize or dilute certain minority rights and liberties?

Voters in some states have occasionally used these devices to express nativism, racism, and sexism against specific minority groups. Yet the overall record suggests that American voters have in most cases approved measures protecting or promoting minority rights, almost as often as institutions of representative government, with which they must be compared. "Even non-voting groups—such as women . . . have found the initiative process useful to make their case to end discrimination against them. Male voters signed petitions for state women's suffrage amendments frequently enough, and in sufficient numbers, to qualify suffrage initiatives for state ballots in several states prior to World War I."[13] And all-male electors in several states approved such measures.

Although a majority of people in a 1987 national survey said they believed minorities or minority rights would get a fair hearing in direct democracy elections at the state and local levels, about a third were skeptical or doubtful (see Table 5.1). A significantly higher proportion of blacks said minority rights would not get a fair say, even though almost the same percentage of blacks and whites support direct democracy procedures such as the initiative, referendum, and recall.

If we are to give occasional free rein to majority rule at the ballot box, we shall have to give additional consideration to protecting the rights of minorities. The willingness to be tolerant of ideas or people that one finds objectionable will always depend on an education in appropriate democratic and social values. This idealistic prescription remains our best hope and safeguard; Chapter 9 discusses several practical safeguards and strategies.

Table 5.1. Citizen opinion about the impact of direct democracy devices on minority rights, 1987 (%) (N = 1009)

"If people were allowed to vote directly on important issues at the state and local level do you think that the opinions of minority groups in the population would or would not get a fair say?"

Would get a fair say	58
Would not get a fair say	32
Don't know	10

Source: Gallup Organization, "The Gallup Study of Public Opinion regarding Direct Democracy Devices," conducted for Thomas E. Cronin, (Princeton, N.J., September 1987).

The Influence of Money in Direct Ballot Issue Elections

American politics is based on the competition of groups in a marketplace of ideas, where everyone's right to be heard and everyone's vote are presumed to be relatively equal. Enormous expenditures of money by privileged individuals or well-heeled organizations such as corporations seem to many people to endanger these ideals and to threaten to give some individuals or groups much more powerful voices and "votes" than others. Data from a 1982 election-day poll in California indicate that voters feel one-sided spending strongly influences outcomes (see Table 5.2).

Proponents of direct democracy devices claim that ballot measures allow for robust participation, encourage citizens to become more involved in public affairs, and permit a redress of grievances when either the government or special interest groups abuse the public trust. Yet evidence appears to be growing that these same procedures are vulnerable to well-financed, slick campaigns that may erode voters' faith in the democratic process ("Why bother to vote? The rich guys always win") or serve to limit the number and kinds of proposals put on the ballot ("Why bother? It's too expensive, and we'll lose anyway"). Several erstwhile proponents of the initiative and referendum have accordingly tempered their enthusiasm for direct democracy.

The traditional view of American politics is that it takes three things to win elections: money, money, and money. Another old saw simply states: "Money talks." Yet students of both candidate and ballot issue elections conclude that money is merely one of several factors that affect election results. In candidate elections, incumbency, party registration rates; the candidate's experience, visibility, person-

Table 5.2. Voter perceptions of money's effect on initiative campaigns, California, 1982 (%) (N = 6345)

"In those proposition races where only one side of an issue has enough money to pay for expensive campaign advertising, the outcome does not usually represent the will of the people but the interest of the big campaign contributors."

Agree	82
Disagree	16
No opinion	2

"How much of an effect does spending have [in proposition/initiative elections]?"

Great deal	63
Some effect	28
Only a little	6
No effect at all	2
Don't know	1

Source: November 1982 election-day survey of California voters, reported in the Field Institute's *California Opinion Index,* 1 (February 1983), 3.

ality, and integrity; newspaper endorsements; campaign organization; and issues can also be significant in legislative and executive campaign outcomes. In ballot issue elections, many of these same factors plus the existence of long-standing opinions, grass-roots interest group strategies, and the strategic errors of one side or the strategic skills of another can help explain why a measure wins or loses.

Although no one would deny that money is a factor in ballot issue elections, it remains to be seen how much and in what ways it influences outcomes. Champions of the initiative and referendum generally downplay the role of money. One political analyst says the "expenditure of money for an initiative does not necessarily correspond with its success or failure."[14] A law professor who advocates the initiative at both the state and national levels writes that there is little evidence to substantiate "the fear that monied interests will be able to use the initiative at the national level to their advantage by hoodwinking the people."[15] Another advocate asserts that "spending appears to give no advantage at all in most initiative campaigns."[16] He acknowledges that in campaigns in which opponents spend more than twice as much as supporters, only one out of five initiatives wins approval. But he concludes that although it is more difficult to win an initiative in the face of massive opposition spending, it is not impossible. "Even assuming that money had a decisive effect on defeated initiatives where there was one-sided opposition spending . . . such campaigns accounted for only 36 percent of all initiative campaigns. Are voters to be prevented from voting on *all* initiatives just because they exhibit massive opposition to *some* initiatives? To do so would be analogous to abolishing candidate races because third-party candidates so rarely get elected."[17]

Those who believe that direct democracy devices may serve as a check on the power of special interests also have to believe that the financial power of special interests cannot control the process.

Financially powerful special interests have strenuously opposed the adoption of the initiative and referendum in states such as Minnesota, New Jersey, and Rhode Island. The AFL-CIO, business groups, and chambers of commerce in recent years have nearly always condemned the initiative—sometimes, ironically, by pointing out that these elections can be costly and that the initiative will benefit only the extremely well-heeled organizations. A vice president of a New Jersey business association testified before a 1986 hearing that citizens would lose the opportunity to be heard if direct democracy procedures were used:

> In the legislative process, any citizen can be heard at committee hearings and through contact with individual legislators. We lament the fact that in place of the present ability of every citizen to be heard—for the price of a stamp, a phone call or an appearance before a committee of the legislature—reaching lawmakers in the initiative process (the 4 million registered voters in New Jersey) would be a prohibitively expensive process, geared to glossy media campaigns and beyond the financial means of average citizens.
>
> Only the well-heeled can afford the multimillion dollar, slick public relations campaigns that are typical of the debate on initiative and referendum questions in other states.[18]

Although this industry lobbyist made valid points, he overlooked the reality that few citizens have paid full-time lobbyists such as himself who regularly press their views before the legislature and enjoy disproportionate access to legislators.

The Bellotti *Decision*

The Supreme Court has supported the notion that one-sided spending is not a crucial factor in ballot issue elections. Before 1976, eighteen states had laws prohibiting or limiting corporate contributions or spending in initiative campaigns. But the Court overruled most of these laws in controversial decisions. Perhaps its most important was its five-to-four decision in April 1978 on *First National Bank of Boston et al. v. Bellotti.*[19]

The *Bellotti* case arose over a Massachusetts law that prohibited corporations from contributing to ballot issue campaigns not materially affecting any property, business, or assets of the corporation. Massachusetts state legislators—spurred and supported by progressive interest groups—had repeatedly placed on the ballot constitutional amendments that would have instituted a graduated personal income tax. These proposals had been consistently defeated, with much of the opposition's money coming from Massachusetts-based corporations. After a 1972 defeat, the legislature amended the laws to prohibit corporate expenditures on ballot proposals concerning "taxation of income."

In 1976 the legislature again put the proposal on the ballot; again it was defeated, but not before the First National Bank of Boston and four other corporations decided to protest the corporate expenditure law in court. The Massachusetts Supreme Judicial Court upheld its constitutionality. Distinguishing between a person and an artificial entity, such as a corporation, the court decided that a corporation's rights were more limited and limited freedom of speech to "when a general political issue materially affects a corporation's business, property, or assets." The court also ruled the income tax proposal did not meet the test of "materially affecting" these banks and corporations.

The corporations appealed to the U.S. Supreme Court, arguing that the law should be declared unconstitutional for the following reasons:[20]

Corporate speech is protected as a right under the First and Fourteenth Amendments. The due process clause of the Fourteenth is the source from which a corporation's rights are derived, including the right to free speech. Media corporations are allowed to voice opinions without interference by the state.

An important part of the First Amendment is the right of the public to hear public debate on political issues without government interference. The Massachusetts law interfered with the voter's ability to obtain information on an important issue. If the right of the listener is the main concern, the business of the speaker should be irrelevant.

There is no clear purpose behind the law. If the law is to prevent "undue influence" by corporations, such a purpose has been ruled insufficient grounds for state interference in an earlier Court ruling (*Buckley v. Valeo,* 1976). This raises the issue of whether one voice should be stifled to enhance the relative voice of another.

The restraint of a corporation's expression to protect shareholders who do not hold similar views does not make sense, because there are no restrictions on corporate expenditures on lobbying. To allow businesses to spend money to persuade state legislators but to forbid funds spent to persuade or influence the public is absurd. Indeed, to prohibit either is unconstitutional.

It is unconstitutional to prohibit speech on a particular subject, unless there is an overriding state interest in doing so. So also it is unconstitutional to prohibit political activity by corporations but not by labor unions.

Lawyers representing Francis Bellotti, attorney general for the Commonwealth of Massachusetts, argued for upholding the constitutionality of the Massachusetts law:

Corporations are artificial entities and as such do not have and are not entitled to the same First Amendment rights as individuals— unless they are in the business of speech or communications. Incorporation laws give corporations certain advantages (limited liability, accumulation of capital) but also impose certain limitations. Corporations do not have all the rights individuals have, such as privacy and freedom of association. Their right to express political opinions is not necessarily as broad as an individual's.

A corporation cannot have an opinion when it is composed of many owners. The opinion is often that of the managers. It is unfair to use corporate money to advance the personal opinions of certain corporate officers.

The public's right to hear diverse views is not infringed upon. Managers may always use their own funds to air their views. What is outlawed is giving managers the advantage of the corporation and all its resources to air their views. The Massachusetts law merely forbids corporate managers from spending corporate funds to express their personal views.

Since the corporation derives its First Amendment rights from the Fourteenth Amendment, which protects property, these First Amendment rights should apply only to protecting a corporation's property. Such advocacy when a corporation's property or business is at stake is not outlawed.

There is a compelling state interest in prohibiting the expenditure of large sums of money by corporations on ballot proposals: voters' confidence in the democratic process. Financial domination of such direct legislation campaigns by corporations might erode the voters' democratic faith. Their vote might appear less consequential. The right to vote is given to individuals, but not to corporations.

Unions are prohibited from using compulsory dues for political purposes; similarly, stockholders should not have to fund causes they may not espouse.

The complexity of the issues involved was reflected in the closeness of the Supreme Court's decision. In an opinion with broad implications for direct democracy and corporate political activity, the majority held the Massachusetts supreme court had addressed the wrong issue: "The Court below framed the principal question in this case as whether and to what extent corporations have First Amendment rights. We believe that the [Massachusetts] court posed the wrong question . . . The proper question . . . must be whether [the Massachusetts law] abridges expression that the First Amendment was meant to protect." In short, the real issue was not the right of the corporation to speak, but the right of the people to listen.

Associate Justice Lewis F. Powell, speaking for the majority, wrote that the First Amendment goes beyond protection of the press and the self-expression of individuals to prohibiting government from limiting the stock of information from which the public may draw. On the basis of this reasoning, the Court rejected the "materially affecting" requirement of the Massachusetts law, calling it "an impermissible legislative prohibition of speech based on the identity of the interests that spokesman represents."

Moreover, the Court found baseless Attorney General Bellotti's fears of an erosion of voter faith in the democratic process: "According to the appellee, corporations are wealthy and powerful and their views may drown out other points of view . . . But there has been no showing that the relative voice of corporations has been overwhelming or even significant in influencing referenda in Massachusetts, or that there has been any threat to the confidence of the citizenry in government."

Finally, the Supreme Court held it was unlikely that the Massachusetts law served the interests of the shareholders, for the law was "both under- and overinclusive." The inclusion of a specific type of ballot question "undermines the likelihood of a genuine state interest in protecting shareholders." On the other hand, the law was over-inclusive, for it prohibited a company from supporting or opposing a referendum proposal even if its shareholders unanimously authorized the contribution. The Court did leave the door open, however, for laws that did take the interests of the shareholders into account, since such interests were "legitimate and traditionally within the province of state law."

A dissenting opinion by Associate Justice Byron White, joined by his colleagues William Brennan and Thurgood Marshall, held that corporate funds should not be used to circulate the opinion of top management. Justice White distinguished between organizations whose ideological causes are shared by all the members and corporations, whose primary purpose is to make money. Under the first case, "association in a corporate form may be viewed as merely a means of achieving effective self-expression." In the second, however, "shareholders in such entities do not share a common set of political or social views, and they certainly have not invested their money for the purpose of advancing political or social causes or in an enterprise engaged in the business of disseminating news and opinion." White went on to say that although states confer special privileges on corporations, they need not allow corporations to use these privileges "to acquire an unfair advantage in the political process . . . The state need not permit its own creation to consume it." White concluded that the interests in protecting a system of freedom of expression "are sufficient to justify any incremental curtailment in the volume of expression which a Massachusetts statute might produce."

A second dissenting opinion, by then Associate Justice William Rehnquist, was based on the contention that corporations are not entitled to the same rights as individuals. Rather than trying to make the case that the state has a compelling interest in not extending First Amendment rights to corporations, Rehnquist merely denied the state is required to endow a business corporation with the power of political speech. Rehnquist supported his argument by quoting Chief Justice John Marshall in 1819: "A corporation is an artificial being, invisible, intangible, and existing only in contemplation of law." Rehnquist concluded by denying any basis for the belief that the liberty of a corporation to engage in political activity with regard to matters having no material effect on its business "is necessarily incidental to the purposes for which the Commonwealth permitted these corporations to be organized or admitted within its boundaries."

Corporations especially applauded Justice Powell's view that free speech is indispensable to decision making in a democracy, whether the speech comes from a corporation or an individual. They also endorsed Powell's view that the inherent worth of speech for informing the public does not depend upon the identity of its sources, whether a corporation, association, union, or individual. Herbert Schmertz, a vice-president of Mobil Oil Corporation, approvingly noted: "What these [Powell's] words mean, as I read them, is that corporations should be accorded the same First Amendment rights to free speech as the press or individuals."[21]

Critics of the *Bellotti* decision held that the Court minimized the impact of corporate spending in initiative campaigns. Political scientist John S. Shockley wrote that corporate expenditures in initiative campaigns "have influenced, if not bought, public opinion, and managed, if not corrupted, the democratic process."[22] Daniel Lowenstein puts it in a somewhat larger context, but he plainly disputes the *Bellotti* decision: "The institutions of direct democracy were indeed introduced into our system to effect a 'shift of power' and a 'shift of influence' in favor of causes whose adherents were numerous and passionate but not well-financed or well-connected. [My study] demonstrates [that] the power of some groups to raise enormous sums of money to oppose ballot propositions, without regard to any breadth or depth of popular feeling, seriously interferes with the ability of other groups to use the institutions of direct democracy as they were intended to be used."[23]

Other critics disputed Justice Powell's reasoning on the grounds that corporations are not minds that formulate ideas, or even voices freely expressing them. On the contrary, corporations serve as megaphones in political campaigns for the views of some of those who own or control them.[24] A Common Cause leader complained that the Supreme Court's decision set the stage for massive corporate spending in initiative campaigns throughout the country and seriously undermined the integrity of the initiative process.[25]

The *Bellotti* decision does set an unusual precedent and is in marked contrast to the general prohibition against direct corporate spending on candidates running for office. One impact of this decision may be to encourage even more spending by corporations to block direct legislation they dislike. It may also encourage some to advocate ballot issues they like. Certainly, the 1980s witnessed an increase in ballot question campaigns involving a million dollars or more. Although the precise effects of these rising expenditures are debatable, it may become too expensive for some groups to place a proposal on the ballot. In addition, it may become less expensive for corporations to spend so much money: some corporations used the *Bellotti* decision to claim that such expenditures should be tax deductible.

Justice Powell did leave the door open for his decision to be narrowed or modified when he implied that if and when the arguments put forth by Attorney General Bellotti were supported by findings that business advocacy threatened to undermine the democratic process, this controversy would merit reconsideration. Most studies, many of them made after the *Bellotti* decision, do suggest that one-sided spending on ballot issue elections can influence initiative voting outcomes.

A similar dispute reached the Supreme Court in 1981. Three years after the *Bellotti* decision, it struck down a Berkeley, California, statute limiting contributions to direct campaigns by individuals or corporations.[26] The California Supreme Court had upheld the Berkeley ordinance, noting that although campaign spending involved First Amendment rights, the city had a legitimate interest in limiting the size of donations to prevent undue influence. Critics of the *Bellotti* decision hoped that a favorable Supreme Court ruling on the Berkeley decision would help modify the impact of *Bellotti*. But Chief Justice Warren Burger, writing for the majority, held that "there is no significant state or public interest in curtailing debate and discussion of a ballot measure." In reversing the California decision, Burger cast doubt on whether local government could ever devise reasons important enough to restrict contributions. Not all his colleagues went that far, but only Justice Byron White dissented from the overall ruling.[27]

The *Bellotti* decision was based on the right of individuals to hear and obtain information. In doing so they equated political spending with speech. The Court, in essence, confirms that money talks. However, with the infusion of vast sums of money into initiative campaigns, the voices of some may be drowned out by a deluge of money. This nullified one of the historical advantages of the initiative process—that citizen groups might on occasion bypass the legislature, particularly when corporate, union, or other special interest lobbying prevented action on certain issues.

The *Bellotti* decision also leaves uncertain the means by which states may regulate corporate influence in ballot issue campaigns, although several ways remain to regulate corporate expenditures or at least counterbalance their influence:

1. Require full disclosure of contributions to ballot issue campaigns.

2. Enact some type of limited public financing for groups that are being outspent by opponents or for both sides in a ballot issue campaign.

3. Require some type of proxy vote by corporate shareholders for authorizing political expenditures by corporate management.

4. Encourage more widespread use of a highly readable and thorough voter pamphlet as a means of reducing the influence of corporate political advertising.

5. Require legislative committees to conduct highly publicized public regional hearings on ballot measures in an effort to make available more complete and objective information than voters might otherwise get.

6. Require the Internal Revenue Service to enforce more strictly the tax code, according to which money spent on grass-roots corporate lobbying is *not* a deductible expense.

7. Encourage or require free airtime for debate and discussion of ballot issues along the line of the Federal Communications Commission's (now terminated) "fairness doctrine" in such a way as to permit a fair response and at least some airtime from groups being noticeably outspent in issue elections.

Difficulties exist with almost all of these suggestions. For example, although almost everyone agrees that full financial disclosure is a sensible state practice in these kinds of elections, it is clear that many or most voters decide on most ballot questions in the two weeks before election day. Thus a one-sided, negative spending blitz is likely to be most effective in the last ten days—and most or all of the money spent might not be disclosed until after the election.

Requiring the media to give equal time and a fair hearing or fair coverage to both sides of a debate also sounds reasonable and sensible. Yet sometimes the well-financed side in a ballot question election will refrain from radio and television ads altogether so as to minimize the free time that might be given to opponents. Still, in various combinations these reforms may achieve more fairness and integrity in direct democracy procedures.

Although the expenditure of large sums does not automatically guarantee the outcome of a ballot issue campaign, money well spent or one-sided spending on ballot propositions has about the same effect as in candidate elections.[28] Just as in candidate races, money buys crucial resources, including sophisticated public opinion tracking surveys, telephone banks, get-out-the-vote drives, experienced public relations and media consultants, mass mailings, and shrewd media ads. However, money spent well in the last ten days probably makes more of a difference in an issues election.

So-called big money has only about a 25 percent success rate in promoting ballot issues. For example, a 1984 Rhode Island initiative to raise vast revenues for "reindustrialization," heavily supported by big business, suffered a landslide defeat at the polls. A 1980 California effort to repeal and modify rent control laws failed despite massive expenditures on a media campaign to win approval. A 1980 Colorado initiative to encourage branch banking, backed by savings and loan institutions, also failed. Similarly, business efforts to enact right-to-work laws have usually failed despite heavy funding on the "Vote yes" side.

However, when big money (usually, though not always, business money) *opposes* a poorly funded ballot measure, the evidence suggests that the wealthier side has about a 75 percent or better chance of defeating it. This is where money counts the most.[29]

Opponents generally try to create confusion in the minds of voters. In controversial campaigns, money can do much to define or redefine the issues, as one elections analyst explains:

> Big spending can have a significant impact upon citizen attitudes, overwhelming opponents with fewer financial resources. In one instance . . . roughly a third of the electorate was repeating the precise arguments of the corporate media opposition ("The right problem, the wrong solution"). And this was occurring at the very time polls were showing a precipitous decline in support for the measure. While this does not necessarily mean that voters were "bought" rather than "educated" by the money, or that the "wrong" side won, it does mean that those with money had enormous advantages wherever they had the wisdom to use it cleverly.[30]

Because most citizen-initiated ballot measures lose, it is difficult to prove that money rather than poor strategy or the voter's natural proclivity to vote no when in doubt is the chief or even a significant reason for defeat. Explaining outcomes over a broad range of issues and in diverse states is a challenge that defies tidy causal analysis.

Yet there are noteworthy findings. In 1976 political scientist John S. Shockley conducted studies of the role of money in twelve initiative campaigns concerning mandatory deposits and the regulation of nuclear energy. In the twelve proposals, industry opponents outspent the proposals' proponents by margins ranging from 3 to 1 to 200 to 1, and in nine of the twelve cases—in every one in which corporate money had been poured into an opposition campaign—the initiatives were defeated (see Table 5.3).[31] Shockley noted: "First, on these measures early public opinion polls showed voters in the various states favored the measures initially, but by election day nearly all the measures were defeated, often resoundingly. Second, money created enor-

Table 5.3.   Reported expenditures and outcomes in nuclear energy and mandatory deposit initiatives, various states, 1976

Issue and state	Expenditures ($)		Final vote in favor (%)
	Proponents	Opponents	
Mandatory deposit			
Colorado	19,000	511,000	31
Maine	26,000	404,000	58
Massachusetts	59,000	1,572,000	49
Michigan	117,000	1,316,000	63
Nuclear energy			
Arizona	25,000	2,200,000	30
California	1,257,000	4,033,000	32
Colorado	119,000	621,000	29
Missouri	21,000	350,000	63
Montana	580	134,000	41
Ohio	25,000	1,755,000	32
Oregon	280,000	1,100,000	42
Washington	120,000	1,005,000	33

Source: John S. Shockley, Testimony in U.S. Congress, House of Representatives, *IRS Administration of Tax Laws Relating to Lobbying: Hearings before a Subcommittee of the Committee on Government Operations,* 95th Cong., 2d sess., May and July 1978, p. 259. Shockley provides the sources of his data in detailed footnotes and makes clear that the accuracy of some of these figures varied because the financial disclosure laws and their enforcement varied among these states.

mous differences in the campaigns waged by the proponents and opponents on these measures."[32] In short, although it would be incorrect to argue that corporate money in *all* cases was the most important factor in the success or defeat of initiatives, corporate lobbying had a powerful effect on public opinion and in a number of cases was a deciding factor.

The Council on Economic Priorities has also analyzed the role of money in ballot elections. In studies of direct legislation elections in 1978 and 1980, the council found that the corporate-backed side virtually always outspent its opponents and won about 80 percent of the time. It concluded: "It is difficult to single out money alone as the single factor which tips the scale in such campaigns. The clear advantages which unlimited funds can make immediately available—from professional polling to unlimited media time to consultants experienced in campaigns on a given issue—are nevertheless quite clear and obviously very powerful. The advantages which money can provide in such campaigns are almost certainly greater than the advantages which any other single factor can provide."[33]

In a study of the role of money in direct legislation elections the Council on Economic Priorities offered these general findings:[34]

Initiatives that affect business interests continue to provoke very expensive campaigns.
Financial dominance in a campaign appears to give a clear advantage.
In some local initiative campaigns, the business-backed opposition in effect eliminated their weakly financed proponents from one of the primary means of redressing a spending imbalance—free media time obtained under the FCC's fairness doctrine. Instead, they concentrated their funds on direct mail, newspaper, and telephone campaigns.

When corporations spend vast sums of money to dominate discussion and debate via the media and mailbox, the voting public often hears only one side of an issue. The advantages that opposition money in large quantities can buy can rarely be overcome. The Media Access Project (MAP) arrived at strikingly similar conclusions in a study of ballot proposals on nuclear safety, mandatory bottle deposits, and public utility regulation reform in Colorado. These proposals were chosen because they were all staunchly opposed by corporate interests and corporate money, and all, after seeming headed for victory, were defeated on election day. MAP found a strong correlation between the amount of money spent in a campaign and the number of votes received. "Corporate finances dominated television and radio advertising especially in peak audience periods." Moreover, the "Federal Communications Commission's 'fairness doctrine' . . . provided inadequate protection for outspent advocates."[35]

Political scientist Betty H. Zisk has provided additional evidence that money counts in direct legislation campaigns. She examined fifty major ballot questions in California, Massachusetts, Michigan, and Oregon from 1976 to 1982. Unlike most students of issue elections, Zisk also examined alternative factors that might explain success and defeat at the ballot box, taking into account spending levels and endorsements by newspapers or major political figures. Her findings are:[36]

Campaign spending is the single most powerful predictor of who wins and who loses.

In fifty-six of the seventy-two measures, the high-spending side won, or a total of 78 percent of the time. (A few of the cases in which the high-spending side lost involved issues such as restoring the death penalty or changing the drinking age—issues on which people's views are likely to be relatively fixed and thus immune to spending campaigns.)

In seventeen of the thirty-two cases in which survey information was available, voter preferences were reversed in the high-spending direction in the course of the campaign: in all but two, this was enough to change the outcome. In nine other cases, money went to the side the public favored from the beginning.

A causal relation was found to exist between high spending and the ballot outcome in the seventeen issue elections mentioned above— mainly because of the lack of any powerful alternative cues (such as party label) available to the voter.

In the nuclear freeze campaigns of 1982, liberals rather than corporate interests enjoyed the spending advantages. Twelve times as much was spent to pass as to defeat these measures, and most passed comfortably in what was plainly a major political victory for freeze advocates.

Law professor Daniel H. Lowenstein examined twenty-five California ballot campaigns involving significant one-sided (over $250,000) spending between 1968 and 1980. He was initially cautious about contending—at least, in the abstract—that money changes voters' preferences in direct legislation elections:

There can be no certain answer to the question whether big spending "bought" a victory for or against any particular ballot proposition. To attempt to ascertain the effects of spending on the election result, one must make such judgments regarding the decisions of millions of individual voters, based upon only fragmentary evidence of what communications took place during the campaign and, to the extent such information can be gleaned from public opinion polls, what voters were thinking.

Even then, the difficulties are not exhausted. For to say that an election was "bought" is to make an implied comparison between the actual result and the result that would have occurred under some hypothetical set of circumstances.[37]

After examining additional data, including opinion polls, financial contributions, and ballot outcomes, Lowenstein concluded that one-sided spending in support of ballot propositions is usually ineffective but in opposition is influential or dominant. Although he did not view the prospect of special interests "buying" favorable legislation as cause for alarm, his case-by-case examination of the role of money in opposing ballot initiatives yielded a different conclusion. Ninety percent of the initiatives Lowenstein studied with one-sided "no" spending were defeated, even when the propositions were popular and were presented under favorable circumstances.[38] Because voters' basic attitudes cannot usually be significantly altered in a direct legislation campaign, he found that opponents attempted to shape or recast voters' perceptions of what a specific initiated measure might do. In what can only be characterized as efforts at deception, they concentrated on peripheral or irrelevant matters in order to confuse or frighten voters. Frequently they used advertisements whose tricky and subtle messages suggested that just the reverse of what proponents said would happen would indeed be achieved if a measure was enacted. Lowenstein concluded that many of these ballot issues would have succeeded if spending by the two sides had been closer. The first three initiatives shown in Table 5.4 demonstrate the apparent linkage between spending, public opinion, and electoral outcome.

When and Why Big Money Can Lose

Although big money influences the voters most of the time, in about 20 percent of cases the "underdog" or more weakly financed side wins.

Sometimes the poorly financed side wins because money, espe-

Table 5.4. Effect of corporate expenditures on public opinion and outcome in 4 initiative campaigns, 1980

Initiative	Expenditures ($)		Public opinion favoring initiative (%)	Final vote in favor (%)
	Proponents	Opponents		
Montana bottle deposit initiative, Nov. 4, 1980: "Shall a mandatory five-cent deposit be placed on beer and soda cans and bottles if, by 1983, 85 percent of such containers are not being voluntarily recycled?"	12,211	554,961	May 70, June 65, Oct. 4 50, Oct. 28 40	29
California oil windfall tax initiative, June 3, 1980: "Shall a 10 percent surtax be placed on oil company profits from California sales, proceeds from which tax to be used for improved public transportation?"	463,859	5,770,706	Feb. 66, April 58, May[a] 49	44
Missouri nuclear power plant safety initiative, Nov. 4, 1980: "Shall operation of nuclear power plants in Missouri be prohibited until there is a federally approved site for radioactive waste storage in operation?"	59,484	1,790,857	Nov. 1979 77, Oct. 1980[b] 54	39
Oregon nuclear power plant safety initiative, Nov. 7, 1980: "Shall Oregon require operation of permanent radioactive waste storage and voter approval before permitting construction of nuclear power plants?"	34,262	625,561	Aug. 1979 67, Sept. 1980 74	54

Source: Adapted from Steven B. Lydenberg, *The Role of Business in Financing Ballot Question Campaigns* (New York: Council on Economic Priorities, 1981), pp. 70, 49–51, 60–61, 106–107, respectively. Montana opinion surveys provided to Council on Economic Priorities; California: Field Institute polls; Missouri: first poll by proponents under professional supervision, second poll by SRI research for *St. Louis Post-Dispatch;* Oregon: polls by proponents under professional supervision.

a. Undecided: 8, 10, and 18%, respectively.

b. Undecided: 9 and 16%, respectively.

cially money coming from outside the state, becomes a significant political issue itself. In a 1978 Montana ballot contest, advocates of an anti–nuclear power initiative were outspent $260,000 to $10,000 but nonetheless won 65 percent of the vote. Attention had focused on the fact that almost all of the opponents' record-breaking campaign money came from outside the state—and virtually all of it came from the nuclear power or nuclear-related industry.

Sometimes the high-spending side is the union side in a union-versus-business issue. This was the case in Idaho's 1986 "Right-to-Work" referendum, in which labor outspent business interests by nearly $2.5 million to about $1 million. It was also the case in a 1980 Massachusetts property tax reduction initiative. The significantly larger amounts of money spent by unions, especially public employee and teachers' unions, did sway Massachusetts public opinion in a dramatic fashion for a while—but not enough to stop passage of a measure sponsored by a coalition of business and property owners. Some $250,000 of the $355,789 spent on behalf of this measure was corporate money (especially from high-technology industries), and it was spent, apparently very shrewdly, in the last two weeks of the campaign. Public opinion had plainly become divided by mid-October, but a media and mail blitz reversed public preferences. Just as this money was coming into the campaign, the opposition's funds had become exhausted.

Another "low-budget" victory over high-spending corporate opponents was a 1980 Oregon anti–nuclear power initiative; Table 5.4 presents the data on expenditures, public opinion, and electoral outcome. Several factors were apparently at work. The nuclear accident at Three Mile Island in March 1979 was still very much on people's minds. An earlier antinuclear initiative had lost in Oregon, and proponents this time worked carefully to modify the measure, using professional pollsters to help select the wording and focus of their 1980 initiative. Proponents carefully organized a statewide campaign and met regularly to broaden their coalition's base. They also were imaginative in using low- or no-cost resources. Thus they conducted a well-orchestrated yet largely volunteer-based grass-roots literature distribution campaign. And they made effective use of the FCC's fairness doctrine, then still in effect, to obtain free airtime on some 135 Oregon television and radio stations. "Proponents believe this access to the airwaves was critical in the ultimate passage of their initiative."[39]

Similarly, a Michigan mandatory deposit initiative won by a decisive 64 to 36 percent vote in 1976 despite twelve-to-one negative spending by the container industry. Some observers say the Michigan advocates were lucky because their opposition gathered late and was poorly led. But grass-roots organization and shrewd spending by the proponents apparently were critical as well. They mobilized thousands of volunteers and crucial organizational endorsements. They staged colorful media events such as "cleanathons" and generated considerable free publicity.

As these examples illustrate, the side with more money does not necessarily always prevail. Well-organized grass-roots campaigning can make a difference. Sometimes backlash against too much money can be used to good effect. Sometimes a national issue—such as Three Mile Island or the tax-cut fever generated by Proposition 13 in California—can help overcome the influential role that heavy campaign spending usually has. Skillful campaign leadership that develops strong arguments, reaches out for imaginative interest group endorsements, generates free publicity, and takes advantage of as much free media time as possible can partly offset the traditional advantages of money. However, the odds are with the big spenders, and as corporations and their trade associations gain more experience in these direct legislation campaigns, it is likely that corporate spenders will learn to cope effectively with many of the tactics used by grass-roots volunteer activists.

The Influence of Media in Direct Legislation Elections

The outcomes of direct democracy elections are often affected by which side can afford to buy television time. Although Lincoln's Gettysburg Address referred to our system as a "government by the people," many modern skeptics would revise his characterization to read: ours is a government by those who can make themselves heard.

Effective use of the media may often make the difference between failure and success at the polls, and effective use of the media is often a function of money. Besides access, money can buy the expertise of media consultants who know the best ways to allocate the budget and the most effective strategies. There is some evidence that media use is even more important than money.

There is controversy over how much influence media use has on voters. Such an effect is difficult to quantify because people learn about election issues in other ways, too. According to law professor Ronald Allen, "the media appears [sic] to have a limited impact on the formation of public opinion, or at least on how the public votes."[40] However, numerous surveys show that most voters decide on ballot issue questions in the last few days before an election—precisely when media blitzes take place. Media studies acknowledge that although the media are generally ineffective in changing attitudes or ingrained behavior, they can often be influential in informing people and creating initial attitudes. Moreover, "minute changes brought about by the media in final voting decisions or voter turnout may alter the outcome of a close election."[41]

The Media Access Project, after studying the 1976 Colorado initiatives discussed in the previous section, concluded that "political editorial advertising represents the single most effective means of reaching and swaying voters."[42] The director of this research project also noted that "in the multimedia twentieth century, a speaker's ability to influence political affairs is determined not only by the rightness of what he or she says and by the persuasiveness with which it is said, but also by the media campaign that the speaker is able and willing to afford."[43]

Three categories of television and print journalism affect initiative campaigns: editorial endorsements; news coverage; and paid advertisements. There is little research on the effects of editorial policy in direct democracy elections. Political scientist Betty Zisk has noted that big money and editorial endorsements are on the same side only about 70 percent of the time but believes money is the more important variable for explaining victory or defeat. Plainly, newspaper editorials were more effective before the rise of television. Television ads reach more people, including the less well-informed potential voters who typically make up their minds late in a campaign about whether and how to vote. Newspaper editorials have been and are read by the better educated. Editorial cartoons, on the other hand, are somewhat more widely read and can sometimes be devastating, especially in raising confusion or fear in the minds of voters faced with a controversial initiative.

Poor or sloppy news coverage of initiative and referendum campaigns can obscure the issues or avoid them entirely, creating confusion and helping to defeat a ballot measure (especially given the fact that, when in doubt, voters usually vote no). Unfortunately, such coverage

is often the norm. Shockley found in Colorado that "analytical articles
... were extremely rare" and advertising images dominated the media.[44] Similar complaints are regularly heard in other states.

A University of North Dakota researcher examined news coverage
and other feature material of the *Grand Forks Herald* as it treated a
controversial North Dakota health care initiative in 1978. The *Herald's*
editorial and management position was decidedly opposed to the
measure, she noted, and although there was not exactly a sustained
campaign to discredit the health measure, the quality and accuracy
of coverage were poor—not only "inaccurate headlines so clearly incorrect that they required virtual retraction" but also "feeble" and
unscientific use of polls. As for the news stories, "the *Herald* had
many column inches of ... copy, but not as much depth as such a
controversial and potentially important topic warranted." On several
occasions opinions were simply placed next to each other, with no
additional dimension [given] to the story. "Such an approach reduced
the role of a reporter from being the public's watchdog to being the
stenographer for a select portion of the public."[45]

A comprehensive examination of the role of money and media
in four states in the early 1980s found that controversial ballot issues
won extensive coverage in the best regional newspapers (such as the
Boston Globe and the *Los Angeles Times*), but observed what is increasingly obvious: that only a small, usually well-educated, and politically aware segment of the public relies on newspaper coverage as
a guide to making voting·decisions. Thus the content of electronic
media coverage is crucial. And here, the verdict is not reassuring:
"There is relatively little news or electronic coverage by most stations,
except for colorful or highly controversial events."[46]

In many states, the most important aspect of the media in issue
elections is paid television political advertisements. In Idaho's 1986
referendum on a state "right-to-work" law, conservative forces spent
less but won because of their shrewd use of celebrity television ads
from movie stars such as Clint Eastwood and Charlton Heston, as
well as from Ronald Reagan. These presumably donated testimonials
had Reagan saying: "I wholeheartedly support right-to-work legislation and would like to see more states adopt such laws." The Heston
ad read: "I've played men like Tom Jefferson, Andrew Jackson, Lincoln—all heroes defending American freedom. There are Americans
still carrying on that fight in Idaho, where citizens want the right to
work without being forced to join a union. As a former union pres-

ident, I believe Americans should be free to choose. We're watching, Idaho. Strike a blow for freedom. Vote yes on Referendum 1."[47] Union leaders were unable to counter these commercials with anything equaling their impact in conservative Idaho—although they tried.[48]

Can effective media campaigns convert voters from one side of an issue to another? Money well spent can indeed encourage voters to rethink their positions on ballot issues. Political scientist Zisk found, in her study of a sample of ballot issue elections, that heavy spending aimed at changing voters' attitudes usually does so—when there is one-sided spending.[49] She also found, like others, that one-sided high-spending campaigns are indeed associated with deceptive paid advertising aimed at confusing the voter. But she also concluded that even two-sided high-spending campaigns, far from serving as an effective check on each other and focusing on the facts, oversimplified and distorted issues and mounted efforts to confuse the issue.[50] This has surely been the case in recent campaigns in Colorado, Idaho, and other western states.

The previously cited Media Access Project study of Colorado initiatives also sought to discover whether a correlation existed between the amount and frequency of media coverage and shifts in voter opinion. MAP found the degree of corporate dominance in three initiative elections even greater in terms of media spending than in total dollar amount expended. The corporate-financed ads' domination of prime-time television and radio, it concluded, had a critical effect on the election. Although others may contend that there were other factors involved and that early support for a measure often evaporates, John Shockley's study confirms the MAP view. In Colorado's 1976 mandatory bottle deposit campaign, opponents stressed that although litter was a problem, the proposal contained in the initiative was the "wrong solution." Ninety percent of those who voted against the initiative gave reasons mentioned in the opposition's advertisements. In a survey of Colorado's food tax repeal initiative, Shockley found that people had likewise incorporated the arguments of the opposition—"they'd get the money some other way." Indeed, 30 percent of the households Shockley surveyed used this reason, and so did 60 percent of those giving an explicit reason for backing or opposing the measure.[51]

Because money is so important in most initiative campaigns, it is not surprising that supporters of direct democracy advocate fairer access to media coverage and media advertising. From the 1970s to mid-1987, proponents of referendum democracy favored vigorous enforcement of what used to be called the fairness doctrine, a 1949 FCC regulation requiring radio and television broadcasters to devote a reasonable amount of time to covering controversial issues of public affairs and, in addition, to provide reasonable opportunity for the presentation of contrasting viewpoints. This was supposed to be one of several factors taken into account when broadcasters requested a renewal of their licenses. In 1963 the FCC introduced a related regulation, the Cullman doctrine or principle (named after a broadcasting company by that name), which required stations to fulfill fairness obligations at their own expense when no forthcoming sponsored programming would air the other side or sides of controversial issues.

The legal justification of the fairness doctrine was that television and radio frequencies were scarce and thus had to be rationed and monitored to ensure they served the public interest. Freedom of the press, as an old saying goes, should not belong only to those who can afford to own one. The intent of these doctrines was to promote an unfettered and robust exchange of ideas. Properly enforced, these regulations were expected to assure television and radio access for minority opinions and even for unpopular ideas.

Balanced coverage did not mean equal time for both or all sides; a reasonable opportunity may be only one-third or one-tenth of the time given to the other side or sides, depending on the circumstances. Factors that the FCC supposedly considered were: total amount of time allotted each side, the frequency of broadcasts or ads, the time of the presentation, and the size of potential audiences to be reached.

In a 1969 ruling, the Supreme Court held unanimously that the fairness doctrine was a minimally intrusive and largely self-enforcing recognition of the public's paramount right to access to different points of view. In short, broadcasters were asked to cover controversies fairly in exchange for the exclusive right to the public airwaves without a fee.[52] Defenders of the doctrine, in what is perhaps an overstatement, like to say that because a broadcasting license was usually a "license to print money" (referring to the considerable profits usually to be made) the fairness doctrine appeared to be a small price for owners to pay in return. They also implied that access to the public airwaves was too important to leave up to the handful of de facto censors (the owners) who otherwise would decide what Americans could and could not see on the evening news.

In theory, these licenses would have been revoked if the FCC had judged that fairness had been denied. In practice, it was seldom enforced with any rigor, especially in the 1980s. In fact no broadcaster ever lost a license due to a fairness doctrine violation or even for wholesale violations over the years. However, various "reminders" and bureaucratic hassling did occur as well as occasional costly legal efforts by owners to counter complaints or FCC investigations.

In practice also, many broadcasters ignored or violated the spirit of the fair access doctrine, and many financially disadvantaged advocates in direct democracy elections made limited or very poor use of their fair access rights. The Media Access Project found that Colorado broadcasters provided little free access and generally "failed to fulfill their affirmative obligation . . . to afford a reasonable opportunity for the presentation of opposing viewpoints."[53] Moreover, free access, when provided, tended to be during times when the potential audience was smaller. As a result, the MAP report recommended that citizens be better prepared to use the fairness doctrine and that broadcasters be held to tougher access standards in initiative and referendum campaigns, especially to the standard stating that lack of paid sponsorship should not in any way diminish a broadcaster's compliance with the FCC regulations. It also urged that political editorials be included under the fairness doctrine for direct democracy campaigns; that the FCC adopt policies that would meet the special needs of direct democracy elections, including more flexible complaint requirements, weighting the substance of complaints more heavily than technicalities, and allowing citizens to inspect station files and contracts in order to see how much advertising time had been allotted to different sides; and that the FCC conduct educational efforts to inform citizens and broadcasters of their rights under the doctrine.

In 1987 many of the controversies surrounding the fairness doctrine came to a head. Congress, fearing the FCC's inclination to end the fairness doctrine regulations, enacted a law designed to give the doctrine the force of federal law. President Reagan promptly vetoed the law, and Congress failed to override the veto. Within weeks, the FCC voted unanimously to abolish the doctrine on the grounds that it restricted the First Amendment rights of broadcasters, and that, with the soaring number of radio, television and cable stations, the old scarcity-of-airways argument was no longer justified. Moreover, the FCC and its allies (most notably the broadcasters and other journalists) claimed that instead of encouraging variety, the doctrine typically encouraged timidity or blandness. Their studies found that many station managers used the doctrine as an excuse to avoid even superficial examinations of controversial public issues. Fearful of having to provide air time to every special interest with a different view, broadcasters simply shied away from any meaningful coverage. Thus, "it had a 'chilling effect' on the airing and discussion of public issues, since the safest way to stay clear of it was to be innocuous."[54]

Despite the demise of the fairness doctrine, the issue concerning the proper role of television and related issues affecting direct democracy are by no means settled. Many scholars, though acknowledging the First Amendment implications, believe the doctrine is no longer the chilling threat broadcasters complained so much about, but rather a standard every responsible broadcaster should aim for. Moreover, paraphrasing the late Associate Justice Hugo Black, advocates of restoring the doctrine emphasize that freedom of the press from governmental interference under the First Amendment never sanctions repression of that freedom by private interests. Fortunately, the FCC's 1987 decision does not give broadcasters total license. They still are obliged to show they are operating in the public interest.

Still, there are many smaller states or communities where the diversity of television channels is limited and the fairness doctrine did have the effect of encouraging fairness. It is also true that the majority of Americans still get the bulk of their news from just two or three of the major networks and their affiliates. Over the years, the fairness doctrine may have contributed to blandness in some places, yet in modest ways it made it possible in several direct democracy campaigns for the less well-heeled and often the less popular views to get some airtime.

The issues of fairness and access will be debated for a long time. Do broadcasters have the right to air only those matters they deem worthy of their airtime? Can they sell time to proponents of nuclear energy, right-to-work, or economic development issues and refuse access to other viewpoints? One student of the fairness doctrine sees it this way: "The fairness doctrine brings together such strange bedfellows as Phyllis Schlafly and Ralph Nader; and it does so, according to some experts, because the basic philosophical question of what broadcasting, especially television, is to the society has not been answered. Is it a privately owned medium of entertainment and information, or is it a kind of public-bulletin-board-cum-town-meeting leased out for fair maintenance to individual broadcasters?"[55]

Most nations heavily regulate or outright control television. But Americans want management both to be as free as possible and also to make access available to the citizenry, providing a forum for minority views. It is a sobering challenge.

Clearly, it is difficult to separate the effects of the media from those of money: sometimes as much as 60 to 80 percent of a campaign budget is spent on media advertising. Television has changed the rules for elections of all kinds in America. Those who aspire to win either issue or candidate elections must understand the new media policies. In light of the *Bellotti* and *Berkeley* rulings of 1978 and 1981, a reasonably enforced fairness doctrine might have provided one of the chief ways to prevent domination of the media by the well financed. A strengthened fairness doctrine that prevented the most common and dangerous abuses, when combined with full disclosure requirements, effective press news coverage, a readable voter pamphlet, and televised legislative hearings, would have gone some of the way toward curtailing the advantages that big money customarily enjoys. Doubtless we have not heard the last of this doctrine. Eventually it, or something like it, will be revived.

Conclusion

Minority rights have occasionally suffered at the hands of both voters and state legislators. Although the very essence of the representative process seeks to ensure and guarantee minority rights, the practice has not always lived up to the theory. On balance, however, the legislative process with all its checks and balances usually does safeguard the rights of minorities; and voters in direct democracy elections have also shown that most of the time they too will reject measures that would diminish rights, liberties, and freedoms for the less well-represented or less-organized segments of society. Voters and legislators alike can make mistakes, yet the risks for minorities are probably slightly greater from lawmaking through direct democracy procedures than from lawmaking through the legislative process. Still, the voters' judgment has proved to be more enlightened than critics had expected.

It seems clear, however, that the proponents of the initiative and referendum seriously underestimated the effect of money in initiative elections. Although money is not always a decisive factor, it is always an important one, and big money, well spent, can usually defeat ballot questions.

Finally, the role of media coverage and media use is closely tied to the influence and impact of money. In general, the side with the most money can acquire the shrewdest media consultants and thus the best chance of influencing voter thinking and voter preferences. As a result, the rights of those who cannot afford to be heard are diminished in direct democracy elections. And in the absence of imaginative safeguards they are likely to be diminished further, as the importance of money and the media grows.

CHAPTER 6

▼

The Recall Device

▼

[The recall] tends to produce in every public official a nervous condition of irresolution as to whether he should do what he thinks he ought to do in the interest of the public, or should withhold from doing anything, or should do as little as possible, in order to avoid any discussion at all.

—William Howard Taft, 1913

The value of the recall as an instrument of genuinely democratic government has not been sufficiently appreciated . . . Above all else a democratic government must be kept closely in touch with public opinion. The recall makes it more possible . . . without any necessary sacrifice of efficiency.

—Herbert Croly, 1914

RECALL is the procedural democracy device that allows voters to discharge and replace a public official. Fifteen states, the District of Columbia, Guam, and the Virgin Islands provide for recall of elected officials, and at least thirty-six states permit the recall of various local officials. Recall requires a petition process, yet it needs more signatures than citizen initiatives (typically 25 percent of those voting in the last election for the position of the official to be recalled). It almost always also requires a special election (see Table 6.1).

Critics contend the recall gives the voters too much power and undermines the independence and necessary discretion of an elected representative. They stress that the republic's basic constitutional features are aimed at preventing unchecked, unrestrained, and unwise

Table 6.1. State adoption of and provisions for recall of state officials

Year adopted	State	Applicability	Petition requirements
1908	Oregon	All elected officials	15% of votes cast in last election for all gubernatorial candidates in official's electoral district
1911	California	All elected officials	For a statewide officer, 12% of votes cast in last election; for state legislators, judges, and board of equalization, 20% of votes cast in the official's electoral district
1912	Arizona	All elected officials	25% of votes cast in last election for targeted office
1912	Colorado	All elected officials	25% of votes cast in last election for targeted office
1912	Nevada	All elected officials	25% of votes cast in last election for targeted office
1912	Washington	All elected officials except judges of court record	25 or 30% of qualified electorate, depending on unit of government
1913	Michigan	All elected officials except judges of court record	25% of votes cast for governor in last election in official's electoral district
1914	Kansas	All elected officials except judges	40% of votes cast in last general election for targeted office
1914	Louisiana	All elected officials except judges of court record	33⅓% of voters voting in elections (40% of voters in districts of less than 1000)
1920	North Dakota	All elected officials	25% of votes cast in last general election for governor
1926	Wisconsin	All elected officials	25% of votes cast in last general election for governor
1933	Idaho	All elected officials except judges	20% of registered voters in last general election in official's electoral district
1959	Alaska	All elected officials except judges	25% of votes cast in last election in official's district
1976	Montana	All elected and some appointed officials	For statewide officials, 10% of registered voters at preceding election; for others, 15% of registered voters in the last election in official's jurisdiction

Table 6.1 (continued).

Year adopted	State	Applicability	Petition requirements
1978	Georgia	All elected officials	For statewide officials, 15%, with certain geographic requirements; for state legislators, 30%

Note: The District of Columbia, Guam, the Northern Marianas, and the Virgin Islands also permit the recall of certain elected officials. At least 21 states permit recall of all or most local elected officials. Another 15 permit local recalls under certain conditions, such as in home-rule cities or for mayors only. Signature requirements range from 5 to 50% of voters in varying jurisdictions, with 25% the most common as well as the average.

majority will. Recall elections are also costly to a community or state, because they force a special election. Moreover, recall in most instances does not require establishment of the truth or even the merit of misconduct charges. It is primarily, and often entirely, a political rather than a judicial procedure.

The recall also raises questions about the competence, interest, and rationality of the average voter. It presupposes a voter with discriminating judgment and with sufficient attentiveness and information to be able to vote wisely on the question of whether or not to discharge a public official. Opponents of the recall doubt the average citizen possesses the knowledge to make such discerning decisions. Proponents of the recall are inclined to a more idealized and optimistic view of the common sense of the voter.

The recall is used infrequently against elected state officials. Only one governor and a handful of other statewide-elected officials have been recalled. Several state legislators have been recalled, including two in California in 1913, two in Idaho in 1971, two in Michigan in 1983, and one in Oregon in 1988. About forty recalls have been mounted to oust state officials in California, but all except two have failed for lack of signatures. Recall drives against governors have been mounted in recent years but failed to obtain adequate signatures in California, Louisiana, and Michigan.

In Arizona, the recall campaign against Governor Evan Mecham in 1987 obtained far more than the needed signatures and forced the close scrutiny of Mecham that led to his impeachment by the legislature. Had he not been impeached, convicted, and replaced by the legislature, he would probably have been successfully recalled in a May 1988 special election. The Mecham Recall Committee claimed he lacked the knowledge, vision, and unifying leadership necessary to be a good governor. They also asserted he embarrassed Arizonans nationally through his insensitive and demeaning statements about women and minorities. Their list of complaints contained other criticisms about his appointments, integrity, and leadership. The governor and his friends dismissed the recall drive as the work of "fringe elements" and homosexual agitators, a charge that had less credibility when former senator Barry Goldwater and Republican-leaning newspapers throughout Arizona called on the governor to resign. The recall group collected 175,000 more than the 216,000 citizen signatures needed to place the issue of recalling the governor on the ballot.

Probably as many as 2,000 county and municipal officials have been discharged around the country since Los Angeles became the first local government to adopt the recall in 1903. Mayors in a score of cities from Seattle to Atlantic City have been recalled. A citizen movement came close to ousting the mayor of Cleveland in 1978. Some groups tried but were trounced in a recall attempt of the mayor of San Francisco in 1983. Mayor Mike Boyle of Omaha was turned out of office in a 1987 recall election that brought 56 percent of eligible voters to the polls—a city record for Omaha. A school board chairman in Los Angeles was recalled by antibusing foes in 1979, and three Honolulu city councilmen were ousted by the recall device in 1985. An entire five-member school board was removed from office in 1978 in the town of Easton, Massachusetts. Six Grand Junction, Colorado, city council members were recalled in 1986. In 1987 alone, Nebraskans targeted sixty-six elected officials in twenty-five recall efforts that discharged sixteen from office.

Background

The idea of the recall did not originate with the populists and progressives. One of the features of Athenian democracy was the ostracism of a politician by the vote of the citizenry. Intended to protect the *polis* against the overly ambitious individual, ostracism caused an official to be banished from the city-state for ten years. It sometimes had the effect of excluding talented but intimidating would-be leaders from participating in Athenian civic life.

The Swiss also provided for the retirement of their canton officials before their terms had expired. This Swiss recall permitted a specified number of citizens to requisition a vote for the discharge of a councilman. Though not a formal part of Swiss law before the 1850s, the Swiss recall dates back much earlier to a time when citizens occasionally exercised it under the customary law. In practice, however, the Swiss rarely employed this device.

The Articles of Confederation (1781–89) provided for the recall and replacement of delegates appointed by the states even within their one-year terms, although this form of recall was exercised by state legislatures, not by the voters at large. The Constitutional Convention of 1787 considered but eventually rejected resolutions calling for this same type of recall.

The notion of a recall received attention at some of the ratifying conventions called in 1787 and 1788. The New York convention, for example, proposed a constitutional amendment allowing state legislatures to recall either or both of their senators and to elect others to serve for the remainder of their terms. In Virginia Patrick Henry praised the recall, saying that one of the defects of the proposed constitution was that although states were allowed to instruct their senators, the latter could simply disregard such instructions if they deemed them unwise or unworthy.

Opponents of the recall at the Virginia and New York ratifying conventions argued that a senator should consult the interests not just of his own states, but also of the Union as a whole. The power of recall, they claimed, might render a senator a slave to the shortsightedness or emotionalism of the people. Federalists such as Alexander Hamilton emphasized that, far from being the servant delegates of a particular state, members of the newly proposed national senate should be in some measure a check upon the state governments and above the misconceptions or narrowmindedness that they might receive from their states.

In the end, the idea of placing a recall provision in the Constitution died for lack of support—at least from those participating in the ratifying conventions. The framers and the ratifiers were consciously seeking to remedy what they viewed as the defects of the Articles of Confederation and some of their state constitutions, and for many of them this meant retreating from an excess of democracy.

The framers, while also deliberately avoiding monarchical forms, designed representative processes by which qualified voters could select representatives to rule over them but could select others only at the expiration of the stated terms of office.

The Populist and Socialist Labor parties urged adoption of the recall in several of their national and state platforms in the 1890s. They saw state capitols and city halls infested with the privileged, the sinister, and the corrupt. They saw how money, secrecy, and lobbying could subvert the otherwise noble intentions of representative democracy. Thus they began to hold that a representative is an agent or servant, not a master. A representative who failed to understand the will of the represented or grossly misinterpreted the needs, wants, and aspirations of the general public should be recalled. "He holds an indeterminate franchise, or what is sometimes called a tenure during good behavior, within the limits of a maximum fixed term," wrote one of the Progressive-era defenders of this practice. "It is a continuing control, calculated to preserve at all times the relation of master and servant between the people and their representatives."[1]

Populist and progressive reformers viewed existing impeachment provisions as inadequate or useless. Impeachment punishes only malfeasance in office, not misfeasance or nonfeasance, and graft is hard to prove. Moreover, there is an area of activity just beyond graft that the impeachment process did not affect. Moreover, those who wish to oust an official via impeachment must prove a crime was committed. Recall charges, on the other hand, can range from assertions of corruption to the presumption that an official is unrepresentative, unresponsive, wasteful, or indifferent to the responsibilities of office. And unlike impeachment, a recall arises from the political action of citizen groups, not from legislative deliberations.

The recall idea is based on the political theory that voters should retain the right of control over their elected officials. Candidates may be elected for a wide variety of reasons, including some that bear little relation to their ability to perform their public duties effectively. The premise of the recall is that if people can be elected for non-job-related reasons, they can also be removed for a variety of reasons.

By 1900 a few small communities in the West had implemented the recall. Los Angeles, then under the control of party bosses who in turn were understood to be under the control of business interests (most notably those of the Southern Pacific Railroad), was the first major jurisdiction to add the recall to its city charter. A local physician, Dr. John R. Haynes, concluded that ordinary remedies could not re-

verse the tide of corruption and organized a several-year educational
and political campaign to restore integrity to the Los Angeles government.

Dr. Haynes had seen the Swiss recall firsthand, and, like other
professional democrats of his day, he also had read about the recall
in socialist, labor, and populist manifestos. His adaptation of the recall
to Los Angeles, though patterned after some of the provisions found
in Swiss canton constitutions, was a case of local invention and initiative. His proposal to institute the recall in Los Angeles shocked
California politicians, who called it radical, revolutionary, and of
questionable constitutionality. Haynes merely replied that honest, responsible public officials had nothing to fear. The recall would
strengthen the hand of all the fine and able people in public life and
permit the political discharge of the occasional bad apples. Haynes
and his supporters asked why citizens should be required to suffer
for two, four, or even more years for relief from public officials who
had won election yet subsequently proved to be incompetent, unfaithful, or corrupt.

The recall in the United States thus had its origins in a notably
corrupt political system. None of its advocates ever viewed it as a
substitute for representative government. They merely hoped for the
restoration of relatively honest representative government as they had
known and enjoyed it in the eastern or midwestern communities where
they had previously lived. The recall arose to remedy the worst possible
side effects of representative democracy—namely, when so-called
representatives sold out to privileged interests at the expense of the
public's interests.

Under the circumstances it is little wonder that Los Angeles voters
approved the recall by a four-to-one margin when it was put to a
vote in early 1903. Subsequently, recall was adopted by similarly impressive margins in several other California cities. Oregon voters approved it for their state in June 1908.

The battle to win approval for the recall of state officials in California proved to be more difficult. Even progressives were split over
the recall of state judges. Opponents raised fears of tyranny by the
majority, the defilement of representative government, and the de-
basement of an independent judiciary. Critics warned that the judges,
along with other officeholders, would violate their oaths of office in
trying to curry favor or too hastily to serve the mob. Progressive leaders
decried the influence of special interests, especially those of the South-

ern Pacific, on even the judges. They would rather, they said, have judges "keep their ears to the ground than to the railroad tracks in California."[2]

The California legislature approved the statewide recall, including its provision for recalling judges, and referred it to the voters. When all the shouting subsided and the votes were tallied, the recall received greater support than the initiative and referendum and far greater support than women's suffrage, all of which were on the ballot in 1911. Four more states—Arizona, Colorado, Nevada, and Washington—adopted it in 1912. Since then another nine states have adopted it at the state level, and about a score more permit it for certain local officials (see Table 6.1).

Since the first tide of adoption during the Progressive era, recall has made little headway in gaining acceptance elsewhere in the nation. A national recall for federal officeholders is occasionally proposed, typically in the wake of scandals such as Watergate, yet little official action is ever mounted toward this end despite the notable support this idea commands.[3] A 1987 Gallup Organization poll commissioned for this book found significant support for amending the Constitution and permitting the recall of members of Congress and even the chief executive (see Table 6.2). Sixty-seven percent of the nationwide sample said they would like to have the Constitution permit the recall of members of Congress. A somewhat smaller percentage yet still a majority, 55 percent, favored amending the Constitution to permit the recall of the president. Nearly 20 percent more of those polled favored

Table 6.2. Public support for a national recall, 1987 (%) (N = 1009)

"In many states and communities if a large number of people sign a petition, citizens can vote to remove an elected official who is unresponsive or doing a poor job. This is called a recall election. Other states and communities do not provide for recall elections, believing such elections lessen the independence of elected officials. What is your opinion: would you favor or oppose changing the Constitution to permit national recall elections for:"

Office	Favor	Oppose	Don't know
Members of Congress	67	27	6
The president	55	38	7

Source: Gallup Organization, "The Gallup Study of Public Opinion regarding Direct Democracy Devices," conducted for Thomas E. Cronin (Princeton, N.J., September 1987).

recall of national legislators than favored a binding national referendum. Nearly 10 percent more favored the recall of members of Congress than favored a national advisory referendum (see Chapter 7). As Table 6.2 shows, only a third or so of those interviewed found the idea of recalling national elected officials undesirable.

From time to time reformers have advocated advisory recall elections, the recall of judicial decisions, or the recall of appointed officials.[4] None of these suggestions has gained even limited acceptance, although Theodore Roosevelt briefly gave a certain visibility to the notion of recalling judicial decisions.[5] The idea of applying the principle of recall to appointed officials has always met with disapproval—in large part because most people believe appointed officials should be accountable to the elected officials to whom they report.

The Case for and against the Recall

Few democratic "reforms" have sparked such sharp division of opinion as the recall. The fact that the arguments are by no means new does nothing to diminish the controversy. Advocates advance the following arguments.

1. The recall provides for continuous accountability, so that voters need not wait until the next election to rid themselves of an incompetent, dishonest, unresponsive, or irresponsible public official. The recall helps elected officials retain a candidate's state of mind. With the sword of a potential recall hanging over them, elected officials will remain alert, honest, and responsive. In this sense, the recall can be viewed as a remedy for defects in representative government. Whereas the initiative and referendum are mere modifications of representative government, recall is plainly an attempt to make government more representative in a more dramatic way—by increasing the responsiveness of elected officials to the will of the majority. Advocates claim too that the voters should have a right to discharge their public servants, just as a business executive or farmer can get rid of hired help. In short, voters should have a right to direct, explicit, and continuous control over elected officials, especially if these officials are granted long terms. The right of the people in a representative democracy involves more than the mere right to elect their leaders at stated intervals. "The recall," wrote one of its strongest defenders, "holds that a representative is a servant, an agent, not a master. To be sure, like an ambassador plenipotentiary, he is a servant with power, but he has had his specific instructions or is presumed to be acquainted with his master's will, and if he fails to recognize his responsibility or if he misinterprets his instructions, he may be recalled at any time."[6]

2. **The recall helps check undue influence by narrow special interests.** The recall makes public officials accountable not to their campaign donors, but to their constituents. It negates special interests, forcing officeholders to consider the people before any mutual back-scratching begins to take place. To be sure, this power derives from the recall's potential rather than from its actual use, but most of the time this threat will motivate officials to represent broad rather than narrow interests.

3. **The recall enables jurisdictions to permit their officials to serve longer terms.** Because of the check provided by the recall, officeholders can be trusted to longer terms in office that will, as they gain greater experience, increase their effectiveness and provide more time to plan and see things through to completion.

This argument was far more common at the turn of the century, when terms of office were generally shorter than they are today. However, modern advocates claim that the recall has helped to make longer terms more accepted today. These longer terms save taxpayers considerable election costs.

4. **The recall gives the average person a reason to stay informed about civic developments between elections.** The potential use of the recall encourages citizens to keep abreast of significant contemporary public issues and to monitor the conduct of the officeholders they elected. Citizens move toward involvement and activism and away from frustration, demoralization, and dependency.

5. **Recall offers a safety-valve mechanism for intense feelings.** A political system is generally organized and designed to contain and manage political conflicts. And, by and large, American political institutions have performed their functions well. The recall can be viewed as yet another guarantee of such stability. Although a recall election may create friction and factionalization in the short run, in the long run it usually provides a means of settling conflicts that might otherwise have intensified and caused even greater polarization.

6. The recall provides a sensible alternative to impeachment. Incumbent officeholders can often thwart efforts to impeach them. Thus President Nixon made extensive claims of executive privilege and used varied cover-up and legal maneuverings for a year and a half before he resigned to avoid impeachment proceedings. At the local level incumbent resistance can be just as extensive and sometimes even more intimidating. Local judges, district attorneys, and mayors often have considerable behind-the-scenes influence in their communities.

Obtaining official records and all other necessary evidence in an impeachment trial can be most exacting and sometimes impossible, and political corruption is often extremely difficult to prove in a court of law. The recall provides for a means to the same ends *without the extraordinary legal work.* "There are many men liable to the recall," one Progressive-era writer said, "but there are very few to whom impeachment could be successfully applied, or widely or humanely applied. The recall is a workable, practical, common sense, just measure, while impeachment is an utter failure."[7] A prudent use of the recall requires that the number of signatures be sufficiently high to protect elected officials from the irritation of fringe groups or mere partisan opposition. Since 25 percent signature levels are common, the use of the recall is, like impeachment, looked upon as a last resort. The recall's safeguards prevent popular excess. A small group would be hard pressed to force its view on the majority. Moreover, popular passions frequently cool during the required interims between petition circulation and the special recall election, providing people with more time to consider what they are doing.

▼ ▼ ▼

Opponents of the recall advance the following arguments.

1. **The very premise of the recall is antagonistic to republican principles, especially to the idea of electing good lawmakers and officials and then allowing them a chance to govern until the next election.** They should be held to account only at the next election. Lawmakers and other properly elected officials need a certain leeway and an independence within which to work. Moreover, a responsive and responsible government is not a government of a majority, by a majority, for a majority, but a government of the whole people elected

by a majority under such rules and checks as will secure a wise, prudent, and just government for all the people.

Recall weakens the fabric and the practice of representative government, encouraging short-term over long-term thinking; officials would act only according to what seemed acceptable to the public at the time. An honest and able legislator could be prevented from performing effectively when the recall's use is threatened by unsavory aspiring rivals who seize the opportunity of a temporarily unpopular decision to deprive the public of a creative public servant. At precisely such times, the recall "takes away the probability of independence and courage of official action in the servants of the people."[8]

2. Recall makes public office less attractive to the most able individuals. Since any official can be recalled on just about any grounds, it amounts to a constant and legal means of intimidation. Strong-minded persons who have convictions of their own and do not want to be mere mirrors of public whim may say no when asked to run. "The recall," wrote A. Lawrence Lowell, an early critic, "assumes . . . the representative is essentially a delegate, whose duty consists in giving effect to the prevalent opinion of his district, instead of a public servant charged to exercise his own judgment on the evidence brought before him."[9]

Every time a controversial problem is solved by elected officials, a potential critic or group of critics is likely to be aroused. Recall allows for political retribution and retaliation against officials—officials who necessarily have to make controversial decisions. Instead of being rewarded, an official is embarrassed or punished. "A strong leader with a positive program may find that some interest group will stand in his path, threatening him with a recall action if he seeks to carry out a program, even if it is the one upon which he was elected."[10]

President Taft argued against the recall of local and state officials because he feared it would inevitably lead to the recall of presidents, with pernicious results.

> Look back, my friends, through the history of the United States and recount the number of instances of men who filled important offices and whose greatness is conceded today, and tell me one who was not subject to the severest censure for what he had done, whose motives were not questioned, whose character was not attacked, and who, if subjected to a recall at certain times in his official career when criticism had impaired

his popularity, would not have been sent into private life with only a part of his term completed. Washington is one who would have been recalled, Madison another, Lincoln another and Cleveland another. These were the highest types of patriots and statesmen, who adhered to a conscientious sense of duty to the public ... Indeed the recall is nothing but the logical outcome of the proposition embodied in the referendum and the initiative, to wit that government must follow the course of popular passion and momentary expression of the people without deliberation and without opportunity for full information.[11]

3. Recall elections are divisive, disruptive, polarizing, and subject to a myriad of abuses and unintended consequences. Recall elections are invariably emotional, bitter, and sometimes even tumultuous events. Rather than solving problems, they increase tensions, dividing communities along lines of old versus new, north versus south, one ethnic group versus another, and so on. They provide instability and discontinuity. Recall elections also tempt rival factions to use smear tactics.[12] A recall election sometimes takes on the appearance of a military skirmish, with casualties and "rematches" and the escalation of retaliation. Those thrown out of office often regroup and either threaten or actually start a recall of the original recallers.

Illustrative of the turmoil, confusion, and pitfalls in recall elections is what took place when four of five school board members were removed from office in San Juan, California, in 1978. Local voters were upset by the old board's unwillingness to abide by a recently approved statewide initiative to cut property taxes. The school board apparently was challenging the law that had been put into effect by a statewide initiative and was trying to ignore or get around it. So four members were recalled. But soon a new majority was making decisions that also upset the community, and these eventually led to the firing of the school superintendent. The ensuing outcry set in motion yet another recall drive. The result of these two recall elections was a community more divided than ever.[13]

4. Recall elections are confusing, often unfair, and place too much burden on the voters to keep informed between elections. Recall elections generally stir up the citizenry and bring out a high turnout— often a larger one than at regular elections. But although the recall device assumes voters have extensive knowledge of technical finance, personnel, and administrative matters, the average citizen seldom follows community or state matters closely between elections and sometimes not even at election time.

Many if not most recall elections involve clashes of factions. The average citizen becomes confused, especially because in most areas the recall movement does not have to prove charges against the targeted official. Indeed, a recall group will sometimes use a ruse or some phony or marginal issue as a pretext for getting someone removed when its real complaint is about an altogether different issue. The voting public is unaware of the real motives that prompted the circulation of a recall petition.

Serious debate on the merit of the charges of misconduct may or may not take place. This language in the Michigan constitution indicates the political rather than judicial or deliberative character of the recall: "Laws shall be enacted to provide for the recall of all elective officers except judges of courts of record upon petition of electors equal in number to 25 percent of the numbers of persons voting in the last preceding election for the office of government in the electoral district of the officer sought to be recalled. The sufficiency of any statement of reasons or groups procedurally required *shall be a political rather than a judicial question*" (emphasis added).[14]

Further confusion arises if a recalled official wins the election in a second race (although some states prohibit an official from seeking the same office immediately). Sometimes, too, a poorly organized or poorly funded recall, defeated either at the signature level or at the election, results in a vindication of or vote of confidence in a person who really should have been recalled. Someone who wins such an undeserved vote of confidence could become even more irresponsible than before and also harder to remove at the next election.

5. Recall elections are costly, unnecessary, and directed against the wrong target. One of the strongest arguments against the recall is the expense of conducting a special election, especially when it involves a large city or an entire state. Moreover, the resulting political turmoil and expense are unnecessary given the existence of provisions for impeachment by the legislature or similar actions by the executive or judicial branch. Finally, because citizens do not always understand which level of government affects them in what way on what issues, recall is sometimes used against local officials who are merely implementing federal policy. Thus, a Los Angeles school board chairman was recalled because he helped implement a federal court order concerning school integration. Voters were unable to retaliate against the federal judge or Supreme Court, so they vented their frustrations on the official closest to them.

In sum, according to opponents, the recall device causes more problems than it solves. It robs elected officials of the independence and detachment that enables them to weigh conflicting values and longer-range considerations. It adds to the voters' already burdened political obligations. Voters are already asked to vote at national, state, and local elections; to choose among hundreds of candidates for scores of offices; and to pass upon the merits of proposed constitutional amendments, bond issues, and often ordinary legislation as well. Citizens perform these already multiple tasks indifferently or grudgingly, and frequently 50 to 70 percent of them refrain altogether. Moreover, recall can be wrenchingly divisive for a community. Finally, if people would only elect virtuous and competent persons to office in the first place, recall would never be necessary. In that sense, recall approaches the problem from the wrong direction and emphasizes the wrong concerns.

How the Recall Works

San Franciscans experienced a highly publicized recall election in April 1983. In late 1982, after Mayor Dianne Feinstein had pushed for the adoption of a strict handgun control measure and succeeded in getting it approved by the San Francisco Board of Supervisors, a small band of pro-gun leftists, called the White Panthers, began circulating petitions to recall the mayor. People generally ignored it as just another fringe protest, since the White Panthers controlled no political offices and had a small membership of at most several dozen. Some of them had served jail sentences for violent activities.

Yet the Panthers persisted in their crusade to get the mayor's and the public's attention. Over several months they collected nearly 24,000 valid signatures, considerably more than the low signature requirement of 10 percent of those who voted in the last election. They enlisted the support of others—some neighborhood groups aroused by the mayor's support of downtown business and development interests, and some gay groups disaffected by her lack of support for gay rights measures. People involved in obtaining the signatures were too disparate to forge an effective strategy, and they had little money. They knew they would lose the election, but they wanted to keep the mayor's margin of victory down to about 60 percent, in the hope of encouraging serious opponents to run against her in the November 1983 regular election.

Mayor Feinstein was initially startled and viewed the recall drive as a personal insult. "Why me?" she asked. The politically ambitious mayor believed other mayors and political figures around the country would view it as a sign of her ineptitude. All in all, it was embarrassing, and she most assuredly did not want to be the first San Francisco mayor to be recalled.

In San Francisco the recall petition drive only places the question on the ballot. A second election is held for voting on the replacement only if the petition drive is successful.

The mayor hired an imaginative California campaign consultant to handle this special election. He based his strategy on the premise that the mayor was popular and could win if the recall was turned into a referendum on her record. The mayor and her closest aides thought she should go to the voters and vigorously defend her record and performance.

Yet the campaign consultant rejected that strategy. Popular as the mayor was, she was not *that* popular. Better, he believed, not to get trapped into having the recall serve as a referendum on her performance. There are always enough people who are dissatisfied with any mayor, at least on one or two policy areas, that she might just get a 50 or 55 percent approval rating—or less.

Early polls verified the consultant's fear. People, he found, were more upset with the waste and unnecessary costs of the recall election than they were positive in their approval of the mayor's performance. Thus, to win by the largest margin and to scare off possible challengers in the upcoming November election race, the mayor's strategists decided to make it a referendum on the recall itself, not on the mayor. Feinstein and her advisers framed the debate and developed the campaign with that theme; they had the necessary money to set the agenda. The overall strategy was to get a high turnout; to portray the mayor as a hardworking, incorruptible victim of a small, single-interest faction; and, above all, to emphasize that the recall election was unnecessary: it was wasteful (it would cost $450,000 in public funds), irresponsible, improper, and an abuse of an important democratic device. Said the mayor in the voter information pamphlet prepared for the election:

The recall is an invitation to chaos. If I am recalled, it is possible San Francisco could have four Mayors within a period of one year. I would serve until early May. Then the President of the Board of Supervisors would act as Mayor until the Board elects a Mayor to serve out the remainder of my term. Then, in November, the voters would elect a Mayor.

No major city should be pitched into such uncertainty. In 1979, the voters elected me to a four-year term. The recall election in April comes just seven months before the November election and pits me against an unknown.

There is no candidate against whom to compare my record. There is no choice, no alternative, just a question mark as to who will administer this complex city until January 8, 1984, when the next four-year term begins.

Orderly government cannot prevail on the shifting sands of a recall brought, not because of any corruption or incompetence, but because of a difference of opinion on an issue. Recall for such a narrow purpose becomes an instrument to stalemate decision-making and disrupt government. Government should not hinge on the virulence of single-issue groups.[15]

On recall election day, 81 percent of San Franciscans who voted (about 45 percent of the city's registered voters) voted against the recall, indicating they were persuaded such a device should be reserved for more appropriate occasions. As the *San Francisco Examiner* observed in an editorial two days later, "There was no conceivable reason to recall Feinstein; she was guilty of neither crime nor incompetence." Moreover, she ought not to have been subjected to this ordeal and diverted from her duties on such frivolous grounds. "The people recognize the injustice of it, and the offense to the process of democracy."[16]

A year later, in March 1984, the recall was used to remove the mayor of Atlantic City, New Jersey, a community with a signature requirement of 25 percent of the electorate. The law in New Jersey, though not permitting recall at the state level, provides for the recall question to be on the ballot in various cities, followed by a second question on who should be the mayor if the majority of voters favor the recall. No transition period is allowed.

The Atlantic City recall election pitted against each other two men who had run for mayor two years earlier. It also pitted a black

Republican challenger against a white Democratic incumbent who was a former state senator. The challenger had campaigned for a recall of the mayor for more than a year, saying the mayor was not communicating with black neighborhoods and was failing to solve several other city problems. He defeated the mayor despite being outspent nearly two-and-a-half to one, in part because the mayor was under federal investigation for accepting illegal campaign contributions. In fact, after the recall the mayor was indicted.

Political analysts generally viewed the Atlantic City recall as a justified use of the recall process. It was, to be sure, a polarizing election, yet it served to remove a mayor who was increasingly viewed as failing to do the job, who had more than two years remaining in his term, and who was also under a cloud of suspected wrongdoing. The voters, by a three-to-two margin, brought his public service to an abrupt end.

The Recall Record

Frequency

Perhaps as many as 4,000 to 5,000 recall elections have been held; several thousand more have been begun but have failed to qualify for lack of signatures. Countless recall drives fail because of technical and legal difficulties that arise even after signatures have been obtained. Incumbent officials often frustrate a recall drive by raising technical objections to the validity of signatures, the form of the petition, or the lack of specificity in the complaint against the officials. "Even if the proponents are vindicated in resulting litigation, they may have lost much of the momentum and organization needed to sustain a recall drive. Moreover, a recall petition is frequently directed against precisely those officers (e.g., incumbent county supervisors or city council members) who are charged with the duty of ordering a local recall election; the officers under attack have the opportunity to persuade a majority of the board or council not to call the election, or to influence the clerk not to certify a sufficient number of signatures."[17]

A survey of existing research suggests that nearly 50 percent of the recalls that get to the election stage succeed in removing at least some of the elected officials targeted for removal. (In about a third of recall campaigns, more than one official is being recalled.) A 50 percent success ratio seems high unless one remembers that the recall, like impeachment, is a cumbersome, complicated, last-resort procedure that requires significant organizational stamina, drive, and intensity to reach the ballot box stage.

The recall device is ideologically neutral. No prototype public official gets targeted for recall. "Recall victims," concluded a political scientist who surveyed California counties and their recall patterns, "spanned the ideological spectrum, and recall efforts were directed by liberals against conservative incumbents nearly as often as conservatives were going after liberal officeholders. Issues such as corruption, unresponsiveness or extravagance tended to generate recall efforts."[18]

A study of recall efforts in Los Angeles, where more than forty-five recall elections have occurred, found voters generally have rejected "politically inspired" recalls—movements in which sour grapes or personal feuds and ambitions were the chief reason behind the recall. "Los Angeles voters have generally preferred to reserve the recall for its originally intended use (to weed out malfeasance and corruption) and to settle political questions at regular elections."[19] The same can be said of most citizens elsewhere who have exercised the right of recall.

Finally, judges are occasionally recalled in those states extending the recall to that office. In 1977 a state judge in Madison, Wisconsin, Archie Simonson, was quickly recalled by irate citizens who were aroused by a statement he had made in a rape case. He had suggested the sixteen-year-old young woman in question had been dressed in such a way as to tempt or invite sexual assault, and he placed the offending fifteen-year-old male youth on probation. Simonson quickly learned about the growing capacity of the feminist movement and its allies to mobilize public sentiment. He was recalled, and a woman judge was elected as his replacement. Another Wisconsin judge barely survived a recall election in 1982 after he said from the bench that a youthful victim of sexual assault had been unusually promiscuous.

Voter Turnout

Even though most recall elections are special elections, they have high voter turnout—indeed, usually higher than in the regular general election that first brought the candidate to office. In small or medium-sized communities these turnouts are often impressive (see Table 6.3). Thus a 1974 Boulder, Colorado, recall election generated the second-highest voter turnout for an election in that city's history—47 percent. A 1981 city council recall election in Manitou Springs, Colorado, wit-

Table 6.3. Eligible voter participation in selected recall elections, 1924–1987 (%)

Year	Locality and office	%
1924	Anaheim, Calif., city council trustees	93
1935	Lane County district, Ore., state legislator	about 50
1959	Little Rock, Ark., school board	58
1978	Pueblo, Colo., district attorney	49
1978	Easton, Mass., school board	47
1978	Cleveland, Ohio, mayor	42
1979	Los Angeles, Calif., school board chair	21
1980	Basalt, Colo., mayor	75
1981	Woodland Park, Colo., mayor and two councilmen	47
1983	San Francisco, Calif., mayor	45
1983	Colorado Springs, Colo., city councilman	18
1983	Cripple Creek, Colo., school board member	60
1987	Omaha, Neb., mayor	56

Source: Various state publications, newspaper articles.

nessed a 43 percent turnout on a subzero February day. A 1987 Omaha recall had a 56 percent turnout.

At least two factors contribute to this phenomenon. One is the passionate emotions ignited in such campaigns, not only in those who have launched the recall effort but also in the threatened incumbent. A recall campaign incorporates all the tactics, strategies, and cunning of an ordinary election, but with added intrigue. The incumbent inevitably feels bitter, resentful, and humiliated: no one wants to be thrown out of office in disgrace—especially before the end of a normal term. The other factor is closely related and intensifies some recall elections: the incumbent's use of subtle (or not so subtle) intimidating influences of his or her office. Thus in Cleveland's 1978 recall election involving Mayor Dennis Kucinich, "Hundreds of municipal employees were directed to spend evenings and off-time on the streets so that city-homes of every registered voter could be personally canvassed by a Kucinich loyalist."[20]

Other Effects

A few additional aspects of the recall deserve consideration.

▼ ▼ ▼

Has the recall discouraged talented people from running for elective office? No evidence exists to support the claim that the recall device deters would-be candidates for public office. Individuals often cite reasons such as privacy, family, financial considerations, health, and business or professional demands for declining to run for elective office, yet few have ever cited recall as a serious reason for not "throwing their hat in the ring."

If people decide not to run for political positions because of recall, they should not run for office. This specter of the recall turning potential elected officials into cowards unwilling to run is an exaggeration.

Thus it is improbable these same officials would warn friends against running because of the existence of the recall. Also, the negligible percentage of officials involved in recall elections suggests that most would-be candidates believe they would have reasonable leeway in exercising their judgment in making most policy decisions. Most hardworking, civic-minded citizens who are interested in public service believe either that their actions and decisions in a public office would be agreeable to their community or that they could educate the community to go along with them.

The recall has been used most often when arbitrary or incompetent officials have angered the public. It has sometimes been used when an emotional issue such as school integration or dramatic tax increases has divided a community. But although there have been occasions when the recall was used for the wrong motives, there is no evidence it has led to any loss of talented volunteers for elective office.

▼ ▼ ▼

Has the recall led to more representative and more responsive government? "I think recall keeps officeholders a bit more responsive and accountable," said a local judge whom I interviewed in 1983. "Frankly, I think more highly of the recall than I do of the initiative and referendum despite the potential for abuse in the use of the recall," he added.[21]

Because of its relatively infrequent use, the recall has not usually been a disruptive factor in representative government. On the other hand, it is exceedingly difficult to prove that its availability has improved the responsiveness of public officials. Polls indicate that citizens favor the recall device, and it generally wins easy approval when put to the people for a vote (an exception is Utah, where it was narrowly defeated in a statewide vote a few years ago). Still, no one can prove that the recall has actually reduced corruption in those state and local governments providing for it. Corruption may still exist in Oregon, California, Colorado, and Arizona despite the early institutionalization of the recall in these states (although these are generally regarded as good-government states).

▼ ▼ ▼

Does the recall intensify political conflicts? The recall is plainly a procedure involving confrontation rather than conciliation. It creates and sometimes amplifies political turmoil in a community, county, or state. A recall contest provides little or no occasion for bargaining between opponents as in legislative or even some regular candidate elections, but instead requires a no-compromise, either/or choice by the voter.[22] By inhibiting conflict resolution strategies such as bargaining and compromise, many recall campaigns do intensify rather than reduce conflict.

Although in some cases intensity and political upheaval continue after a recall election, this result is not entirely surprising: factions are a normal phenomenon and usually persist regardless of election arrangements. A recall election is almost always a symptom or by-product rather than a direct cause of political conflict. And in most recall situations, the community is able to resolve the political conflict occasioned by the recall.

▼ ▼ ▼

Is the recall used in a reckless way that harms the rights of citizens and officeholders? The chief purpose and historical use of the recall has been to remove corrupt or irresponsible officials, but inevitably the recall has sometimes also reflected a campaign to remove an official because of his or her policy views: one person's responsible official is another person's irresponsible official; one person's "statesperson" is another's "bum." Thus, Boulder's city council in 1973 approved an ordinance prohibiting discrimination based on sexual orientation. Indirectly, if not explicitly, this was a gay rights measure. Some displeased citizens launched a campaign against those who had been on the council long enough to be recalled. Signatures were quickly gathered, and a special recall election was held in 1974. The mayor barely survived with a 51 percent vote. One member of the city council was recalled. Policy and value differences sparked the recall.

Who was right in Boulder? From a civil liberties standpoint the city council was right. Yet a large number of citizens were unready for and indeed intensely opposed to the council's stand. They believed their council was too far ahead of the citizenry and hence unresponsive. Were they not entitled to express their views and to expect their representatives to heed them?

Another example of a recall caused by policy differences occurred in Los Angeles in 1979, when voters recalled school board president Howard Miller entirely because he had become the symbol of public school busing. Miller's opponents raised no credible accusations of personal misconduct, criminality, or dishonesty in the conduct of his performance. Rather, they stressed their political or policy differences. Miller was recalled with a 58 percent vote favoring his removal.

About a year later I interviewed Miller in Los Angeles. What did he think of the recall process? He responded that "recall clearly serves a purpose," noting that, unlike a parliamentary system, with its votes of no confidence, the United States has a system of fixed terms. In light of this he accepted the recall process as a valid and practical tool of accountability. "On balance, I'd still stick with it [the recall process]," said Miller.[23]

Others who have been recalled or threatened with recall because of policy differences believe the recall laws should be changed. Thus Oregon state senator Charles Hanlon said in a 1980 interview that although he favored the initiative process, recall was a different matter. Hanlon worried that voters could recall officials "for no reason at all," and he thought the device was occasionally abused. He tried in vain to get a bill passed in the state legislature requiring a specific reason, such as malfeasance or misfeasance, to be documented before a recall could be brought to the ballot stage. Although many of his colleagues said recall "had not been abused that much," most of the opposition to his bill came from Oregon newspapers, according to Hanlon.[24]

Hanlon had himself been subject to a recall soon after his election to the state senate in 1975. Later he had the legislature's legislative research staff conduct various studies on the reasons given by recall campaigners. Their studies revealed a marked lack of specificity in the reasons cited in recall petitions. Subjective or emotional factors were the motivation in a majority of cases. According to the legislative council staff, the recall, as used in Oregon, "is becoming an increasingly popular means by which the general public can remove a public official from office for whatever reason they see fit."[25] In March 1988, however, voters in and around Medford, Oregon, recalled state senator

Bill Olson despite his pleas for forgiveness after he had pleaded guilty to sexual abuse of a thirteen-year-old girl.

▼ ▼ ▼

Does the recall turn elected officials into cowards, depriving them of the independence of their convictions and their purpose to make necessary but sometimes unpopular leadership decisions? A spokesman for the National Municipal League told me in an interview in 1980 that recalls diminish civil rights and civil liberties. He cited as an example one southern city whose whole governing body was once recalled because it ordered the city swimming pools desegregated. "An undesirable consequence of the recall," he emphasized, "is that elected officials may be unwilling to deal with tough controversial issues. They merely become, because of the recall, more cautious and conservative."[26]

Some evidence does exist that recall elections have been used to remove officials who held or displayed unpopular views. In 1917 Anna Louise Strong was apparently recalled because of her pacifist and "radical" views concerning America's involvement in World War I. Two Idaho state legislators were recalled in 1971 over the always controversial and usually unpopular issue of legislative pay raises. An attempted petition drive to recall three members of the Tempe, Arizona, city council was pushed by reactionary interests after whispered general rumors were spread that they were communist sympathizers. In 1979 the president of the Los Angeles school board was recalled primarily because of his moderate support of school desegregation plans. Two Michigan state legislators were recalled because they voted for a controversial hike in state taxes in 1983. A Colorado Springs city councilman survived a 1985 recall by neighborhood activists aroused at his and the city council's aggressive progrowth and development policies.

Because voters choose officials as much on the basis of character, party affiliation, and name recognition as on the basis of policy views, persons with unpopular views often get elected and even reelected. Moreover, America's fondness for a "profiles in courage" tradition often lends legitimacy to the holding of a particular unpopular view, so long as the official is viewed as acting in the public interest most of the time.

A few officials probably minimize risktaking because of the recall.

It is doubtful, however, that the recall device encourages this any more than the fact that they must stand for reelection. Politicians are generally cautious. By definition they want to retain majority and plurality support. Democratic elections encourage this. Recall is merely an additional device—a form of insurance.

The question is whether or not the recall deprives an elected official of the sense of independence necessary to exercise imagination, initiative, and prudent thinking about the public interest. Most of the people interviewed for this study say the recall does not dampen these desirable traits. Most would agree with the city official who told me: "Despite what I went through, I'd keep the recall—it's useful to have and it's needed. I certainly wouldn't do away with it, but some things can be done to improve the recall process."[27]

A related question is whether the recall has undermined the possibility of long-range planning at the state or city level. "In those commonwealths (states) where it [recall] has not been adopted, a governor or other officer is free to use the methods that seem to him best suited to the solution of each problem, even though the reasons for his choice are not immediately apparent to the casual observer," wrote one public administration specialist. "He knows that he will not be required to give an accounting until election day, and that the intervening months or years will make the wisdom of his course apparent to all except the blindest partisans. But the governor who is subject to the recall is not so fortunately situated . . . He must shift his course to meet every passing thrust of public fancy."[28] No evidence exists to support this assertion. No one can say with any assurance that governors, state legislators, or mayors in New York, Massachusetts, or South Carolina act with any less sensitivity to the public's mood than officials in the western "radical" states. Surely Governors Ronald Reagan and Edmund G. Brown, Jr., in California, Richard D. Lamm and Roy Romer in Colorado, and Bruce Babbitt in Arizona, to name some recent ones, acted with just as much independence and freedom as their eastern counterparts.

Progressive writer Herbert Croly long ago concluded that recall would not turn elected officials into cowards. It would not, he predicted, deprive them of their needed independence. If it produced any such effect, he wrote, the ultimate failure of democratic government would be tolerably well assured. Croly believed a person of independent yet unpopular convictions had every right and should be given full opportunity to convert fellow citizens. Yet this official had no right to force voters to accept the consequences of his convictions, or those of any other individual or minority.

> An elected official, endowed with a long term and with effective powers, yet subject to the recall, would have a far better chance of being independent than an official who had an indefensible title to an impoverished office for a comparatively limited term. The fact that he would constantly be threatened with the loss of popular confidence would act upon a man of independence of convictions as a stimulus to personal initiative. He would possess an extraordinary opportunity of recommending his own opinions to the public. He could make himself independent just insofar as he was capable of maintaining his leadership of public opinion; and only to that extent would he as a representative official be entitled to independence. Whenever under such conditions he ceased to be independent, the fault would be his own . . . Doubtless the very conditions which might afford a strong and shrewd man an opportunity of guiding public opinion would convert a weak and unscrupulous man into a mere demagogue; but such a danger is inseparable from any system of organized popular political leadership.[29]

Croly presents the paradox of the recall as well as anyone else before or since. The recall provides protection against demagogues yet allows constitutions to provide for longer terms and more robust powers for public officials. These latter provisions permit and can even encourage strong, forceful leadership willing to shape opinion in an enlightened direction.

Regulating the Recall Device

No uniform procedure exists for the recall. In many states and localities there is only one election—for both recall and replacement. If the officeholder survives recall, he or she remains in office and there is no vacancy. If the officeholder loses, a second election is held on the same recall ballot that allows voters to choose a replacement. Some states—such as Arizona—and communities—such as Massachusetts home-rule cities and Atlantic City—allow the recalled person's name to appear on the ballot as a candidate for reelection; thus the recalled official could conceivably win immediate reelection. In such places, two ballot choices are put to the voter: first, whether the official in question should be recalled; second, a choice of who should replace the official, including (if the person subject to the recall fights to get on the ballot again) the official who is the target of the recall effort. Most jurisdictions—such as Colorado and San Francisco—prohibit the recalled person from running again immediately for the same office.

The considerable variation in these arrangements has caused confusion and extensive litigation. For example, in 1914 the Oregon supreme court held that the questions of (1) whether the person should be recalled and (2) who his or her replacement (if necessary) should be were distinct questions that must be handled separately on the recall ballot. Subsequently procedures were changed, and Oregon voters were given the opportunity to vote yes or no as to whether to recall a person and to vote for one of the possible replacement candidates (usually including the officer whose recall was being sought).

A problem arose with this procedure. On certain occasions the vote to recall was successful, yet the recalled person still managed to win enough votes in the new election to win reelection. As a result, election officials arranged for a period between the two elections, presumably to allow the opposition forces to get behind a serious challenger.

Perhaps the most controversial aspect of the recall process is the lack of specificity required by the law for individuals' or groups' reasons for seeking to recall a public official. Many observers and many victims of recall efforts say an official should be subject to recall *only* when that official has clearly displayed misfeasance, malfeasance, or nonfeasance. "In plain English, that means the politician has stolen from the treasury or proved to be completely incompetent."[30] Others note that the reasons cited are often different from the emotional or subjective reason that really prompts the recall effort. Sometimes those who lose an election try to harass an official, using the recall as merely one of several political guerrilla tactics. Sometimes, too, there are wild charges, just plain unfair charges, or charges that are vague, unspecific and wrong.

At least three-fourths of the recall elections in America take place at the city council and school board level. A main reason for its infrequent use in the largest cities or against elected state officials is the large number of signatures needed to trigger a recall election. Generally this figure is 25 percent of those voting in the last election. Yet even in California, where the signature requirement is only 12 percent, recall is difficult to instigate on a statewide basis. Attempts to recall three California governors (in 1940, 1960, and 1968) all failed for lack of enough signatures. A recall of the governor of California in the 1980s would require about 800,000 signatures.

Two other reasons why recall is not used more against state legislators are that most are elected for two-year terms and that it is difficult to fasten the blame for the work of the entire legislature on a single legislator. Legislators can often justify their position on a measure by saying they were powerless to pass (or defeat) it in this session or that it was the people in committee who really "bottled it up." Or they might say, "I was for the general principle but not for the particular measure in question because of the way it was written." Then, too, much legislation is passed in the last few weeks or even days of a legislative session. By the time their work is done, at least in many of the smaller states that still hold short sessions, legislators are already back home before the voters can become aroused enough to rally behind a recall movement. By that time the legislative session is over and voters can just as effectively "punish" a legislator by voting him or her out at the next general election.

In contrast, school board or county commissioners or members of city councils are in constant session and are making decisions all the time. There are fewer of them, and they are nearly always on the spot. Moreover, irate citizens can see them right there in their home community and watch how they vote. Whereas bicameralism may confuse accountability in a state legislature, the smaller unicameral local legislatures are subject to far more open scrutiny and hence a more direct, explicit accountability.

Recall elections often occur in communities where factions have already formed and dissatisfaction is high. In most recalls that reach the election stage, a valid grievance exists; an official or officials have been excessively rude, extravagant, unresponsive, or incompetent. A grievance often stems from the neglect of a certain segment of the community.

The arbitrary or wanton exercise of the recall to displace or harass conscientious officials usually backfires, as it did in the San Francisco recall effort of 1983. A few years ago a Des Moines, Iowa, police official was threatened with recall by gambling interests. He immediately publicized this threat in the local papers, and the recall failed to materialize. In 1975 a Seattle mayor was subject to a recall organized in large part by public employees. The mayor spoke directly to the public about the issue and won a resounding 63 percent of the vote—a margin that allowed him to treat the election as a virtual vote of confidence in his performance.

The sponsor of a recall election bears the burden of proof for justifying removal. In regular elections campaigners strive to make the best possible case for why their candidate should win. In a recall the main strategy for the recallers is to convince people that "the rascals," "crooks," or "incompetents" should be thrown out of office. "The factual alignment of interests, the shrewd political manipulators, and the crowd with its gregarious inertia are ever-present factors," wrote Frederick L. Bird and Frances M. Ryan. But "the circumstances of an emergency referendum on the question of summarily dismissing a public official charged with betraying his trust arouses a tension and an excitement developed in regular elections only when vital issues are at stake."[31]

Most states have instituted safeguards intended to minimize abuses of the recall device. Additional safeguards are suggested from time to time.

Most states, in addition to signature requirements, prohibit the initiation of a recall against an official until he or she has held office for at least six months. Several states also prohibit a second recall attempt during the same term, or for at least the next year; other states and communities merely prohibit a repeat recall for three to six months. Such restrictions are designed to prevent "sour grapes" recalls and to reduce the risk of needless harassment.

Regulations for the recall vary considerably. One study of recall provisions in thirty-three Massachusetts cities and towns found marked differences in the number required to sign an affidavit for recall (from 1 to 200), in the number required to sign the recall petition (from 5 to 25 percent of those who voted in the last election), in the timing of the recall election (from 25 to 110 days), and in prohibitions against a repeat recall (from no prohibition to one year).[32]

Other regulations in effect in some states include:

Criminal penalties for misrepresenting or making false statements about the petition to gain signatures, for filing or circulating a petition known to contain false signatures, and for using a recall petition as a threat to extort money

Requiring sponsors of a recall, through their treasurer, to file documents listing those who contributed to their effort, as well as all expenditures

Requiring sponsors to circulate and file the completed petition within ninety days

Requiring verification of petitions in state recalls by the secretary of state, using a statistical sampling technique

Additional regulations occasionally suggested, especially by those who have experienced a recall, include:

1. Requiring a "cooling-off" period between the deadline for petitions and the election itself.

2. Requiring a public hearing at which both sides could state their cases and debate and deliberate on the recall charges. A variation on this would be to require a preliminary trial by a citizen body or jury after a certain percentage of petition signatures had been gathered. A jury would be selected by lot and asked to decide impartially whether or not adequate grounds existed for recall. The petitioners could present their case, and the official would have the opportunity to defend his or her record. If the jury absolved the official, the recall petitioners might be required to obtain an additional 5 to 10 percent of signatures in order to justify their case for a recall election. If the jury agreed that there was just cause for a recall election, an election would be set for a date perhaps thirty to fifty days later.

3. Requiring greater specificity in recall charges in order to allow the targeted official to answer them.

The first suggestion would be easier to implement than the other two. Yet a properly designed public hearing, either during or after the petition gathering, could enhance the quality and quantity of information available to voters. The idea of a jury hearing appears to be too cumbersome in a process that is already awkward, but it would provide an additional safeguard. It would also check one procedural democracy device with yet another procedural democracy device.

The problem of providing for more specificity in recall charges probably remains the most frustrating aspect of the recall. Vague or flimsy charges or even charges different from those that really motivated the recall characterize about a third of the recall elections I have studied. On the other hand, requiring more specific justifications might well defeat the reason for making the device available. Some tightening can and should be achieved, but dissatisfaction is likely to continue.

Conclusion

The recall is sometimes called the "gun behind the door" that keeps officials responsive, yet in practice the "gun" is heavy, complicated, and requires countless people to aim and fire it. And, like a gun, it occasionally backfires.

In numerous recalls, as in San Francisco, those who triggered a recall have witnessed a landslide vote of confidence for the targeted official. And the reverse has also happened. Thus in Oregon's Rogue River School District in the 1970s, criticism of four school board members grew so intense that their wives started a recall move against them. "Its purpose was to clear the air by having their husbands win the election and reaffirm the support of the community," according to the *Oregon Statesmen*. "The election was held, and their husbands lost."[33]

The recall device, often viewed as a direct democracy device, has not significantly improved direct communication between leaders and led and has not ended corruption in politics. Neither has it produced better-qualified officeholders or noticeably enriched the quality of citizenship or democracy in those places permitting it. Whether it has strengthened representative government in any measurable way seems doubtful.

The recall device has sometimes served as a tool to weed out an incompetent, corrupt, or arbitrary official or as a catalyst of increased sensitivity to a segment of the community. Properly used, the recall device can instruct a legislative body or other officials about the changing mood of the citizenry and can be a constructive form of a vote of no confidence. It can be a positive device that reminds elected officials they are the temporary agents of the public they must serve. When improperly used, it can encourage demagogues or excessive majoritarianism.

How one views the recall, writes political scientist Charles M. Price, depends "to a large degree on how one views the American electorate. Are voters uninformed, indifferent, prejudicial and easily manipulated? Or, are American voters basically reasonable, well-educated, capable and interested?"[34]

Today's critics of the recall device continue to view it as an invitation to unruly, impatient action and as a potential hazard to representative government. They also say it is yet another media-age factor that could weaken the party system. No evidence exists to support either contention.

Power may not always corrupt, yet it does have this tendency. The recall strikes at incumbent arrogance. "Given all of the advantages of name recognition, availability of money and staff, incumbents normally win reelection in the American system. This, in turn, means that some officeholders can become smug or disdainful in their attitude toward the public. Incumbents in recall-vulnerable communities are forced to be more responsive to the public since they cannot assume they have a lock on their offices."[35]

Thus the recall device, so long as there are stiff signature requirements and proper safeguards, remains a helpful yet crude safety valve at the state and community levels. It permits citizens to eject those officials who violate the public trust. It has not, in any essential way, lessened the independence of well-intentioned public officials.

The best safeguard is to educate voters to the potential pitfalls and undesirable side effects of the recall device. Voters, when confronting recall petitions or a recall election choice, need to be encouraged to ask who started the recall and for what reasons. Was there a legitimate grievance? Who is financing and promoting the effort? Have other less formidable and less costly methods of correcting the situation been tried? Will the recall provide an effective remedy? Can the matter wait until the next election? Is this an appropriate use of the recall device? The mere asking of these questions will help to guard against gullibility and undue haste.

CHAPTER 7

▼

A National Initiative and Referendum?

▼

America needs more direct democracy. It is a way in which we can restore meaning to our democracy and truly give people the opportunity to control their destiny.

—Mark Hatfield, 1979

The track record of representative government—of the U.S. Congress in particular—is abysmal, particularly in comparison to the record of direct democracy. In California . . . the people have acted deliberately, rationally, purposefully, and responsibly through the process of referenda and initiatives . . . Why not adopt the California system of direct democracy at the national level? In economic matters, at least, it is hard to imagine that the people could do worse than their elected representatives.

—Arthur D. Laffer, 1983

THE NATIONAL initiative and referendum have not been advocated nearly so often as these devices have been proposed at the state and local levels. Yet they are regularly proposed and enjoy support from the general public. Although most political and elected officials either oppose or refrain from supporting them, some leaders across the political spectrum actively champion different versions of the idea.

I do not think either device is now necessary or desirable at the federal level, although either would probably help attract more voters to the polls. According to most of the proposals, issues of war and peace would be off limits for a national initiative, as would most issues concerning the Bill of Rights. One wonders whether complicated economic and budget issues should be left to occasional yes-or-no referendum verdicts. Regular federal elections every two years, however imperfect, already serve to send a message on general national issues. And tax-slashing measures or environmental state ballot measures, if they succeed in enough states, also now serve to send a message to officials in the national government. But perhaps a central reason to oppose a national initiative is that its expense would nearly always restrict its use to large, well-financed organizations, some of them perhaps extremist political, social, or religious groups.

Still, it is a proposal that seems to be here to stay. It has been proposed and defeated a number of times in Congress. Most recently, in the late 1970s, the U.S. Senate held hearings on a proposed amendment to the Constitution that would have permitted a national voter initiative. That proposal died in committee, yet debate about the general idea of a national referendum continues.

The same arguments are heard that have been advanced at the state level. It is, say its advocates, the only way to make government truly responsive, to make sure officials keep promises after they are elected. Champions of the national initiative have a strong Jeffersonian faith in the people. "I think the country would have been a hell of a lot better governed over the past fifty years if we had a national initiative," said the godfather of modern-day polling, George Gallup, Sr. He did not mean that the voice of the people was the voice of God. "It's more a question of who's more likely to be right. On the most major issues we've dealt with in the past 50 years, the public was more likely to be right . . . than the legislature or Congress."[1]

Contemporary critics of direct democracy for the nation echo the sentiments of the Constitution's framers in 1787: they believe there is often a difference between public opinion and the public interest. Prudent judgment about national policies should be shaped by deliberative bodies in representative institutions. Moreover, to ask average citizens to pass complex domestic and economic planning matters is to overburden their knowledge and their interest except on highly emotional issues—and these are the very issues that cry out for sensitive debate and deliberation.

Times have changed, however. Americans are used to being regularly polled and to reading public opinion poll results. Technology makes it easier and easier to discover the public's policy preferences.

Telephone companies and television and radio programs regularly combine their resources to conduct "instant" media referenda. Although the thinking of the framers still has considerable merit, new and different political realities make it important to reevaluate the call for a national initiative or referendum.

How Would a National Referendum Work?

Reformers have proposed several different types of initiatives and national referenda, ranging from purely advisory or consultative measures—which would operate much the same as a national public opinion survey operates—to measures that would be binding and have the full force of federal law.

Some commonly promoted national referendum processes would allow citizens to vote on issues that are already before or have already been acted upon by the Congress. Here are two examples:

> Whenever the president and Congress are in conflict or deadlock on domestic legislation, either or both may submit the question at issue to a referendum vote of the electorate.

> The people of the United States may petition for referendum on national legislation, after passage by Congress . . . When 10 percent of registered voters in more than one-third of all states sign a legal petition for referendum, the proposed law shall be put to majority decision of the electorate at the next regularly scheduled election.[2]

Another version is the proposed national initiative that was much discussed in the late 1970s. Its chief sponsor was U.S. Senator James Abourezk (D.–S.D.), and it was also championed by Congressman James Jones (D.–Okla.). Their measure, supported at the time by at least fifty members of Congress, allowed advocates of a policy measure eighteen months to gather a number of signatures equal to 3 percent of the ballots cast in the preceding presidential election, including 3 percent in each of at least ten states—that is, about 3 million signatures. After these requirements were met, the measure would be voted on at the next regularly scheduled national election. If a majority of people casting votes on the ballot question approved, the proposed law would be enacted and would take effect thirty days after the election, or as mandated in the law itself.

According to this proposed amendment, the initiative could not be used to amend the Constitution, call up troops, or declare war. Laws adopted by the national voter initiative would, like the laws passed by Congress, be subject to review by the federal courts. The Abourezk–Jones national initiative also gave Congress the right to repeal or amend the public-enacted law by a two-thirds vote in both houses within two years of its adoption. After this period Congress could amend or repeal the measure by a simple majority vote.

Initiatives and Referenda in Other Nations

Direct democracy elections or plebiscites are nearly as old as the idea of democracy. The notion of a plebiscite goes back at least to ancient Rome. A plebiscite is a direct vote in which voters are invited to accept or refuse the measure, program, or government of the person or party initiating the consultation, and is a consultation whereby citizens exercise the right of national self-determination. It derives from the Latin *plebiscitum,* "the people's decree"—from *plebs,* "common people," and *scire,* "to approve, to seek, to know."

Plebiscites have been used in Europe to unify disparate city-states (Italy), to create new nations (Norway's separation from Sweden in 1905), and to settle boundary disputes (Schleswig in the early 1920s). Napoleon Bonaparte used plebiscites to demonstrate support of successive annexations and constitutional revisions. Hitler, de Gaulle, and Nasser used plebiscites to demonstrate their popular support. Hitler used an existing referendum process to get Germany out of the League of Nations in 1933 and to gain approval for merging the powers of president with his role as chancellor in 1934. But his use of this device on these and other occasions was plainly an effort to win fresh popular mandates for his dictatorial authority; they were extraordinary examples of Nazi propaganda efforts and a controlled one-sided media campaign. De Gaulle used the plebiscite to obtain a vote of confidence on his policies and to weaken his political opposition. One of his more notable plebiscites was on the Algerian question; France's decision to pull out of Algeria was legitimized by a 1958 plebiscite.

Proponents of the plebiscite conclude it is a useful device in expressing the people's self-determination. It has also been used successfully to settle territorial disputes, although it has never completely been accepted for that purpose. Opponents of the use of plebiscites to settle self-determination fear that its incorporation with international law would mean recognition of the right of secession and thus might threaten the unity and sovereignty of nation-states. "It is this fear, alarming to pre-war German writers because of Schleswig and Alsace-Lorraine, to American writers because of the Civil War and the Philippines, and to British writers because of Ireland and India, which has colored and still colors much of the comment on the plebiscites."[3]

The notion of the right of the people to approve constitutions or policy measures began to spread in Europe in the sixteenth century. In revolutionary America, Massachusetts circulated its 1778 and 1780 state constitutions for approval by direct vote at town meetings. In 1788 Rhode Islanders voted in town assemblies to reject the U.S. Constitution. Later, the referendum idea was shouted about on the barricades of the French Revolution.

The Swiss constitution of 1848 provided for a popular constitutional initiative. Anyone who could muster at least 50,000 signatures on a petition could propose a constitutional amendment that would be put to the Swiss electorate as a whole. When the Swiss constitution was revised in 1874, direct democracy procedures were extended with the introduction of the legislative referendum. If, within ninety days of adoption, a petition was signed by 30,000 voters in eight cantons, a law or treaty had to be put to the voters, and a simple majority of those voting could reject it. The Swiss have held more than 300 referenda and launched more than 135 initiatives since the mid-1800s.

Swiss citizens sometimes complain they have to vote too often. Critics also say the submission of highly complicated policy issues to the voters has sometimes yielded unclear or muddled results. Still, analysts regularly report that the Swiss like their direct democracy procedures. The Swiss claim it permits citizens who so desire to express opinions on the laws that affect them. Such nationwide devices, advocates claim, encourage hundreds of thousands to learn about the business of government. Switzerland "has made referendums an integral part of its political life. It has shown that, at least in a small, sophisticated country, direct democracy can work with almost none of the ill consequences which have been ascribed to it in political argument elsewhere."[4]

Australia, Italy, Spain, the Scandinavian nations, Canada, Ghana, and the Philippines have all used referenda. Parliament submitted an advisory referendum to British voters in 1975 to determine whether it would remain in the Common Market, and referenda played a role in Spain's and Greece's returns to constitutional democracy.

Although the United States is one of the few democracies without a nationwide initiative and referendum, the State Department has sometimes recommended its use to settle political questions in other nations. Thus in 1978, U.S. mediators (along with mediators from Guatemala and the Dominican Republic) urged President Anastasio Somoza to allow Nicaraguans to vote on the question of whether he should remain in office. Somoza initially rejected the notion of a plebiscite; after agreeing to it later, he was forced from power by a military coup before it was implemented. The irony that the United States prescribed a direct democracy device for others but does not permit its own citizens the same right went largely unnoticed. U.S. diplomats also praised the fact that the 1987 Philippine constitution was submitted to the public for its approval.

Although the initiative, plebiscite, and referendum have usually been used sensibly to settle ad hoc political problems in other nations, their use has almost always occasioned heated objections that they are a threat to representative government, and in particular to parliamentary democracy. These devices have therefore been used sparingly except in Switzerland and Australia. And, precisely because of their infrequent use, they have seldom weakened national legislatures. They have helped to overcome difficult political deadlocks and enhanced nations' abilities to govern. According to a conservative member of Britain's House of Commons, even a cursory look at the use of the national referendum in democratic nations shows it to be compatible with parliamentary or representative democracy: "It is plain that if it is used sensibly the referendum can buttress rather than destroy a Parliamentary system."[5]

A survey of the uses and effects of referenda in modern democracies yields the following generalizations:[6]

The referendum appears to be a politically neutral device that generally produces outcomes favored by the current state of public opinion.
Partisans of either the left or right are well advised to examine carefully the state of public opinion on the issues that especially concern them before they embrace the referendum as the sure pathway to the policies they want.
The referendum has been useful in the settling of boundary issues, perhaps because the old Wilsonian principle of self-determination still strikes most people as the just basis for determining sovereignty over territories and peoples.
The greatest deficiency of the referendum is its tendency to force voters

to choose between only two alternatives: they must either approve or reject the measure referred. No opportunity exists for continuing discussion of other alternatives, no way to search for the compromise that will gain the widest acceptance.

Conversely, a great advantage of the referendum is that it compels a decision at times when some decision is better than no decision, when continued delay is itself disruptive, and when the likelihood of working out a sensible and electorate-pleasing compromise that will please everyone is slim or nonexistent. In such a situation the decision produced by a referendum is likely to be regarded as legitimate.

In sum, referenda have often proved to be useful devices for solving or setting aside problems too hot for representative bodies to handle. They have often given legitimacy to new regimes or boundaries or constitutions that these would otherwise have lacked. Clearly, they have been valuable adjuncts to representative democracy.

Proposals for a National Initiative and Referendum in the United States

Politicians and theorists have debated the merits of representative versus direct democracy since 1787 and the subsequent ratification conventions. Advocates of direct democracy believe the people should have a greater say in the decision-making process. They agree with Jefferson that government degenerates if entrusted solely to the ruling elites, and they quote Jefferson's assertion that he knew of "no safe depository of the ultimate powers of society but the people themselves."[7] However, to the framers of the Constitution, direct majority rule was an odious concept, and they would have opposed a system of initiatives or referenda even at the state level, let alone at the national level. Article 1, Section 1 reflects their sentiment: "All legislative powers herein granted shall be vested in a Congress of the United States, which shall consist of a Senate and House of Representatives."

It was not until the 1880s and 1890s that the idea of a national initiative or referendum was discussed and advocated with any seriousness. By then both the theory and practice of direct citizen involvement in deciding issues at the state level were winning at least grudging acceptance; all but five states were governed by constitutions that had been submitted to the people by referendum. Once the constitutional referendum became accepted as a standard practice, amendments to state constitutions were also referred to popular vote.

Connecticut had begun this practice as early as 1818. Next, referenda were held on certain statutory questions such as the location of a state capital (Texas in 1850), the location of state universities, and state debt limitations. After 1898 states began to experiment with statewide initiatives and referenda of nearly every kind.

There have been three major waves of advocacy for nationwide direct democracy devices: during the populist and progressive movements (1890–1912), during the isolationist and peace movements (1914–1940), and during the issue activism on both the left and the right (1970–1988).

Early supporters of the initiative and referendum were influenced by their use in Switzerland. Labor and socialist activists were the first to publicize the cause. Although their initial objective was to gain approval of these measures at the state level, some called for the initiative and referendum at the national level as well. Populist activist Nathan Cree, in his 1892 *Direct Legislation by the People*, proposed a complicated two-step method for permitting voters to enact national laws. First the government would hold an election so voters could recommend a proposed law. "If at any such election a majority of the whole number of ballots cast in the United States shall contain a proposal for the enactment of any particular law, the Congress, as soon as may be, shall pass a bill proposing the enactment of such law, which bill need not be signed by the President . . . but shall be submitted to the electors of the several states for approval or rejection."[8] Cree recognized that his form of national initiative was cumbersome, yet he wanted to protect against hasty action. He was in fact almost indifferent to the form; he wanted to bring about a change in the system. "But all this is but a matter of detail," he wrote, "which need not be further noticed here, our main object being to show the necessity and advantage of providing new modes for the formation and expression of the public will."[9] The National People's party platform, adopted in Omaha in July 1892, supported the initiative and referendum: "Resolved we commend to the favorable consideration of the people and the reform press the legislative system known as the initiative and referendum." The Socialist Labor and Nationalist parties also endorsed it that year and again in 1896.

Before 1900 the idea of a national initiative and referendum was viewed with considerable suspicion by moderates and the two mainstream political parties, the Democrats and Republicans. Around 1900, however, certain activists began the Non-Partisan Federation for Securing Majority Rule. Leaders of this group won support from labor leader Samuel Gompers, and the 1902 national convention of the American Federation of Labor (AF of L) passed a resolution calling for the initiative and referendum at the national level. The resolution was subsequently passed at several AF of L conventions through 1912.

In 1906 a new group called the National Federation for People's Rule was formed to demand nationwide initiative and referendum. Together with the AF of L they mailed questionnaires to congressional candidates at election time in 1906. The questionnaires asked whether or not, if elected, the candidates would favor an advisory initiative applicable to several policy questions of the day and an advisory referendum applicable to all laws passed by Congress. They also asked: "Will you obey instructions from your constituents when given a referendum vote?" Less than a third of the candidates responded favorably. Yet possibly as many as fifty or sixty who won election indicated at least some support for an advisory initiative and referendum at the national level.[10]

One reason the national initiative and referendum failed to win widespread support during this period is that it is difficult to amend the U.S. Constitution. Further, the national government had been functioning for over one hundred years, whereas most of the states that adopted the initiative and referendum were much younger. The established national parties, the Republicans and Democrats, also enjoyed more influence and party discipline at the national level, and they opposed the idea of a national initiative and referendum, viewing it not only as unnecessary but also as a threat to traditional representative principles and to their own role as policy agenda-setting organizations.

The Proposed War Referendum, 1914–1940

A proposed American war referendum, now largely forgotten, enjoyed considerable popular and at least some political elite support from 1914 to 1940. The proposal was to amend the Constitution to require a popular vote on whether the nation should go to war, except when the country was attacked or invaded. Sometimes called the peace referendum by its advocates, it was supported by former secretary of state William Jennings Bryan and by U.S. Senator Robert La Follette (R.–Wis.). Scores of prominent writers, educators, and religious leaders embraced it. The proposed Ludlow Amendment, as it was best known in the mid-1930s—named after its sponsor, Congressman Louis Ludlow (D.–Ind.)—failed in a test vote in the House of Representatives by only twenty-one votes.

The popular control of declarations of war had occasionally been mentioned at the time of the French Revolution and in nineteenth-century America. Popular control of defense was an important issue in the early days of the republic; during the early 1800s New England states fought for local control of the militia as well as for local determination of when it should be used. In 1809 the Reverend John Foster preached that the power of war must be based literally on "the collective wisdom of the nation," and he stressed that nothing should be done in a republic unless the people vote on and approve it.[11] The Civil War prompted additional calls for a war referendum, and in 1864 pacifist writer Robert E. Beasley proposed a national referendum on whether the Civil War should be continued. Under Beasley's ingenious if defective plan, those who did not vote would be prosecuted and, along with those voting to continue the war, would form the army if the war were continued.[12] Nothing came of his plan.

The rise of American adventurism and commercial expansion abroad ended the nation's long-standing policy of isolation, although isolationist sentiment enjoyed surges of support right through the 1930s. The expansionary policies of Presidents William McKinley and Theodore Roosevelt gave rise to a growth in anti-imperialist groups that advocated popular control of the nation's foreign policy. One of the more prominent anti-imperialists was populist Democrat William Jennings Bryan, who became a leader of the war referendum movement. These anti-imperialists did not want to commit the United States to the political and defense responsibilities that accompanied territorial expansion. The American Anti-Imperialist League even suggested a "consent of the governed" referendum in the late 1890s at the time of the Philippine annexation controversy.

The first congressional proposals for a war referendum amendment to the Constitution appeared as war loomed in Europe. On July 21, 1914, Congressman Richard Bartholdt (R.–Mo.) proposed the first, and when war began the next month, many people wanted to prevent U.S. involvement. Several groups and public officials supported the idea of a war referendum. They believed that the ultimate commitment to go to war should not be decided by representatives of the people—few of whom would have to do the fighting—but by the people themselves.

In September 1914 Allan L. Benson (who would be the Socialist party's presidential candidate in 1916) published an article not only calling for a referendum on the war but also urging that in the event of a favorable vote, those who voted for it, regardless of age or sex, be sent to the front first.[13]

Benson's plan won support from some moderate political figures, and in 1915 Senator Robert Owen (D.–Okla.) proposed a new war referendum amendment that was influenced in part by both the Bartholdt and Benson plans. Primary support for these early proposals came from a coalition made up of populists, socialists, pacifists, and groups such as the American League to Limit Armaments, the Women's Peace party, the National People's Sovereignty League, and the Socialist party. But the galvanizing force for the war referendum soon became Bryan, who, because he opposed Wilson's war-preparedness policy, resigned in protest as secretary of state in June 1915. Within days after his resignation, Bryan was lamenting the absence of a referendum mechanism in the Constitution, and a few months later he was urging that the Constitution be amended to provide for public votes on matters of war and peace.

In 1916 Senator Robert La Follette proposed a bill that would enable one percent of the voters in each of twenty-five states to petition for a national advisory referendum on the question of declaring war. He proposed that a ballot be sent out by the director of the U.S. Census Bureau, which would read: "Shall the United States declare war against the Government of _____, with which government the president has severed diplomatic relations? Yes ___ No ___ ." Every qualified voter would get a ballot. La Follette was confident that the people who did the actual fighting and dying should master their own destiny and decide who would do the fighting and dying. "They themselves are going to decide whether they shall spill their blood out upon murderous battlefields. They themselves shall decide what questions of 'defense,' of 'aggression,' of 'national honor' may be involved, compelling enough to make them desire to kill and be killed."[14]

La Follette even took his war referendum to the national Republican convention in the summer of 1916, but it failed to win endorsement. Several other members of Congress and the Hearst newspaper chain proposed similar advisory or compulsory war referenda.

In early 1917, as American involvement in the war seemed more and more likely, calls for a war referendum increased. In February alone, nine war referendum proposals were introduced in Congress, and one explicitly mentioned how the actions of a president could simply force the country down the road to war. One pacifist group, the Emergency Peace Committee, surveyed 12,000 voters in Massachusetts and found 62 percent against U.S. intervention and 60 percent against conscription.[15] Evidence suggests a majority of American voters might have vetoed American entry into World War I if it had come to a vote at that time.

Once the decision had been made to enter the war, many pacifists and almost all moderates, Bryan and La Follette included, halted their opposition and backed President Wilson. Serious attention to the war referendum was next raised during the debate on the League of Nations in 1919. One senator proposed a war referendum to the League Covenant to allay fears the United States would be committed to wars that were not in its vital interest. Many people believed America's entry into the Great War had been instigated by powerful groups such as the munitions industry and certain corporate interests. The high point of the war referendum movement was the inclusion of war referendum planks in both the Democratic and Progressive party platforms of 1924.

From 1925 to 1935 war referendum resolutions were regularly introduced in Congress, most of them modeled after La Follette's advisory referendum. Supporters said wars were begun by governments or special interests, not by people. Congressman James Frear (R.–Wis.) led the war referendum movement in the early 1930s, advocating continental self-defense and divorcing military force from diplomacy. He based his approach on a three-point program: passage of a war referendum, a prohibition on conscription for fighting outside North America, and taxation to control war profits. Interest in a war referendum increased after hearings held by the War Policies Commission, a precursor to the Senate munitions investigation chaired by Gerald P. Nye (R.–N.D.). Both investigations encouraged the view that the arms or munitions industry was responsible for American entry into the war.

Congressman Frear retired in 1934, and Louis Ludlow, a New Deal Democrat from Indianapolis, became the next self-appointed champion of the war referendum. Ludlow, a former newspaper reporter, had covered Congress for many years. He won election in 1928. Although he favored most of the progressive New Deal measures, he opposed Franklin Roosevelt's foreign policy. His war referendum measure, first proposed in 1935, included a provision against war profits. The following text was the first of seven "Ludlow Amendment" variations he urged Congress to consider.

> *Section 1*. Except in the event of attack or invasion the authority of Congress to declare war shall not become effective until confirmed by a majority of all voters cast thereon in a Nationwide referendum.
>
> *Section 2*. Whenever war is declared the President shall immediately conscript and take for use by the Government all the public and private war properties, yards, factories, and supplies, together with employees necessary for their operation, fixing the compensation for private properties temporarily employed for the war period at a rate not in excess of 4 percent based on tax values assessed in the year preceding the war.[16]

In 1936 Congressman Ludlow published *Hell or Heaven,* a passionate book that created more publicity for yet another version of the war referendum proposal, one without the antiwar profits provision. In a speech to Congress on January 14, 1937, Ludlow outlined the rationale for his war referendum resolution: "When the war pressure from a thousand directions is on and the heat is applied and the propaganda is in full swing, Members of Congress are likely to crack under the strain and vote for war when they would not want to do so. Members of Congress are, after all, human. No Member wants to be called 'yellow' and no Member wants to be seared and burned by the opprobrious epithet of 'traitor.' "[17] Thus it was wrong to ask members of Congress to vote on a declaration of war. This most vital of questions, Ludlow insisted, should not be decided by the public's agents but by the people themselves. His proposed peace amendment was based on the philosophy that "those who have to suffer, and if need be to die, and to bear the awful burdens and heartaches of war, should have something to say as to whether war should be declared. What could be more elementally just than that?"[18]

Public opinion, at least on the surface, endorsed Ludlow's amendment. In a November 1937 survey by the American Institute of Public Opinion, 73 percent of the voting-age public supported it— almost equally in both parties, in all regions, and in both cities and rural areas.[19] Sixty-five college and university presidents publicly endorsed the Ludlow measure, as did the national convention of the National Education Association. The noted historian Charles Beard signed on. Peace groups and several unions joined the movement. Congressmen Everett Dirksen (R.–Ill.) and Warren Magnuson (D.– Wash.), both of whom would later become "strong defense"–oriented and influential U.S. senators, also supported the war referendum idea.

Though slow to make their views heard, opponents rallied and advanced serious arguments against the Ludlow measure. They stressed its paralyzing effects on national defense and executive initiative in national security policymaking. They argued too that the president and his advisers along with Congress were in a better position to decide on sensitive war declaration matters than the people, for the reason that they have better and more extensive information on foreign policy developments. In a letter to the *New York Times* on December 22, 1937, former secretary of state Henry L. Stimson warned that Ludlow's proposal was dangerously experimental:

> The greatest evil would be its psychical effects upon the people themselves. When a nation faces the mortal test of war, those psychical elements constitute the most important factors in its chances of success . . .
>
> At best, when the referendum was over, the President would have behind him the support of a people temporarily delayed and distracted by irrelevant local appeals. At worst, we might enter the war with a popular support which had been openly divided and weakened in the face of our enemy. No more effective engine for the disruption of national unity on the threshold of a national crisis could ingeniously have been devised.[20]

More than anything else, external developments and a forceful statement of opposition from FDR halted the growing support for the war referendum idea. On December 12, 1937, the Japanese attacked the American gunboat *Panay,* and, as before World War I, the clouds of war brought increased support for the president and diminished support for the proposed war referendum. On December 14, the discharge petition for the Ludlow Amendment, a technical congressional procedure for permitting a matter to be voted on, was approved. At the same time, however, an increasing number of opponents, including former president Hoover, former presidential candidate Alf Landon, and journalists such as Walter Lippmann and Arthur Krock, joined with FDR in charging that the referendum would have the undesirable effects of undermining presidential prerogative and tying the president's hands in critical foreign policy decisions.

Roosevelt wrote to the Speaker of the House on January 6, 1938, and his letter was read by the Speaker to the assembled representatives three days later:

> I must frankly say that I consider that the proposed amendment would be impracticable in its application and incompatible with our representative form of government.
>
> Our government is conducted by the people through representatives of their own choosing. It was with singular unanimity that the founders of the Republic agreed upon such a free and representative form of government as the only practical means of government by the people.
>
> Such an amendment to the Constitution as that proposed would encourage other nations to believe that they could violate American rights with impunity.[21]

On January 10, 1938, the major test vote came for the Ludlow Amendment. The actual vote was on a procedural matter—whether to bring it to the floor from a committee where it was bottled up. Although more than 250 members had indicated their willingness to discharge the measure, the vote was 209 to 188 not to discharge.

Public support waned after this vote, and especially after Hitler expanded the war in Europe. Ludlow vainly proposed a conscription referendum in 1940, but the country was already adopting Roosevelt's internationalist views. When the Japanese attacked Pearl Harbor on December 7, 1941, a central premise of the war referendum—America's invulnerability to attack—was destroyed.

The war referendum's popularity, at its peak in the mid-1930s, was based on a populist belief that the power to declare war should rest with the citizens. One way to prevent needless wars was to consult the wishes of those who must, in case of war, defend the nation with their lives or the lives of their sons and husbands. Begun as an effort to prevent American entry into World War I, it was proposed again as a solution to European problems in the early 1920s. The war referendum was the product in part of pacifist, anti-imperialist, and neutrality sentiments, in part of the earnest libertarian belief that Americans should mind their own business and merely defend their own continent. Plainly, however, another factor was an idealism, perhaps misplaced or unrealistic, that the general public could and should weigh the merits of any decision to commit the United States to an all-out war.[22]

Proposals in the 1970s and 1980s

The next wave of political advocacy in behalf of a national initiative and referendum began in the late 1960s, swelled throughout the 1970s, and persisted with diminished force into the 1980s. Support came primarily from individuals and groups on the political left and right, but a variety of polls suggested that, as with the war referendum in the mid-1930s, the idea of a nationwide referendum still enjoyed widespread popular support. A handful of moderates in Congress and at leading universities also gave strong support to a constitutional amendment for a national voter initiative.

Support on the left came from consumer advocates such as Ralph Nader and a California group known as the People's Lobby. "What the national initiative does," said Nader, "is to say to the electorate, 'listen, you have nobody to blame but yourself because you now have a direct tool of decision-making, namely the ability to propose and write your own laws.' " And Governor Tom McCall of Oregon heartily endorsed the national referendum idea in the belief it could result in the addition of an essential and reassuring fresh dimension to the flawed right of the people to run this country. "Adoption of the Voter Initiative Amendment will serve to wrest the controls of public policy from the hands of special interest groups and hand it over to those it affects, the people."[23]

A spokesperson for the People's Lobby testified before a 1977 Senate hearing that a national initiative is basically the citizens' tool of self-government. "It is the nagging little voice which speaks above all others to elected officials, establishing the will of the majority."[24] The group's representative argued that the national initiative and referendum were a much-needed balancing force among interest groups. They would enable citizens to compete, at least on occasion, with the well-financed lobbyists who customarily enjoy great influence in Congress.

In early 1977 an organization was formed in Washington, D.C., with the objective of getting a national initiative adopted. Called Initiative America, its activist officials said they were disenchanted with "personality politics." They helped double the number of cosponsors of the national voter initiative in Congress and helped instigate the first Senate hearings ever to be held on the national initiative and referendum idea. They also sought and won over 200 endorsements from congressional candidates in the 1978 campaign, about one-quarter of those on the ballot.

This support by modern-day populist standard-bearers was matched by support from conservatives and populist-conservatives. Congressmen Jack Kemp (R.–N.Y.), Barry Goldwater, Jr. (R.–Calif.), Phil Gramm (a Democrat from Texas who later turned Republican), tax-cut crusaders Howard Jarvis and Arthur Laffer, conservative pundits Kevin Phillips and Patrick J. Buchanan, and leaders of the Committee for a Free Congress all supported the national initiative. Kemp stressed that it would "allow you to vote yes or no on such issues as a balanced budget, reducing your income taxes, tax limitations and much more."[25] Two-time White House aide Buchanan wrote: "For years now my right-wing brethren have been talking about a natural conservative majority 'out there,' whose will is frustrated by an elitist establishment ensconced in the bureaucracy, the judiciary, the Congress, and the media—an establishment with a game plan all its own for America, over which we exercise little control . . . Well, the . . . [national voter initiative] offers the people an unimpeded end-run around that liberal establishment. Now is the time for the brothers to put up or shut up."[26] In the view of supply-side economic theorist Arthur Laffer, citizens believe "their desires have no effect on the course of the nation. With the extension of the referendum and initiative to the federal level, this political deterioration would be quickly reversed. Direct democracy would supplant a faltering, overburdened system of representative democracy."[27]

Traditional Republicans generally viewed the national referendum with alarm because it tampered with the representative system and the provision for indirect lawmaking celebrated in *The Federalist*. But certain populist or libertarian conservatives and those more concerned with the explosion of government subsidies and entitlement programs looked upon a nationwide referendum as a possible cure for the ills of modern government.

Much of the support from both left and right appeared based on the premise that the people would make the correct decision more often than Congress. It was as if these supporters had lost faith in national politicians and felt the national initiative permitted them to bypass the national legislature, or at least occasionally compel it to be more responsive.

Political moderates who supported the national referendum appeared to do so less because they had some urgent policy proposals in mind that Congress had been unwilling to support or because they wanted to bypass Congress than because they saw direct democracy as a means to invigorate democracy in America. As Congressman James Jones of Oklahoma put it: "This is not a partisan issue. It is not a philosophical issue. To me it is the basic issue of whether or not you trust the American people with their own destiny."[28]

Political scientist Henry J. Abraham, another supporter of nationwide direct democracy devices, believes the initiative and referendum would revive interest in public affairs. These devices would not supplant representative democracy, he says, but augment it.[29] Political scientists Benjamin R. Barber, Larry Berg, Harlan Hahn, and John R. Schmidhauser have supported the Abourezk–Jones nationwide initiative and referendum.[30] Law professors Ronald Allen, Daniel Lowenstein, Arthur S. Miller, and Clement Bezold have also advocated, with some reservations, a national initiative.[31]

At the height of the support for the 1970s version of a national initiative and referendum, polls revealed considerable approval for this constitutional change. Pollster Patrick Caddell's survey firm, Cambridge Reports, Inc., interviewed people across the country in late 1977, and most people liked the idea and said they would be inclined to vote on the issues as well as on the candidates (see Table 7.1). Gallup polls in 1978 and 1981 found that Americans supported

Table 7.1. **Public support for a national initiative, 1977 (%) (N = 1500)**

"Would you favor a Constitutional amendment, similar to the laws which 23 states already have, that would permit the citizens of the United States to place a proposed law on a national ballot by collecting a specified number of signatures on a petition and have that law take effect if approved by a majority of the nation's voters at the next general election or not?"

Yes	57
No	25
Not sure	18

"Would you be more inclined or less inclined to actually go to vote if you could vote on issues as well as on candidates?"

More inclined	74
Less inclined	7
No difference	13
Don't know	5

Source: Cambridge Report, Fourth quarter 1977, cited in U.S. Congress, Senate, *Voter Initiative Constitutional Amendment: Hearings before the Subcommittee on the Constitution of the Committee on the Judiciary, on S.J. Resolution 67,* 95th Cong., 1st sess., December 1977 (Washington, D.C.: U.S. Government Printing Office, 1978), p. 17.

a national referendum by a two-to-one margin (see Table 7.2), with remarkably little difference across party lines, by region, or by age and occupational group. The 1981 poll also found that about half of the nonvoters in their samples said they would be more likely to vote if there were national initiatives or referenda on the ballot. The Gallup analysts interpreted their data as lending support to the view of proponents of the initiative and referendum "that offering citizens an opportunity to vote on major issues of the day would encourage greater participation by giving them a greater voice in national affairs."[32]

Los Angeles County voters were presented with an advisory question in their 1978 state primary on the subject of a national voter initiative. By a two-to-one margin, voters said they would like to see a nationwide initiative.[33]

As Table 7.2 indicates, those surveyed in 1978 and again in 1981 were merely asked whether they favored the general notion of a national referendum as it was being discussed in the U.S. Senate. In 1987 I commissioned the Gallup Organization to ask a somewhat more balanced question about the idea of a national referendum—one that suggested reasons both to oppose and to support the idea. Because support in the Congress had also faded by 1987, I anticipated diminished public support. As Table 7.3 shows, support had leveled off, but not much. Opposition, however, was significantly higher, probably in large part because of the wording of the question. Still, 48 percent of those responding indicated their approval, and the idea plainly attracts more support than opposition.

Table 7.2. Public support for a national initiative, 1978 and 1981 (%)

"The United States Senate will consider a proposal that would require a national vote—that is, a referendum—on any issue when 3 percent of all voters who voted in the most recent presidential election sign petitions asking for such a nationwide vote. How do you feel about this plan—do you favor or oppose such a plan?"

	January 1978 (N = 1536)	May 1981 (N = 1553)
Favor	57	52
Oppose	21	23
No opinion	22	25

Source: Gallup polls, January 1978, May 1981.

Table 7.3. **Public support for a national referendum, 1987 (%) (N = 1009)**

"First there is the idea of a national referendum to permit voters to vote on some proposed laws. An issue would be placed on the ballot if a large number of voters from around the country signed a petition. Some people favor this change in the Constitution, believing it is important to give voters a direct say in making laws. Others oppose such a change, believing it would undermine the independent judgment of elected officials. Which comes closer to your view?"

Favor a national referendum	48
Oppose	41
Don't know/no answer	11

Source: Gallup Organization, "The Gallup Study of Public Opinion regarding Direct Democracy Devices," conducted for Thomas E. Cronin (Princeton, N.J., September 1987).

A National Advisory Referendum?

Another proposal in the debate over a nationwide initiative and referendum is the *nonbinding* advisory referendum. In one sense, the advisory referendum is a strange hybrid of direct and representative democracy: it utilizes the electorate but does not actually give voters the power to make law. It is not really direct democracy as much as it is a government-administered advisory opinion poll on a certain issue.

Advisory referenda have been used on occasion in a few states (such as Illinois, Wisconsin, and Massachusetts), in numerous cities, and in several other Western democracies. The rationale is that by allowing input from voters while preserving the deliberative legislative process, it prevents the enactment of hastily conceived or emotional laws. States occasionally allowed advisory referenda on special issues, as Oklahoma did when debating where to locate the state capital, and as Texas did in 1987 on two issues, one a gambling measure and the other pertaining to school board election procedures.

Advisory referendum by petition was an idea proposed at the local government level around the turn of the century. In 1895 Winnetka, Illinois, adopted a procedure that was to become known as the "Winnetka System." Candidates for city council pledged they would agree to refer issues to the voters when enough petitions were submitted. The candidates also pledged to vote in accordance with the voters' wishes, as shown in the advisory referendum. The Winnetka

System soon spread to several midwestern cities, including Detroit, but was never supported with any measurable strength at the national level.

A national advisory referendum has gained support throughout the twentieth century. Some of the proposed war referenda were advisory. In 1924 the Democratic party platform included a plank calling for an advisory referendum on whether the United States should join the League of Nations. And in 1939 Senator La Follette offered an advisory war referendum as an amendment to a neutrality resolution; it was defeated by a vote of seventy-three to seventeen.

The Agricultural Adjustment Administration used a national advisory referendum to determine market quotas for several basic commodities from 1933 to 1936. Farmers were encouraged to vote on farm programs, partly as a way to get them to meetings at which farm programs were explained. Over 500,000 voted on a wheat referendum. Later, Congress required that farmers approve government quota systems by a two-thirds vote in periodic referenda. In 1963 over 1,200,000 farmers participated in a referendum on wheat quotas.[34]

In the early 1960s Congressman Charles Gubser (R.–Calif.) introduced a resolution calling for a "nationwide advisory opinion poll" to be conducted each December by the Bureau of Census. The majority and minority leaders of each house would each select two issues, and the president could also select two, for a total of ten. Gubser's resolution generated some public and media interest but little political support.

In 1980 Congressman Richard A. Gephardt (D.–Mo.) urged adoption of a national advisory referendum. His proposal, which emerged from the Missouri Public Interest Research Group (MoPIRG), sought to make representative government more representative by giving people an opportunity to participate before legislative decisions are made. "There is a growing feeling among the American people that their votes no longer count, that politicians fail to respond to legitimate concerns, and that they have little or no impact on policy decisions. People are frustrated. Voters stay home on election day and yearn for a clear choice on issues. When people are given clear choices," Gephardt stated, "the evidence points to increased participation in the democratic process. A National Referendum will provide the vehicle for the re-expression of public sentiment for or against critical issues facing the Nation."[35]

Gephardt's proposal called for up to three issues to be placed on the ballot every two years; issues would be selected following public hearings around the country, and a voter's guide would be published providing the public with information and arguments for and against the issues. The referendum would be nonbinding, but issues not acted upon by Congress would be resubmitted to the voters within a reasonable period.

According to Tom Ryan, codirector of MoPIRG, the advisory referendum is better than an initiative process, for it gets public input before a decision is made and then allows a more deliberative approach to lawmaking. In essence the referendum allows the public-hearing stage of the legislative process to be opened up to the country as a whole for a national town meeting. However, "the detailed language of legislative proposals would be worked out in congressional committees . . . Congress would still perform its responsibility to carefully consider both the policy and the practicality of implementing the expressed desires of the voters."[36]

Many advocates of an advisory referendum think the mandatory or binding initiative process is too rigid, allowing little or no room to compromise, refine, improve, and amend. And one important advantage of the advisory referendum is that it can signal a lack of consensus on an issue in the case of a close vote, whereas a binding initiative may be enacted by as slim a majority as 50 percent. Advocates of the advisory approach believe this would be an advantage over an initiative process in protecting minority rights.

When asked in my 1987 Gallup survey whether they would support an advisory referendum at the national level that would *not* force Congress to act, an impressive two-to-one majority (58 percent) said they liked the idea (see Table 7.4). Women supported the national advisory referendum somewhat more than men, as did those who believe voters are informed enough to vote on complicated policy issues. Greater support for a national advisory referendum came from those living in the West, where direct democracy opportunities already exist at the state level; less support came from residents of the South, where these devices are rare.

An interesting question regarding the advisory referendum is whether its results would be any different from those of a true referendum. Common sense would suggest that elected officials would carefully heed the returns on advisory referenda; yet they do not always heed public opinion poll data. And there are some examples of legislators' ignoring the advisory will of the people at the state level.

Table 7.4. **Public support for a national advisory referendum, 1987 (%)**
 (N = 1009)

"What if we changed the Constitution to permit what is being called a national advisory referendum? This type of a referendum would allow voters to vote directly on a few proposed laws every two years. The results from this voting would be 'non-binding' and would not require Congress to vote in a certain way. Would you favor or oppose having a national advisory referendum?"

Favor a national advisory referendum	58
Oppose	29
Don't know	12

Source: Gallup Organization, "The Gallup Study of Public Opinion regarding Direct Democracy Devices," conducted for Thomas E. Cronin (Princeton, N.J., September 1987).

Thus in 1906 the Delaware legislature submitted this question to the people: "Shall the General Assembly of the State of Delaware provide a system of advisory initiative and advisory referendum?" The proposal was overwhelmingly approved by the voters, 17,248 to 2,162, but the Delaware legislature has never enacted such measures.[37] Still, voters could doubtless on occasion send a loud and clear message.

The advisory referendum is more in line with theories of representative government than are other direct democracy procedures. It allows for more deliberation and compromise in the decision-making process and is also useful in indicating a lack of consensus. It is, however, debatable whether the advisory referendum is actually a direct democracy device, for the final lawmaking power plainly does not rest with the people. In a sense, too, advisory referenda are not very different from national public opinion surveys already regularly conducted on public policy issues by scores of private polling companies.

What Issues Might Appear on a National Issues Ballot?

What issues might people place on the ballot if a nationwide initiative and referendum were ratified? Judging by the kinds of issues that appeared most frequently on state initiatives and referenda from 1970 to 1986, the proposed balanced-budget amendment and related tax or spending limitations would undoubtedly be pressed on the voters. Affirmative action and busing issues might also appear. The death penalty, gun control, draft registration, clean air, public financing of congressional campaigns, pay raises for Congress, and prayer in public schools would all be possible candidates.

Several observers have claimed that an advisory referendum is the next logical development in American democracy, or at least that it is an idea worthy of serious debate and examination.[38] The Gallup Organization has sometimes claimed that a national advisory referendum such as its periodic polls could be a workable and valuable indicator of public opinion on issues. The organization asks such questions as: "Suppose that on Election Day . . . you could vote on key issues as well as candidates. Please tell me how you would vote on each of these propositions." Gallup stresses that the results not only are national in scope, but also, and perhaps even more important, reflect the views of *all* adults—both those who do *and* those who do not actually go to the polls on election day. "The judgment of the American people is extraordinarily sound," said George Gallup, Sr.[39] On the basis of his five decades in the polling business, Gallup believed the American people could and should be trusted. Hence he championed the idea of a government-run national referendum. Results from a 1982 Gallup poll reveal that several propositions that have not been acted upon by Congress enjoy popular approval. And many of these issues engender strong emotional support and opposition (see Table 7.5).

Although 1982 saw many gains for Democrats, these Gallup data show Americans to be conservative on several critical issues. They

Table 7.5. Gallup poll referendum on contemporary issues, 1982 (%)
(N = 1486)

Proposition	Favor	Oppose
A constitutional amendment to balance the federal budget	75	25
The Equal Rights Amendment	61	39
Busing children to achieve better racial balance in public schools	28	72
The death penalty for persons convicted of murder	72	28
A constitutional amendment to permit prayer in public schools	73	27
A ban on federal financing of abortions	44	56

Source: Gallup poll, September 1982. This poll was a sample of all adults, not just of those who would vote.

also suggest that both conservative and liberal positions might win support and that Congress would probably be pressured, depending on the issue, by both the right and the left. Civil rights and affirmative action issues advanced in the mid-1960s, but they were set back or modified in the early 1980s. A bilateral nuclear freeze would not have won support in the 1950s, but it won decisive support in the early and mid-1980s, both in the Gallup polls and in actual advisory, non-binding referenda held in numerous states and cities.

Civil libertarians have often worried that emotional and prejudicial issues would find their way to the referendum ballot and win majority votes. Some say the people at large are not sufficiently educated or thoughtful to protect the rights of the weak, minorities, or those accused of wrongdoing. Evidence exists to confirm at least some of these suspicions. However, as was noted in Chapter 5, legislatures and executives sometimes have not been much better (examples include Senator Joseph McCarthy's reign of intimidation and FDR's Japanese-American internment program during World War II).

Other issues that might be placed on a national ballot are:

Increase (or decrease) Social Security spending
Reduce the federal bureaucracy
Stop the MX missile program or the Strategic Defense Initiative (Star Wars)
Abolish the Electoral College
Institute same-day election registration
Adopt a six-year single term for presidents
Adopt either nationwide or regional primaries to nominate presidents
Limit tenure of members of Congress and the judiciary to a maximum of twelve years
Approve the proposed item veto for presidents
Enforce antipollution and antitoxic waste laws more strictly
Increase (or decrease) restrictions on gun ownership
Terminate tobacco and dairy subsidies
Make English the official national language

Proponents of a national initiative tend to believe that most citizens hold views similar to theirs and would surely endorse their proposal if they made their case adequately, although some worry about adequate financing to do so. A close examination of the state experience suggests, however, that people are unpredictable. Both liberal and conservative stands win, yet opinions can and do swing from one side to the other.

All kinds of issues could eventually wind up on a national ballot—limited only by the restrictions spelled out in the enabling legislation. Some proposals would rule out any changes in the Constitution—while advisory referenda would presumably permit this type of measure. Most proposals for a national initiative and referendum rule out the issue of whether or not to go to war, but the history of the war referendum and Ludlow Amendment suggests that pressure could once again grow to force some new variant of that measure. Proposals for a nationwide initiative and referendum would have to allow for judicial review and, in most instances, for some kind of legislative override by a two-thirds vote of Congress; hence certain safeguards against tyranny by the majority would remain available.

The Case for a National Initiative and Referendum

Proponents offer the following claims in behalf of a national initiative and referendum.

1. Democracy should not be static. As the nation expands and as educational levels rise, so also should we continue to expand and amplify the opportunities to participate in self-government.

2. Self-government is more than simply electing governors and representatives; it should involve meaningful citizen participation.

3. A national initiative and referendum would signal a new and healthy respect for citizen responsibility in the United States. Citizens who are upset, disappointed, or alienated would realize that in addition to running for office, voting individuals out of office, or petitioning Congress and the White House, they also have the chance to devise their own proposals and try to get others to join in support.

4. A national initiative and referendum would allow voters a direct means of self-expression and a more direct voice in the shaping of some of the laws that affect our lives and opportunities.

5. A national initiative and referendum would encourage citizens to become more interested in the affairs of government, would encourage self-education about controversial public issues, and might increase voter turnout.

6. A national initiative and referendum would help offset some of the influence that special interest groups have on many members of Congress.

7. A national initiative and referendum might increase a sense of political responsibility in elected officials and the mass media.

8. A national initiative and referendum would allow controversial issues to be brought forward more readily, and a decision through national debate and vote would bring increased legitimacy to the resulting policy resolution.

9. A national initiative and referendum, and perhaps especially an advisory one, would provide a public forum for debating critical national issues and letting public leaders know the views of the nation.

10. Initiative and referenda have worked well for at least three generations in several states and, in various forms, in nearly a dozen other democratic nations.

The Case against a National Initiative and Referendum

Opponents of a national initiative and referendum offer the following as reasons to reject these devices.

1. A national initiative and referendum would weaken the essential fabric of representative government. It would so undermine the representative idea of debate, deliberation, and judicious compromise as to reduce legislative responsibility and discourage qualified leaders from running for the national legislature.

2. A national initiative and referendum would encourage division and polarization of the nation. Highly emotional issues would be debated in superficial media campaigns, and hate and scare tactics would often be employed.

3. Most citizens are not prepared and do not want to devote the time that a national initiative and referendum would require to study the complexities of issues.

4. A national initiative and referendum would diminish the rights and liberties of minorities.

5. A national initiative and referendum would often produce legislation drafted by well-financed special interest groups not satisfied with congressional action. Groups with great financial resources and political organizational skills would dominate the process. National initiatives would usually be won by those who could afford the best media coverage and thereby change, if not "buy," the minds of confused or indifferent voters.

6. A national initiative and referendum would be abused by single-interest groups attempting to circumvent the normal legislative process.

7. A national initiative and referendum would foster sectionalism. Under the terms of the congressional resolution for a national voter initiative, groups would have to fulfill a signature requirement in only ten states to qualify a self-serving initiative. Thus, an issue of great interest to southerners or to unions might readily gain ballot access while sponsors of a more generic issue might find it more difficult to get on the ballot.

8. A national initiative and referendum would not allow for prudent compromise. It would force an unfortunately rigid yes/no choice on typically unmodified and unmodifiable ballot propositions.

9. A national initiative and referendum could inhibit Congress from acting on controversial matters. "Let the people decide this one!"— an excuse sometimes used in state legislatures—could become a common rationale for representative timidity.

10. An initiative or referendum would be immensely more complicated at the national level than it is at the state level. Not only would it be far more costly to administer, but citizens voting on individual issues would be even more handicapped than members of Congress in trying to consider policies with reference to other policies.

The States' Experience with the Initiative and Referendum

Decades of experience with the initiative and referendum at the state level yield some indications about the possible effects of a nationwide initiative and referendum in terms of the issues that might be presented, voter composition and turnout, the groups that initiate ballot measures, the general outcomes, and voter competence.

Issues on the Ballot

State-level issues presented for voter approval have included bond issues and debt authorization, taxing and spending limitation, legalized gambling, smoking in public places, the death penalty, extension of suffrage, nuclear freeze, nuclear-free zones, U.S. intervention in Central America, and regulation of alcohol sales, the drinking age, voter registration, land use, public utilities, the environment (such as bottle deposits and nuclear power plants), gun ownership and registration, terms of office for state officials, and unions and working conditions. Issues of war, peace, international economics and trade, and foreign policy have seldom been on state ballots, and when they have been, as in the case of the nuclear freeze, they have been advisory. We can expect that many of these same issues, especially environmental and tax matters and questions of political rights and law and order, might be placed before voters via a national initiative or referendum.

Voter Composition and Turnout

Generally speaking, the older, the better educated, and the better informed vote in state direct legislation elections. As discussed in Chapter 4, initiative and referendum voting typically drops off at least 5 percent from the vote for president or governor—which is generally around 95 percent of the vote cast. Voting for ballot issue measures approximates that for state legislators and congressional candidates.

Initiators and Outcomes

State legislatures have frequently put issues before the voters. In some cases they prefer to "pass the buck" to the voters—especially on controversial matters such as daylight saving, the drinking age, and the death penalty. In other cases they are appropriately seeking public legitimation of a measure or a constitutional change. About 60 percent of the measures proposed by state legislatures are approved, compared with 35 to 40 percent of measures proposed by outside citizen groups who gain access to the ballot by initiative petition.

In the early days of the initiative and referendum, populist groups advocating issues such as the single tax, direct presidential preference primaries, and women's suffrage placed their priority measures on the ballot in several states. Labor interests were also early supporters of the state initiative and referendum. But these devices produced few benefits for the labor movements. Gradually, a disenchantment set in, and in recent years labor leaders, especially leaders of public employee unions, have opposed initiative and referendum procedures lest the general public curtail existing rights to organize or public employee wages and pension benefits.

Corporate or big business interests have rarely brought issues to the ballot. Fearing an antibusiness backlash, they have preferred to deal directly with elected state officials. In the early 1980s corporate interests encouraged the founding of the National Center for Initiative Review, with an implicit goal of discouraging additional states from adopting the initiative and referendum; an explicit goal was to keep corporations informed of "the increasing tendency of special interest groups across the political spectrum to see the initiative process as something that will 'work for them in enacting their special agendas.' "[40] Business interests have been in the forefront of successful efforts to defeat the initiative and referendum in Minnesota, Rhode Island, and New Jersey, states that seriously considered adopting these direct democracy devices in the 1980s.

Although progressives and liberals were the first champions of the state initiative and referendum, today it is difficult to predict or identify the ideological or political motivations of the groups that use these devices. Conservatives, together with the established political parties and business groups, have learned to use them for their own issues and have almost always been able to defeat opponents' proposals. Such questions as Sunday baseball, prohibition, required reading of the Bible in public schools, hunting, tax cuts and tax increases, and a ban on leghold animal traps indicate the involvement of a diversity of interests in the initiative process.

Moreover, it is often difficult to say whether liberals or conservatives have won a particular measure. Cutting taxes is in the progressive or populist tradition, although the upper-income segment of the population may be the main beneficiary. An analyst who found that 1980 initiatives produced a modest four-to-three margin of victory for liberals over conservatives conceded that "those scores may well be an artifact of my coding—and, even more, of the fact that most voters and most referendum measures are much less concerned about what is the 'liberal' or the 'conservative' position than with what is the right or wrong position."[41] Another analyst found that over a five-year period in the late 1970s and early 1980s conservatives were more successful than liberals in placing ballot measures before the voters and getting them adopted.[42]

Overall, the results from the states suggest a wash between liberal and conservative victories. Clearly, timing and public political sentiment play significant roles in the outcomes.

Voter Competence

Perhaps the most disquieting lesson learned from the state-level experience is that voters often vote on partial or even misleading information. The studies discussed in Chapter 4 provide evidence that voters are sometimes confused, often make up their minds at the last minute—perhaps as much on the basis of a television campaign blitz as on any detailed knowledge of the issues—and realize they may not always be as well informed as they would like to be when they vote on issues. Yet most studies of the state-level experience with direct democracy devices have also found that voters discriminate between what they perceive as reasonable and unreasonable initiatives and are fairly selective in the measures they approve or reject.[43]

Prospects and Recommendations

The immediate prospects for a nationwide initiative and referendum are dim. Its chief sponsor in the 1970s, Initiative America, went out of existence in 1981. Roger Teleschow, one of the organization's founders and codirectors, explained how the movement lost impetus:

> We were mainly active in the 1977 through the 1980 period. We were never that optimistic we could get the national initiative adopted. In fact, we were really surprised that it got as much attention and went as far as it did in 1977 and 1978. For a while it really was catching on. But after the 1980 election, interest seemed to wane, and those of us involved in the campaign could only go on so long living off our savings . . . we think we did a pretty good job and we still favor it as strongly as we ever did. [But] it will have to await another time, perhaps . . . when a new president supports it in the same way Governor Hiram Johnson made it an issue and won acceptance for it in California during the progressive era.[44]

But history has shown that the national initiative and referendum is an issue that emerges in cycles, and it is likely to return again. Moreover, it still enjoys impressive popular support. Therefore, it is important to consider its virtues and liabilities and the various modifications suggested by its proponents for making it a more realistic or feasible device for self-government.

The virtues lie in the potential for getting citizens more interested and involved in the decision making of their nation. In one sense, adoption of the national initiative and referendum would be another extension of suffrage, this time in a qualitative rather than quantitative way. It would be a vote of confidence in the people.

In the states the initiative and referendum have generally promoted a helpful public dialogue on issues that would also be welcome at the national level. In a 1987 nationwide survey of 1,009 adults, 59 percent of those not registered to vote claimed they would be more likely to register and vote if they were able to vote on a few proposed laws in state and national elections.[45] A national initiative and referendum would serve to tell Congress and presidents the wishes of the public, especially of those less able to afford the high-priced lobbyists and public relations firms in Washington, D.C. Used selectively, these devices could on occasion help resolve a deadlock on a decision of national importance.

We must ask, however, whether we really want to make national laws based on taking the national popular temperature of the moment. Effective political leaders must shape public opinion, not just mirror it. They must also be willing to disregard current public opinion when situations call for vision. Elected leaders are usually in a better position to be sensitive to cherished constitutional principles and minority rights. Notable American leaders have sacrificed their personal and political popularity for what they knew was right.

What would the initiative and referendum do to this concept of statesmanship or leadership? Clearly, those who devised our national institutions believed that public opinion would not always be identical with what was right for the nation. They constructed a system that would allow representatives to concern themselves primarily with what ought to be done rather than with what the majority of the public might temporarily want or think was best. They created some distance between the people and their leaders in order to provide some scope for leadership or statesmanship.

The sternest critics fear that a national initiative and referendum would greatly diminish the checks that have generally worked well. In bypassing bicameralism, the presidential veto, and judicial review arrangements, direct democracy devices at the national level would enable majority factions to enact their favored policies. "Through an initiative in the whole nation, the cellular structure that interferes with national faction formation [would be] cracked."[46] A mistake made in a single state can be far more easily corrected or checked than those of a national-level measure with the force of a majority behind it.

There are also the twin problems of money and media access. The qualms people have about fair play in initiative campaigns at the state level would necessarily multiply at the national level. As was discussed in Chapter 5, money has had a strong impact on initiative outcomes in the states. Corporations and unions have spent huge sums on issues they thought would affect them. Unlike citizens' groups or even political parties, well-funded interests can dominate issue advertising. Experience in the states indicates that voters are often bombarded with commercials that spew catchy rhymes or gloss over differences without really educating them on the issues. The manipulation of symbols and images often frightens or misleads voters, especially those who are apt to make up their minds at the last moment.

Voters are painfully aware that one-sided expenditures would undermine the integrity of national direct democracy elections. Nearly two-thirds of a national sample told the Gallup Organization in 1987 that if direct democracy devices were permitted at the national level, they favored government restrictions on how much money groups could spend to support their side of the issue. Among college-educated respondents, 75 percent favored government restrictions on campaign contributions to ensure the fairness of these elections (see Table 7.6).

Those who have studied initiative election outcomes are also nearly unanimous that money can make a difference, especially because so many people make up their minds at the last minute. Media advertising is often crucial and would be far more so at the national level. Advocates of the 1977 and 1979 National Voter Initiative Amendment invariably recommended the related passage of some type of campaign finance reform to ensure fairness. But as matters stand now, the *Bellotti* precedent means that the Supreme Court would rule this provision as unconstitutional.

The fact that money would be a major factor in national initiative and referendum campaigns, combined with the *Bellotti* precedent, is enough to diminish support for the initiative and referendum among

Table 7.6. **Public support for restrictions on expenditures in national direct democracy elections, 1987 (%)**

"If we permitted national referendums and recall elections do you think that the government should restrict the amount of money organized interest groups and wealthy persons could spend to support their side of an issue, OR do you think that people should be able to spend as much as they like in order to support or defeat an issue?"

	General population (N = 1009)	College graduates (N = 287)
Favor	63	75
Oppose	28	20
Don't know	9	5

Source: Gallup Organization, "The Gallup Study of Public Opinion regarding Direct Democracy Devices," conducted for Thomas E. Cronin (Princeton, N.J., September 1987).

many progressives. Available research at the state level demonstrates, as one legal scholar has put it, that the power of some groups to raise vast sums of money "to oppose ballot propositions, without regard to any breadth or depth of popular feelings, seriously interferes with the ability of other groups to use the institutions of direct democracy for their intended purpose."[47]

Political scientist John S. Shockley, who supported the national initiative in the late 1970s, foresees a difficult future for direct democracy because of the *Bellotti* decision. A consequence of *Bellotti*, he says, is to invite the continued actual or potential domination of ballot proposals by wealthy groups and individuals. "As long as wealth is as unequally distributed as it is in American society, and our political interest groups are organized around private rather than public rewards, ballot proposition campaigns, like American politics generally, will reflect the power of the best organized and wealthiest groups in society."[48] In effect, Shockley adds, direct democracy practices are left even more vulnerable to the very abuses they were designed to overcome.

One safeguard in direct democracy elections in five states is the availability to all potential voters of a voter information pamphlet. Such a document would have to be considered at the national level if a national initiative and referendum were established, providing the text of each ballot question, an independent objective assessment of its significance, and arguments for and against it.

Even with a highly readable national voter information pamphlet and innovative assistance from the national media, it is doubtful that voters would feel confident about voting on complicated national issues. In a 1987 Gallup Organization survey 55 percent said they did not believe "most voters would be informed enough to cast a responsible vote" in national direct democracy elections. Only 38 percent believed voters would be informed enough or would inform themselves enough to participate responsibly.[49]

Are there additional modifications or improvements that could make national referendum proposals more acceptable? The most sweeping modification to a national referendum would be merely to permit the national government or its agent to conduct occasional polls on controversial public policy issues. However, the expression of a person's views in a poll and the same person's vote on an actual law would often be different. Poll data, especially in California, indicate considerable change in people's views between advance polling and actual voting a few weeks later. Although a sample survey usually provides a good measure of opinion, it lacks the legitimacy and credibility of a referendum. "The answers a voter gives to an interviewer who unexpectedly raises some issue of public policy may be very different from what the voter would solemnly record in the polling booth at the end of a long campaign on the subject."[50]

Some of the same reservations or limitations might also apply to a national advisory referendum. On the one hand, such a survey might apprise government leaders of public sentiment on certain issues. On the other hand, precisely because it would be merely consultative and not binding, many people might overstate their views in order to "send a message" to officialdom. A binding referendum would presumably make voters more sober and thoughtful.

Proposals for a national initiative and referendum should contain a higher requirement for signatures than exists in most states. Various Senate resolutions in the late 1970s called for signatures from 3 percent of those voting in the last presidential election and from at least ten states. The ten-state provision would allow regional interests to exert an inordinate influence on proposals. Signatures should come from as many as twenty to twenty-five states, and a 7 percent requirement would ensure that a substantial number of people really cared about the issue before it was placed before the entire nation.

Yet another modification involves the type of majority needed to approve a national initiative and referendum ballot proposal. One possibility is to follow the Swiss procedure, which requires a general popular vote majority, plus majorities in a specified number of states. Such a requirement helps prevent domination by any one region.

The premise of this suggestion is that an important measure passed in a national plebiscite that bypasses the traditional checks and balances of the representative system should rest upon a consensus more complete than that required by a majority vote. One scholar who wrestled with this problem concluded there were essentially two solutions. One would be to require a supermajority vote of, say, 60 to 65 percent of the popular vote. An alternative solution would involve a structural formula that parallels the federal arrangement: a proposed initiated law would have to receive both an overall majority and a majority in a majority of the states. "Such an arrangement would ensure that no bill would be enacted without widespread support, and thus it would go far towards solving the problem of regionalism as well as serving the laudatory, although somewhat random, screening function of the Senate."[51] Moreover, each state would maintain its ability to influence the outcome of a proposed statute.

Yet another modification of the national initiative would mandate an *indirect* rather than *direct* process. The indirect initiative, provided for in some states such as Massachusetts and Michigan, allows for a period of scrutiny and potential action by the legislature before a ballot question is submitted to the electorate. As with a direct initiative, completed petitions with the required signatures would be submitted to the Justice Department for validation. Once verified, the measure would be sent to Congress for consideration. Congress would have a specific period, perhaps two or three months, to consider the measure, hold hearings on it, and possibly to act upon it either in its existing form or perhaps in some amended form. Should Congress fail to enact the measure in its original or a very similar form, the petitioners (as in the Massachusetts process) would then be free to place it on the ballot at the next election, if they obtained another 10 to 15 percent in signatures. Some states authorize the legislature to place its own version of the measure on the ballot alongside the initiated one.

The indirect initiative may place a formidable obstacle between the people and the political process. Should the people, in essence, be forced to ask permission of Congress to pass a law that Congress has refused to pass? Supporters of the indirect initiative contend, however, that the people would be allowed to vote on a measure only if the legislature did not act after considerable public sentiment had been expressed on the matter. Indirect initiatives could serve as an incentive to get the legislature to work on a problem of pressing interest. Indirect initiatives might avoid ill-conceived and poorly drafted popular ballot questions and give Congress the opportunity to go through the important consensus-building process of compromise that is really the basis of the American representative system: the indirect initiative would marry democratic and republican virtues.

Still another variation of an indirect national initiative process would require that a national initiative or referendum receive a favorable vote on two separate occasions. "A two-stage process in which the public would be required to vote twice for a given measure (say with a year between each vote) . . . would again protect against hasty or emotionally charged decisions, and also give the public a chance to consider what it did the first time around," according to political scientist Benjamin R. Barber. "An affirmative vote expressed twice, a year apart, would at least demonstrate that the public was acting deliberately and knowingly, with real conviction, and would answer the fears of those worried about mercurial and impetuous actions."[52] This two-stage process would have the additional virtue of permitting Congress to work on the matter during the intervening year. Very often Congress would probably resolve the action or pass some ameliorative legislation, and thus make unnecessary the second-stage vote.

A summary of these and related suggestions or modifications for a national initiative and referendum highlights many of the uncertainties and unanticipated consequences that might arise from this new arrangement. The proposed modifications are:

Full disclosure in advance of money contributed to ballot question campaigns

A readable and widely available national voter information pamphlet

A higher percentage of signatures

Signatures obtained in a greater number of states

Both a national majority and a majority in a majority of states

A period of congressional scrutiny and a waiting period between signature collection and popular vote

A two-stage process in which voters would vote on a ballot question on separate occasions, perhaps a year apart

Initial screening by Justice Department officials of the language of a proposed ballot question before it is circulated, to correct poor or misleading language and to ensure that the measure is constitutional

Although they are not now apparently constitutional, there is a need for campaign finance provisions that would ensure adequate public education and fair access by both sides to the media and prevent the possible domination of campaigns by big moneyed interests. Perhaps some combination of a publicly financed "floor," below which neither side would be allowed to fall, and mandatory television time for both sides would help inject fairness into a national ballot campaign. Such provisions, carefully written, might get around the *Bellotti* decision.

Some will object that all these provisions would make a national initiative and referendum nearly impossible to use—as cumbersome on a national level as the impeachment process. The objection is fair, but the primary consideration must be a national initiative and referendum designed for decidedly prudent use. Perhaps like the impeachment provisions of the Constitution, a restricted, cautious, indirect, and two-staged version of a national referendum might prod decision or action when the nation needs it. Congress has rejected simpleminded and incautious proposals for a national referendum (such as the war referendum, the Ludlow amendments, and, more recently, the Abourezk–Jones, Hatfield, and Kemp resolutions) because they would too seriously alter the representative and mixed system of separated and shared powers. A reform of the existing system requires prudence and a more judicious sense of both America's past and future than are found in the measures reviewed above.

Conclusion

I oppose a national referendum and national initiative. Even though I have outlined a variety of ways to curb their worst effects and to modify their usage to make them more compatible with our present system, I believe these devices are unnecessary and undesirable at the national level. Two fundamental and apparently insurmountable problems remain. Either process would involve making national laws based on general public opinion at a particular moment. Either process would reduce some aspects of political leadership and policymaking in a large and diverse nation to a Gallup-poll approach to public policy. Yet effective political leaders in both the legislative and executive branches have been and should continue to be asked to shape and educate the public's view of what is right and what is in the public interest, not just to mirror momentary moods.

Another reason to oppose the national referendum idea is the fact that members of the House of Representatives are already elected every two years. People who are upset or disappointed by their representatives have frequent enough occasions to vote them out of office despite the advantages of incumbency and the assistance given incumbents by money from political action committees. Should the Constitution be changed to permit members of the House to serve four-year terms, the case for a national advisory referendum would have added merit (as would the recall, as noted in the previous chapter). But term-extension reform appears highly unlikely.

And, although this is of less concern to many people these days, the supporters of a national initiative and referendum largely understate or altogether ignore the implications of these devices for the values and principles of federalism. Rightly or wrongly, this issue, once raised, would diminish support for direct democracy devices at the national level. Great resistance would come from the same people who resist altering or abolishing the Electoral College. Defenders of federalism and those who live in the smaller states, who not unnaturally come to value their disproportionate influence in the U.S. Senate, are likely opponents.

Finally, those who are dissatisfied with Congress should find ways to make it more responsive, accountable, and effective rather than inventing ways to bypass or supplement it with these potentially dangerous devices. Ultimately, as Roosevelt said in 1938, these devices at the national level are fundamentally incompatible with the republican forms the framers wisely devised for national policymaking.

▼

CHAPTER 8

Direct Democracy and Its Problems

▼

The people who rule under direct legislation tend to be those who can understand and use the process. Less educated, poorer, and non-white citizens are organizationally and financially excluded from setting the direct legislation agenda because their own issue agendas are less articulated and because they lack the resources and personal efficacy to attempt a petition circulation and direct legislation campaign.

—David Magleby, 1984

The initiative is worthwhile, because legislators can be ponderously resistant to innovation. But legislators have the time and resources to evaluate the consequences of change. For that reason, the legislature should still be the preferred surgeon of the statute books. For the occasional acute complaint or major public policy question, though, the citizen initiative is an important safety valve.

—Editorial, *Denver Post,*
August 15, 1984

THE American experience with direct democracy has fulfilled neither the dreams and expectations of its proponents nor the fears of its opponents.

The initiative and referendum have not undermined or weakened representative government. The initiative, referendum, and recall have been no more of a threat to the representative principle than has judicial review or the executive veto. Tools of neither the "lunatic fringe" nor the rich, direct democracy devices have become a permanent feature of American politics, especially in the West.

The initiative, referendum, and recall have not been used as often as their advocates would have wished, in part because state legislatures have steadily improved. Better-educated members, more-professional staff, better media coverage of legislative proceedings, and longer sessions have transformed the legislative process at the state level, mostly for the better. Interest groups once denied access to secret sessions now regularly attend, testify, and participate in a variety of ways in the legislative process. Although individuals and some groups remain frustrated, the level and intensity of that frustration appear to be lower than the discontent that prompted the popular democracy movements around the turn of the century.

Still, hundreds of measures have found their way onto ballots in states across the country, and 35 to 40 percent of the more than 1,500 citizen-initiated ballot measures considered since 1904 have won voter approval. About half of these have been on our ballots since World War II. A few thousand legislatively referred measures have also been placed on the ballot, and at least 60 percent of these regularly win voter approval. Popular, or petition, referenda, placed on the ballot by citizens seeking a voter veto of laws already passed by state legislatures, have been used infrequently (for example, one in 1982, four in 1986) (see Table 8.1). Recall, used mainly at the local and county level, is seldom used against state officials. The marvel is that all these devices of popular democracy, so vulnerable to apathy, ignorance, and prejudice, not only have worked but also have generally been used in a reasonable and constructive manner. Voters have been cautious and have almost always rejected extreme proposals. Most studies suggest that voters, despite the complexity of measures and the de-

Table 8.1. State ballot issues, 1982–1986

Issue	Year		
	1982	1984	1986
Initiatives (petitioned by citizens)	52	40	38
Popular referenda (petitioned by citizens)	1	0	4
Referenda (referred by state legislatures)	185	197	184
Total	238	237	226

Source: Initiative and Referendum Report, February/March 1987, p. 18.

ceptions of some campaigns, exercise shrewd judgment, and most students of direct democracy believe most American voters take this responsibility seriously. Just as in candidate campaigns, when they give the benefit of the doubt to the incumbent and the burden of proof is on the challenger to give reasons why he or she should be voted into office, so in issue elections the voter needs to be persuaded that change is needed. In the absence of a convincing case that change is better, the electorate traditionally sticks with the status quo.

Few radical measures pass. Few measures that are discriminatory or would have diminished the rights of minorities win voter approval, and most of the exceptions are ruled unconstitutional by the courts. On balance, the voters at large are no more prone to be small-minded, racist, or sexist than are legislators or courts.

A case can be made that elected officials are more tolerant, more educated, and more sophisticated than the average voter. "Learning the arguments for freedom and tolerance formulated by notables such as Jefferson, Madison, Mill, or the more libertarian justices of the Supreme Court is no simple task," one study concludes. "Many of those arguments are subtle, esoteric, and difficult to grasp. Intelligence, awareness, and education are required to appreciate them fully."[1] Yet on the occasional issues affecting civil liberties and civil rights that have come to the ballot, voters have generally acted in an enlightened way. This is in part the case because enlightened elites help shape public opinion on such occasions through endorsements, news editorials, talk-show discussions, public debates, and legislative and executive commentary. Further, those voting on state and local ballot measures are usually among the top 30 or 40 percent in educational and information levels.

The civic and educational value of direct democracy upon the electorate has been significant, but this aspect of the promise of direct democracy was plainly overstated from the start. Most voters make up their minds on ballot issues or recall elections in the last few days, or even hours, before they vote. The technical and ambiguous language of many of these measures is still an invitation to confusion, and about a quarter of those voting in these elections tell pollsters they could have used more information in making their decisions on these types of election choices.

Like any other democratic institution, the initiative, referendum, and recall have their shortcomings. Voters are sometimes confused. On occasion an ill-considered or undesirable measure wins approval. Large, organized groups and those who can raise vast sums of money are in a better position either to win, or especially to block, approval of ballot measures. Sometimes a recall campaign is mounted for unfair reasons, and recall campaigns can stir up unnecessary and undesirable conflict in a community. Most of these criticisms can also be leveled at our more traditional institutions. Courts sometimes err, as in the *Dred Scott* decision and in *Plessy v. Ferguson* or *Korematsu*. Presidents surely make mistakes (FDR's attempt to pack the Supreme Court, 1937; Kennedy's Bay of Pigs fiasco, 1961; Nixon's involvement in the Watergate break-in and subsequent coverup, 1972–1974; Reagan's involvement in the Iran-contra arms deal, 1986). And legislatures not only make mistakes about policy from time to time but wind up spending nearly a third of their time amending, changing, and correcting past legislation that proved inadequate or wrong. In short, we pay a price for believing in and practicing democracy—whatever the form.

Whatever the shortcomings of direct democracy, and there are several, they do not justify the elimination of the populist devices from those state constitutions permitting them. Moreover, any suggestion to repeal the initiative, referendum, and recall would be defeated by the voters. Public opinion strongly supports retaining these devices where they are allowed.

Important issues have come before the voters (sometimes issues state legislatures may not have wanted to handle or could not resolve). Women's suffrage was approved in several western states because of the initiative process. Abolition of poll taxes was advanced by the initiative. Other initiative-forced reforms include: establishment of the eight-hour work day for women and underground miners, establishment of the nation's first presidential primary system, prohibition and antiprohibition measures, environmental protection measures such as bottle bills, good-government reforms such as "sunshine" open meeting laws, financial disclosure, campaign finance reform, and voter registration reform. Since the mid-1970s many notable initiative efforts have been launched. Voters in some states have rejected initiatives to restrict nuclear power and in other states have approved such restrictions. Those campaigns laid the groundwork for later antinuclear initiatives in several of these and other states. California's 1978 Proposition 13 served as a model or inspiration for dozens of tax-cut measures in about half the states. The most successful of these measures were those to stop tax increases rather than actually cut back on public services.

Nuclear weapons freeze advocates placed nonbinding resolutions on ballots in many states by initiative petition and convinced legislators in other states and several major urban areas to put freeze resolutions on the ballot. In 1982, "with over 30 percent of the nation's voters casting ballots on the question [of a mutual, verifiable nuclear freeze], it was the closest equivalent of a national referendum ever to take place in the United States."[2] In 1986, 58 percent of Alaskans voting favored a nuclear weapons freeze.

Voters in Colorado in 1984 passed the first statewide antiabortion initiative in the nation, while on the same day Washington State voters rejected a similar proposal. Oregonians in 1984 authorized the death penalty and in 1986 increased the rights for victims of crime. Many states in recent years have used the initiative as well as legislatively referred processes to win voter approval for state lotteries. Voters in Massachusetts and Nebraska overturned state laws mandating seat belts in 1986. Eighty-three percent of the voters in the state of Washington in 1986 urged Congress to disapprove a nuclear waste site in their state. And Californians have stiffened the regulations on toxic waste.

Who wins? Critics say organized interests win. Defenders of direct democracy say the voters win. "America wins," says *Initiative and Referendum Report* editor Patrick B. McGuigan. "Conservatives get a fair shake. So also do liberals. Environmentalists plainly have won—it's an effective tool for them . . . it allows people who feel they are not in on the political scene and it gives them a chance to have a say . . . they get their chance to be heard and if they lose, as they often do, they are at least being told no by their fellow citizens."[3] Liberal and conservative direct democracy advocates often disagree about the merits of particular voting results, yet they agree that the initiative process seems to allow them both chances for victory (see Table 8.2).

"The initiative process is used almost equally by liberal environmental citizen groups and by conservatives," according to David D. Schmidt, editor of *Initiative News Report*. Although voters in the early 1980s "seem to have a slight preference for conservative-sponsored proposals, the difference is small enough that if liberals sponsor more initiatives than conservatives in any given year such as 1982, they are likely to have more victories than conservatives. The initiative process itself seems to be unbiased toward either side."[4] In another study Schmidt found that from 1977 to 1984 ballot initiatives classified as "liberal-environmentalist" appeared on state ballots seventy-nine times, "conservative" measures seventy-four times. These liberal mea-

Table 8.2. Liberal/conservative ballot issues and outcomes, 1977–1984

	Conservative	Liberal	Nonclassifiable
1977–1978			
Total initiatives	22	14	11
Approved by voters	50%	36%	91%
1979–1980			
Total initiatives	14	23	8
Approved by voters	29%	35%	50%
1981–1982			
Total initiatives	16	32	12
Approved by voters	56%	50%	8%
1983–1984			
Total initiatives	22	10	15
Approved by voters	41%	60%	53%
Combined 1977–1984			
Total initiatives	74	79	46
Approved by voters	45%	44%	50%

Sources: David D. Schmidt, *Initiative News Report,* November 30, 1984, p. 4; idem, "United States Direct Democracy in Perspective: The Case for Initiative and Referendum" (Paper presented at the American Political Science Association annual meeting, Washington, D.C., September 1986).

sures won voter approval 44 percent of the time; conservative ballot issues 45 percent. Concluded Schmidt, "The results of the . . . study, over five years in the making, show conclusively that *initiatives*—proposed laws or amendments placed on ballots by citizen petition and enacted or rejected by popular vote—are truly the tools of all citizens, from the ideological left to the right, from the grass roots to the corporate suites."[5] Various studies of voting patterns in 1986 likewise found about an even split between liberal and conservative wins, suggesting again that most voters are less concerned with whether a measure is "liberal" or "conservative" than with whether they think it is right or wrong.[6]

Many of the early advocates of these populist devices were socialists, trade union leaders, agrarian populists, and others who viewed themselves as unable to influence their own state legislatures. They favored economic changes such as the single, progressive income, and corporate taxes, increased federal regulatory and antitrust policies, and other governmental intervention to enhance the economic opportunities of the less well-off. But "redistributive" initiatives are uncommon now, and they usually go down to defeat. Somewhat more successful have been some consumer initiatives such as those placing citizens on utility commissions or reducing or eliminating sales taxes on food purchases. Indeed, the two most successful "liberal" efforts to use the initiative process have been for conservation or environmental protection and, in 1982, to advocate a nuclear freeze. Both of these are issues of the educated and are supported by people from all income groups.

"Good-government" civic groups, such as Common Cause and the League of Women Voters, also use the initiative. Most of their efforts are devoted to streamlining state government practices, encouraging open meetings and conflict-of-interest statutes, and expanding suffrage through easier registration laws. Again, these citizen action groups are organized, supported, and funded by members of the educated middle and upper classes.

In the late 1970s and 1980s the initiative and recall began to be used more frequently by conservative groups. Supporters of the death penalty, tax reduction, prayer in school, educational vouchers, tuition tax credits, antipornography and antiabortion measures, and of making English the official language seized upon these direct democracy devices and won enough campaigns to persuade conservatives in other states to try to do even more. "We've just recently awakened to the power that we have to change the direction of government and get the changes we want to come about," said one leading activist. "There's going to be an explosion of efforts on the part of conservatives to use the initiative."[7]

State governors and state legislators are also turning to the initiative. Some wish to bypass the legislature (even though they may be members themselves) out of impatience with the slowness of the legislative process. Republican legislators in California used the initiative process because the Democrat-controlled legislature stymied their bills. California's Republican governor George Deukmejian has used it for the same reason. And Colorado Democratic governor Richard Lamm in 1984 and again in 1986 sponsored an initiative to restructure Colorado's state personnel system. "These initiative wielders are not unaware of the irony of an elected representative circumventing the forum of representative government via ballot propositions," noted Sue Thomas of the National Center for Initiative Review. They "usually offer the defense that an opposing group has a stranglehold on the normal legislative channels."[8]

Lawmakers and state officials have the following incentives to take certain of their proposals directly to the voters:

The lawmaker can draft the measures to read exactly as he or she wants. There is no worrisome wrangling over a bill's language as there might be in a legislature.

Win or lose, the initiative campaign can give the sponsoring lawmaker status as a daring maverick standing up to a self-serving legislature and affords access to a great deal of free publicity.

Using the initiative process sidesteps the need to guide a bill through committees, defend it at hearings and debates, protect it from unacceptable amendment, and hammer out a compromise between houses. There is no need laboriously to construct a fragile coalition, no threat of a gubernatorial veto, no need for horse-trading.[9]

For these reasons other legislators and elected officials are likely to turn to the initiative process, especially when their pet policies are thwarted in the traditional representative processes. Surely this was not the intention of the early proponents of these direct democracy devices, who, understandably enough, assumed these populist tools would be used by the outsiders and groups not normally a part of the statehouse crowd. Still, legislators and other elected officials surely have the right to use them.

Grass-Roots Democracy in the 1980s

Direct democracy devices have been used frequently—more than 200 measures of one kind or another reached the state ballot via citizen-initiative petition during the 1980s. Several hundred others failed to obtain the appropriate signatures or, in the case of perhaps a dozen or so measures, were ruled off the ballot by the courts. About 1,000 additional measures were referred to the voters by state legislatures or constitutional procedures. Scores of recall elections were conducted, resulting in the removal of dozens of mayors, school board officials, county legislators, and even two state senators. Thousands of additional measures were voted on by citizens at the local level.

Public support for direct democracy is strong. Polls at the state level invariably indicate citizens approve of giving themselves the right to vote on selected controversial issues; the idealism long associated with initiative and referendum is alive and well.[10] Politicians either favor initiative, referendum, and recall or keep quiet about it.

Yet one of the ironies of contemporary direct democracy politics is that former supporters and erstwhile champions of the initiative, referendum, and recall are now more cautious and sometimes even opposed to them.[11] Thus union interests now generally oppose the adoption of the initiative, referendum, and recall. The National Municipal League, once a champion of initiative, referendum, and recall, now supports only an indirect initiative and even that with some reluctance. "Unquestionably, the initiative process served a good and valuable function beginning with the Progressive Era," said William Cassella, executive director of the National Municipal League. "However, it has now become apparent that these functions have changed as the system has changed."[12]

A growing number of critics think the initiative, referendum, and recall have become troublesome, expensive, and damaging to the structure of governmental decision making. They are now wondering whether the price of participatory democracy is too high. How do we maintain the special checks and balances that seem to be essential in representative government? The California League of Women Voters was moved by these and other concerns to prepare a thoughtful survey of the initiative and referendum in that state. The subtitle of their report—*A Legacy Lost?*—hints at their concern.[13]

The initiative and referendum mechanisms are used by a variety of interest groups. Their diversity defies easy generalization. It is also nearly impossible to predict how voters in certain states and communities will vote. Voters in normally progressive California and Massachusetts have adopted major property tax reduction measures. Voters in normally conservative Alaska, Montana, and North Dakota voted to endorse the proposed mutual, verifiable nuclear freeze. Voters in normally progressive Oregon have approved the death penalty, while those in traditionally conservative Utah voted against banning pornographic programming on cable television. Liberal Oregon voted no on legalizing the growing of marijuana. Liberal California voted for the questionable "English only" initiative. Year after year, voters produce surprising results. Yet contextual examination of why voters vote the way they do usually provides evidence that additional factors, often specific to the state or locality or to the particular election, help explain and make more understandable the voting results. "A different story in each state" is how one analyst described the initiative results on tax-slashing measures in one recent election.[14] That characterization could just as easily be applied to the overall direct legislation voting results throughout the 1980s.

California legislators now agree the voters were right when twice in the late 1970s they put measures on the ballot (property tax relief and coastal conservation) that the legislature simply failed to consider. In these cases, the "safety valve" really worked.

What is the frequency of initiative petition drives in recent years? Hundreds of measures get circulated, but only about 20 percent qualify to get on the ballot. What types of initiatives have appeared on state ballots in recent years? Tax matters, regulatory policy, government reform, environmental concerns, and public morality issues lead the list.

What can be said of the voters' mood and policy judgment in recent years? Generalizations are difficult. Voters have passed bottle bills in several states but defeated them elsewhere. Voters have streamlined and opened up the political process in a number of instances. Time and again they have endorsed a tougher criminal justice system and have given greater consideration to the rights of the victim. Voters in several states have defeated proposals to prohibit state-funded abortions, although this was approved by a slim majority in Colorado. Voters have approved state-run lotteries as a convenient means to raise revenues despite the view that it is apt to place a heavier burden on low- and moderate-income people. Voters have used the initiative to send a message to their national leaders that they want more arms control progress (although these measures failed in Arizona and South Dakota).

Tax measures have been the most frequent policy issue. A 1984 Michigan campaign deserves note. Michigan was hard hit by the recession in the early 1980s, and its state officials were forced to increase taxes in 1982. These taxes proved extremely unpopular, and some of them were soon modified, but local taxpayer groups wanted further cutbacks and wanted to change the taxing process. Calling their Proposal C measure "Voters' Choice," their proposed constitutional amendment would have: (1) rolled back the state income tax levy to 4.1 percent unless voters approved the current rate of 6.1 percent in a subsequent referendum; (2) required majority voter approval for all new taxes (after being proposed by the legislature); (3) required four-fifths approval by the legislature for any new fee, license, or permit; and (4) limited city income taxes on nonresidents working in those municipalities to 0.5 percent (this was a direct effort to lessen the impact of Detroit's commuter tax).

Michigan voters rejected the measure by a 60-40 percent majority. Political, business, union, and media leaders combined to persuade them that the proposal would severely harm Michigan's economic recovery. Voters will traditionally vote themselves a tax cut, and they are prone, at least on occasion, to punish their state politicians for their role as tax collectors. But antitax campaigns can be stopped, and notable defeats of these kinds of measures have occurred in Ohio, California, and in other states, as well as in Michigan. National columnist Neal R. Peirce cautions, however, that voters someday may make a costly mistake when one of these measures wins approval. When that happens, Peirce says, the price will be "short-term fiscal chaos, potentially long-term economic decline for the state and its people."[15]

Although this warning is appropriate, it appears that over the past decade voters have known when to cut and when to leave tax matters alone. Voters in Massachusetts, California, and elsewhere voted themselves tax cuts when surpluses were present and the legislatures needed to be instructed that they had been too slow to reduce taxes. In Michigan, it is clear that legislators rolled back much of the 1982 tax increases precisely because supporters of the Voters' Choice initiative were gathering so many signatures and they feared the even more drastic tax cutbacks that initiative would bring.

Hundreds of local ballot propositions are decided each year, many referred by local legislatures or councils, some by citizen initiative. Changes in the political process and growth and antigrowth measures get even more visibility at the municipal than at the state level. For instance, Denver in 1984 voted against a new height limit on downtown buildings. Oakland, California, voted against a strict rent control initiative, while West Hollywood voted to incorporate a new city. Laramie, Wyoming, voters approved a measure continuing their one-cent sales tax, and voters in Eugene, Oregon, and in several eastern Massachusetts communities approved an advisory initiative asking an end to U.S. military involvement in Central America. Telluride, Colorado, voted by nearly a two-to-one margin in 1987 to permit the rock music group the Grateful Dead to perform in that resort town.

A study prepared by the Coro Foundation showed that 110 municipal initiatives appeared on the ballot in the San Francisco Bay area from 1974 to 1984. Approximately 40 percent of these measures won voter approval—a ratio almost identical with that at the state level around the country in the same period. The proportion of local initiative petitions qualifying for the ballot, once intent to circulate was filed, was much greater (about 93 percent). No doubt this result reflects

the much greater ease of signature gathering in these more homogeneous communities. Development (for and against), rent control, and
measures affecting public officials and municipal employees were the
most prevalent on local ballots.[16]

Traditional Problems

The enduring problems of direct democracy devices are ballot
access, signature drive deceptions, drafting confusion, voter turnout
and falloff, voter competence, weakening of the legislatures, and minority rights.

Ballot Access

Direct democracy has served the interests of organized groups
rather than the interests of individuals. Too much was made of the
mythical citizen who might resort to initiative, referendum, and recall
as a readily available means to be heard and to protest laws or officials'
actions. Time limitations and costs, especially in large states, make
the collection of thousands or hundreds of thousands of signatures a
serious problem. No band of friends or a small handful of individuals
can mount a serious initiative drive without joining together with existing interest groups. Organization skills are crucial.

Of course the same obstacles face a citizen who wants to run for
office or to encourage legislation at the state level. The American system is designed to represent majorities, and it usually does so rather
well. On occasions when state legislatures are slow to respond or deliberately refuse to respond to majority sentiment, determined individuals will probably have a chance of attracting organized group
support from diverse quarters. For individuals in these circumstances
the direct democracy devices are available and can be made to work.
That the unorganized do not use the initiative, referendum, and recall
reflects in part the fact that state officials are generally responsive and
responsible, and in part the fact that those who designed the initiative
process did not design it for frequent or easy use. They intended it
to be used when large numbers of citizens became upset enough to
join together to supplement the legislative process with this alternative
means.

Ballot access could be made easier, but the result would be to
encourage too many initiative campaigns, and a few state polls indicate
that about half the voters believe there are already too many issues

on their ballots. Although lowering signature requirement levels, providing public funds for signature drives, and other "reforms" could be implemented, these changes are not likely to be enacted soon.

Signature Drive Deceptions

Many observers believe clever and unscrupulous signature gatherers can get virtually anyone to sign any petition. By using slogans such as "Do you want to make politicians honest?" "Let's get tough on muggers," "Don't let the government push you around," and "Sign here to stop big business pollution," signature collectors often talk citizens into signing something they do not understand. Such slogans usually simplify a complicated policy issue. Petition managers usually want and need as many signatures as they can get. They usually do not want potential signers to read the proposed initiative, referendum, or recall statement in its entirety. That takes time, prolongs their efforts, and often leads to discussion and questions. Hence the tendency to oversimplify and mislead.

Some states have passed measures requiring that the full petition statement appear on the petition signature page. Circulators should be required to encourage potential signers to read these statements. To reduce the risk that circulators might be less than truthful when seeking signatures, statutes should be passed making it a fraud for blatant deception, with a fine of $100 or more.

Drafting Confusion

Too many initiatives or propositions unwittingly confuse potential petition signers and voters. Sometimes campaign managers deliberately prepare misleading titles and slogans. Ordinarily, however, too little counsel is sought, and the passion and emotion of the cause make those involved hasty and careless.

Several states have already improved the process. Some provide staff assistance through their legislative counsel's office or through the secretary of state or attorney general. Some, like Colorado, have a state board—consisting of the secretary of state, attorney general, and director of the state's legislative counsel's office—to review wording and to encourage a readable and accurate initiative petition statement. It is helpful at this stage to prepare also a financial impact analysis, providing a note, to appear on the petition signature sheet, briefly stating the probable tax revenue and spending implications of the particular initiative. It is important, too, for the petition to list the names of the groups, individuals, or organizations sponsoring the petition.

Special care is needed to ensure petition statements and titles are accurate and written in clear language that can be grasped even by a high-school dropout. Despite the improvements in some states, too many initiatives still are imprecise and misleading.

Voter Turnout and Falloff

Critics have long questioned direct democracy practices because they presume greater interest in and comprehension of the issues than many voters have. However, the dropoff in issue voting from those voting for governor or U.S. senator in recent years is typically not much more than about 5 percent.

Dropoff is usually a function of education and interest. Voters who are confused and "burdened" by ballot propositions either skip over them or vote against them. This is the rational and indeed the responsible action for them.

Students of direct democracy devices sometimes relate voter turnout to voter competence. When ballot measures are readable, when ample information on the issues is available beforehand, and especially when controversy has created extensive visibility for a measure, voters turn out in large numbers—sometimes in higher numbers than those voting for governor or president. Ballot issue fights on tax cuts, nuclear waste and toxic substances, and right-to-work laws have won more attention than candidate races in states such as California, Idaho, and Oregon. Clearly, however, the presence of too many issues on a ballot can overwhelm the voter. Some voters are intimidated when they confront seven or more ballot measures. Voting lines get longer as voters linger, trying to figure out these issues and how they should decide on them. Even well-educated Californians now despair over the length of their ballots. Ballot measures usually receive almost as much voter attention as the races for state and national legislatures—which is about all that can be expected.

Outside California, however, in many respects the problem of voter falloff is a bogus issue. A comparison of voting rates in direct democracy and in regular legislative sessions shows that many legislators also refrain from voting on certain issues too. It is well known that legislators absent themselves when they are confused, not sure how to vote, or want to avoid taking a stand on a controversial issue. Voters merely act in a similar way. Like professional legislators, they sometimes avoid voting on measures whose outcome seems certain—measures sure to pass or be rejected. They simply do not waste their time on routine or obvious measures.

Defining the voter falloff tendency as a major problem is invalid and exaggerated in yet another sense as well. Few promoters of direct democracy ever claimed that everyone would vote and that the public would vote with equal levels of enthusiasm on all measures put before them. They merely wanted a "safety valve" process for those occasions when some voters believed their professional legislators were not fulfilling their representative obligations. That about 90 percent of those who vote in the presidential elections, and nearly 95 percent of those voting for statewide public officials, regularly take the time to vote on ballot initiatives is a pretty good record.

Voter Competence

Perhaps the greatest fear of the critics of direct democracy was that unsound legislation would get approved because of voter apathy and ignorance. No one would try to argue that voters are as informed as they might or should be. Few voters are textbook voters—constantly reading about candidates and issues, constantly keeping abreast of complex public policies and their consequences. Few legislators, for that matter, are as informed as they might or should be.

It is well known that many legislators vote a relatively straight party line or are sometimes unduly influenced by their peers or senior members. Some legislators are compelled by binding party caucus procedures to vote contrary to their consciences. Sometimes as many as 2,000 issues and personnel nominations come before a state legislator in a given session. Most state legislators become reasonably informed and reasonably competent; few of them become experts on everything. Given that analogue, the typical voter appears more competent than when he or she is held to a false, ideal standard.

Critics of direct democracy are fond of saying that many issues are too complicated to be decided by a simple yes-or-no vote. This too seems to be an exaggerated contention—for legislators, judges, and elected public executives are forced, in the final analysis, to make yes-or-no decisions. Jurors also generally have to arrive at yes-or-no verdicts. To be sure, officials usually have the chance to hold debates or hearings or to hear oral arguments, and jurors have sat through trials; but, properly supervised, direct democracy campaigns and voter handbooks should likewise provide most of the information needed by voters to make reasonable yes-and-no decisions.

Citizen-voters have responded more responsibly than critics anticipated. Although unusual measures and a number of discriminatory issues have found their way onto state ballots over the past eighty-five years, they have rarely won support from the voters. Part of the explanation is that voters are able to make good judgments—especially when an aggressive press, community and state officials, and other leaders make it their civic responsibility to help shape public opinion. The best way to defeat unsound legislation is for the voters to ask good questions, read good newspapers, watch television news programs, compare the advertisements of the proponents and opponents, and hold discussions at home, with friends, and at their workplaces and churches—and this is what often happens.

The process is not foolproof, yet bad legislation probably gets approved about as often in the initiative and referendum process as it does through the legislatures. Both processes could be improved. Both the professional and the occasional legislator could obviously be better briefed, better educated, and better read.

Weakening of the Legislatures

Critics of initiative, referendum, and recall have often said direct democracy devices would, if used regularly, diminish the incentives of those who might run for state legislative positions. Little evidence exists to suggest this is a serious problem. Many observers would say the legislators in office today are the best educated and most professional the country has ever had. Pay is better, staff is better, information systems are improved, and the resources made available by the National Conference of State Legislators are more advanced than ever before.

It is true that legislators sometimes—usually out of frustration with being in the minority in their legislature—work to put initiatives on the ballot. It is also true that some legislatures refer measures to the ballot as a means of "passing the buck" on some controversial, hard-to-resolve policy dispute. But neither of these occasional uses of direct democracy procedures is necessarily a threat or challenge to the value and importance of representative government and traditional legislative procedures. Legislative seats are still hotly contested—especially in competitive districts and when seats are open.

What weakens state legislatures is that the pay is too low in most states, and the advantages of incumbency may thwart an infusion of new blood and fresh ideas. In 1984, for example, all seventy-seven members of the California state assembly running for reelection won.

Only a handful of state legislators have been recalled in the past generation. Few legislators spend much time worrying whether they are going to be subject to a recall movement or cast their votes with an eye to such a possibility. Most recalls occur at the city or county level. No one now claims, as was once feared, that state legislators would be forced to sacrifice their best judgments because of the existence of the initiative, referendum, and recall. Legislators are aware of these devices, but few view them as an impediment to the performance of their responsibilities.

Minority Rights

A perennial fear about direct democracy has been that majorities at the ballot box might be less sensitive than state legislators to the rights of minorities—whether an ethnic, racial, or religious minority or perhaps a small ideological or partisan group. Women, although they now make up at least 50 percent of the population, have also long been viewed, and justifiably so, as a political "minority."

Direct democracy measures in recent years have not generally had the effect of diminishing minority rights. A 1978 California proposition that would have allowed school districts to fire homosexual teachers was soundly defeated.

Women's legal rights and advisory votes on the proposed Equal Rights Amendment to the Constitution have enjoyed mixed success. Some states have passed ballot measures of a progressive kind. Other states, reflecting a more conservative mood, have voted against the ERA. A proposed state equal rights amendment, referred to the voters by the Maine state legislature, was defeated in the November 1984 election. In 1986 a similar measure went down to defeat in Vermont. According to observers in both states, existing statutory protections covered nearly all the rights that would have resulted from adoption of the ERA. Women's groups apparently could not get voters there excited about an existing lack of legal rights and legal standing. Thus the defeat of this measure cannot be viewed as a diminution of rights. Had they passed, the measures would have solidified and slightly extended women's rights. Yet their defeat did not take away rights.

Another 1984 initiative could, had it passed, have had the effect of infringing on the rights of a "minority." In this case it was a Utah initiative seeking to make it a misdemeanor to "distribute . . . any obscene or indecent material by means of cable television." This was a direct attempt to prohibit "playboy" or pornographic cable programming. The 61 percent vote against this "Cable Television Decency" initiative prompted the editor of *Initiative News Report* to ask, "Why didn't Utah's Mormons, who represent an estimated 75 percent of the population, want to apply their strict moral standards to Cable TV?"[17] Mormon Utah voted against this measure largely because an effective campaign effort successfully persuaded voters that the real issue was not pornography, but government interference with individual rights.[18]

Measures advocating prayer in public schools and prohibiting state-funded abortions have also appeared on state ballots. Clearly, the public is divided on these issues. West Virginia voters in 1984 readily approved a state constitutional amendment, referred by the state legislature, authorizing "voluntary contemplation, meditation, or prayer in school classrooms." The Supreme Court in the early 1960s ruled official and required prayers in public schools unconstitutional. In 1985 the Court affirmed the 1960s ruling despite polls showing widespread support of voluntary prayer or "minutes of silence." These rulings presumably protect the rights of religious minorities. Several state legislatures have voted to approve a minute of silence for meditation or contemplation. Until the courts address these highly emotional issues in a definitive way, prayer in school will no doubt continue to be put before the public in ballot measures.

Antiabortion activists have placed initiatives on several state ballots calling for an end to the use of state funds for abortions. So far they have been successful only in Colorado, where such an initiative passed by a slim margin in 1984. Confused wording may have aided its passage: 26 percent of voters in a statewide survey immediately after the election said they wished they had had more information on the initiative; and 10 percent were mistaken about whether a yes vote was for the antiabortion or the prochoice side. Alaskans rejected a similar proposal in 1982, Oregonians in 1984, and other states in 1986. The Arkansas supreme court struck from the state ballot a measure that would have forbidden public funding of abortions and made protection of unborn children official state policy. The court majority said the measure's wording was inaccurate and misleading.

On this highly emotional issue, both sides claim minority rights are involved. Proponents of the antiabortion measures say the rights of the unborn infant are at stake. Opponents say the rights of low-income mothers are involved: if denied public funding, they would be forced either to have unwanted children or to risk their own lives by seeking abortions in less desirable settings. Courts and legislatures will have to confront these issues. Voters at the ballot box are likely to do no worse than their legislatures in approving unconstitutional, unfair, or discriminatory policies on these issues.

A 1984 nonbinding initiative in California has raised additional questions about minority rights. Proposition 38, which won approval from 71 percent of the voters, called for the use of English-only ballots in U.S. elections. It recommended that the governor of California deliver to the president of the United States, the U.S. attorney general, and all members of Congress a written communication urging enactment of an amendment to federal law so that ballots, voter information pamphlets, and all other official voting materials shall be printed in English only. Proponents of the measure claimed that foreign-language ballots are unnecessary because virtually all applicants for citizenship must pass a test for literacy and proficiency in English. They also said the printing of foreign-language ballots is costly. Another argument was: "The United States, a country of immigrants from other lands with differing languages and cultures, has had the enriching experience of living with and learning from other cultures. We learn from each other because we are unified by a common language, English. We must preserve that unity."[19] Many California liberals viewed this initiative as a nativist campaign aimed particularly at Chinese- and Spanish-speaking groups in some sections of the state, as well as an attack on the Voting Rights Act of 1965, which enables all Americans to exercise effectively their right to vote. (Ballots appear in several languages in certain California communities.) Opponents also pointed out that federal laws require only a fifth-grade level of English for naturalized citizens and that voting assistance is especially necessary in California, where so many state and local propositions are written in such complex language that they confuse even some of the educated native-born.

New Challenges

In recent decades, the following new challenges have presented the sternest tests for direct democracy devices: money (especially one-sided campaign expenditures), paid petition circulators, direct mail deception, deceptive advertising campaigns, litigation and court intervention, and video or teledemocracy.

Money

Money is, other things being equal, the single most important factor determining direct legislation outcomes. Well-financed measures enjoy a significantly greater chance of winning than do those that are poorly financed. One study of citizen-initiated measures found that in fifty-six of seventy-two campaigns, or about 78 percent of the time, the high-spending side won the election.[20] In California in recent years the well-financed "Vote no" campaigns have been able to defeat measures 80 to 90 percent of the time.

Money can buy television advertisements, and television time is increasingly crucial to winning direct democracy elections. Critics of unbalanced spending efforts draw an analogy to a town meeting in which one side gets to speak five or six or twenty times as much as the other side. Presumably no town meeting would permit such an imbalance. Hence, critics advocate some spending limits, perhaps $20,000 or $30,000 for corporate or individual contributions, or some provision to enable the grossly outspent side to have access to public funds, and thus to some minimum level of television time to air its arguments.

For reasons discussed earlier, courts are unwilling to regulate the financing of direct democracy campaigns. If and when we did make it fair (in monetary terms) for both sides in initiative and referendum campaigns, would they not also have to be made equal for both or several sides in the state legislature lobbying process and also in candidate campaigns? That, at least, is the view of those who prefer to leave the financing of these processes alone. It would be too complicated as well as undesirable, they say, to try to regulate the role money plays in initiative, referendum, and recall elections. Even proponents of direct democracy campaign reforms are pessimistic about solving the money problem.[21]

Paid Petition Circulators

A few states restrict or prohibit the paying of petition signature gatherers. Yet a court in Oregon ruled this type of prohibition unconstitutional. Critics say laws banning paid petition circulators violate First Amendment rights. Part of the process of obtaining voters' signatures, they say, is speaking to those persons about the merits of the issue. The communication inherent in the signature collection process is political expression; thus it should be protected speech.

A 1984 court case in Colorado raised these questions anew. Colorado defended the prohibition on the grounds that it served the state's compelling interest to protect the integrity of the initiative process. Officials said the law prevented abuses without creating any real obstruction to proponents' efforts to qualify initiatives. Judge John Moore of the U.S. District Court ruled that the Colorado ban is not unconstitutional (and his ruling was upheld by the Tenth Circuit Court of Appeals): "As I understand the contention," said Judge Moore, "it is not that plaintiffs desire to pay for dissemination of their political position, as one would do in political advertising, but that they desire to pay someone else to speak upon a subject which plaintiffs support. Thus viewed, the question arises as to whose rights of speech are involved? Can plaintiffs claim their right to free speech has been invaded because someone else cannot be paid to speak?"[22] Thus he failed to see that the prohibition against payment of circulators constituted an inhibition, especially since, as he noted, Colorado is among the most frequent users of the initiative despite this ban.

Critics of direct democracy applaud this ban on petition circulators, as do some progressives and "good government" advocates. They note that groups who have to pay people to get a measure on the ballot often do not represent the public at large. Moreover, restricting paid solicitation might ensure that only issues with deep and wide citizen support qualify for the ballot. Critics also say paid solicitors often are tempted to mislead the public in order to obtain as many signatures as quickly as possible. Yet observers in California—where to qualify to get on the ballot in the late 1980s a group needs about 400,000 valid signatures for an initiative statute and at least 600,000 for an initiated constitutional amendment—say it would be nearly impossible for most groups to use the direct democracy process without paid circulators. "Banning the use of paid solicitors would mean that no initiative could ever qualify unless it [was] backed by an extensive organization with a cause appealing to a special group of citizens."[23]

In 1988 the U.S. Supreme Court ruled unanimously that Colorado could not prohibit the paying of signature gatherers, thus overruling Judge Moore and both the U.S. District and Tenth Circuit courts. (See Chapter 9 for further discussion of this decision.)

Direct Mail Deception

A related issue is raised by the rapid growth of the direct mail industry and its innovative "high-tech" techniques. Its influence is especially evident in California. Several California firms, precisely because it can be profitable, are now in the business of gathering signatures and simultaneously raising campaign contributions via computer-based direct mail efforts.

A number of critics despair of this method of signature collection. First, they say, it subverts the person-to-person participatory process. Second, it has turned into a business rather than a volunteer effort. Third, some of the mail is alarmist as well as misleading. Finally, opponents say direct mail solicitation gives too much of a head start to well-funded special interests that can afford to hire specialized firms with computerized lists of likely supporters. These firms recover their costs through fund solicitation in the same mailing—and, of course, they take their share before turning the remainder over to the interest group that hired them. In California, the rising costs and new technologies "have made it [the initiative] an instrument primarily left to professionals."[24]

Prohibition of direct mail drives would be considered a violation of First Amendment rights. Moreover, some analysts think voters are far more likely to read a petition statement that comes to them through the mail than at a petition table in front of the supermarket. Californians are especially accustomed to direct mail solicitations. Even some progressives say direct mail is probably a necessary reality in the initiative process in that large state.

Direct mail solicitation, however, could be improved. First, there should be stiff fines for fraudulent and even especially deceptive literature sent along with letters of solicitation. Second, precise information naming the sponsoring groups and individuals should be included. Finally, solicitation of signatures and of campaign contributions should be done in separate mailings. According to one line of reasoning, two separate appeals would necessitate a broader initial base of support for the campaign and might discourage certain abuses of the initiative process by the so-called initiative industry. There should also be thorough and immediate financial disclosure of all activities related to initiative petitions, including the qualification phase.

Deceptive Advertising Campaigns

Nearly every state permitting the initiative has witnessed misleading advertisements in some of the more controversial ballot measure campaigns. Nearly everyone concedes the direct democracy process loses credibility and integrity as a result. Sometimes the deceptions stem from the appropriation of misleading names by the sponsors or opponents. More often the deception takes the form of campaign slogans and thirty-second television spots designed to mislead voters. "For Farmworkers' Rights . . . Yes on 22" was a billboard message in 1972 portraying a measure as one whose adoption would help the farmworkers. But in fact the initiative was sponsored by farm and ranch owners and was explicitly intended to restrict farmworkers' rights. In another flagrant attempt to confuse voters, opponents of a famous 1972 environmental initiative to preserve much of the California coast employed as their basic slogan: "The Beach Belongs to You, Don't Lock It Up."

A classic illustration of a deceptive ad campaign was that against Proposition 11 in the California general election of 1982. The issue was a bottle deposit bill pushed by environmental groups. The anti–bottle bill groups joined together as "Californians for Sensible Laws." In June the deposit bill enjoyed a two-to-one lead in public opinion support. But its opponents raised nearly $6 million, two-thirds of it from out-of-state companies such as the manufacturers of Budweiser, Coke, Pepsi, and container companies.

The Californians for Sensible Laws consistently claimed the bottle bill could destroy California's voluntary recycling industry, even though recycling levels in each of the states with bottle bills were triple those of California. The group ran a television advertisement with a uniformed Boy Scout asking his father why "the grown-ups" behind Proposition 11 were shutting down "Mr. Erickson's recycling center and putting us scouts out of business." Despite protests from Boy Scouts of America and kindred groups, the advertisements continued. Another advertisement presented five Oregonians who claimed the bottle bill law did not work in their state, even though polls have shown that Oregonians overwhelmingly favor their law. The advertising firm for the opponents merely hired four Oregon beer distributor employees and one Safeway employee and paid them to pose as typical Oregonians on the street. Other advertisements described Proposition 11 as a tax, failing to mention this so-called tax was a refundable deposit. "Even the most groundless assertions became lasting campaign themes because they met no early rebuttal," said the director of the group that proposed the bottle bill.[25]

No one can dispute the right of any measure's opponents to mount vigorous opposition. Yet false claims and deceptive ads and arguments cropped up repeatedly in the Proposition 11 campaign. Opponents funded five times as many advertisements as proponents. Thus many of what the proponents believed to be outrageous untruths were never refuted on television. For direct democracy to work, they insisted, room must be made for both sides at the podium. "Fair and full debate cannot occur without two-sided discussion," said a leading proponent in this fight. "And two-sided discussion cannot occur so long as meaningful access to the public is so overwhelmingly dependent on a group's ability to spend millions on advertising."[26]

Students of direct democracy favor state regulation of the "con jobs" and hyperbole employed in selling or defeating initiatives. Surely some of these deceptions warrant litigation, but the attorney general of California doubts state controls are the answer. And his view is persuasive:

> The best way to fight fabrication, half-truth and smears is in the free expression of objection and opposition and in their publication by a press that realizes it is a focal point for sifting out of claims and charges—and counter claims and counter charges.
>
> By and large those who go too far lose not only their credibility but usually lose their measure as well. Not always, mind you, but it's a risk we have to deal with in a society which values free speech under the First Amendment.[27]

Litigation and Court Intervention

Disputes about the constitutionality of the initiative, referendum, and recall invariably wind up in the courts. In recent years an increasing number of initiatives have either been taken off the ballot before an election or been modified or invalidated after they have won voter approval.

In the past the courts usually intervened in the initiative process only after an election. In 1984 the courts in a handful of states ruled several issues off the ballots beforehand. Legal challenges usually come from opponents of a proposed initiative, who question the titling, signature certification, the constitutionality of the measure, or deceptions in information or advertisements. In some states the courts have refused to allow advisory initiatives onto the ballot, saying this was not the intent of the state's initiative and referendum process. In December 1983 the Massachusetts Supreme Judicial Court threw off the ballot a petition that called for reform of the state legislature, on the grounds that it dealt with a subject beyond the intended scope of the initiative.

Conservative spokesman Patrick McGuigan decries this new role for the courts as an obstacle to free exercise of the franchise. "The decision of the California supreme court removing Proposition 35 [a forerunner of the federal balanced budget amendment] from the November 6 [1984] statewide ballot is unfortunate, unfair and unbelievable . . . This is only the latest decision of a state court thwarting the right of citizens to draft legislation through state initiative provisions."[28]

A few states, including Massachusetts and Oregon, provide a mechanism by which state officials, such as the attorney general, can halt an initiative measure as unconstitutional before signatures are collected. Some observers urge that this procedure be adopted in all states permitting initiatives, referenda, or recalls. But the question must then arise whether an attorney general will necessarily know with certainty what is constitutional or unconstitutional. Such a mechanism might tie too much power to a single state officer or board. The editors of *Initiative Quarterly* view the chilling effect of court intervention in a positive light: "such rulings could prevent advisory issues from cluttering the ballot, confusing the voter, and trivializing the initiative process."[29]

The courts will undoubtedly remain involved, as they must whenever majority rule clashes with the rule of law. Preferably, however, these clashes should take place either at the early stages or after the election is over. The handing down of court decisions in the midst of a heated campaign and just days or a week or two before an election will lead to cynicism and diminished confidence in the direct democracy process.

Teledemocracy

Nearly everyone agrees that television-age technology should be a positive force for voter education, especially in informing people about public issues.[30] Since 1974 there have been a number of intriguing experiments in "televoting" and "electronic town meetings." They suggest ways to extend and refine direct democracy. Yet they also threaten the Madisonian notions of checks and balances and indirect representative processes. Nevertheless, the technology is likely to revolutionize the possibilities, and a century from now the whole array of direct democracy procedures being used today may seem innocently unimaginative and timid.

The "televote" system, apparently invented by Dr. Vincent Campbell in 1974, in San Jose, California, is a process that informs citizens by giving them summaries of information relevant to the issues, easy access to more detailed information, and time to think the whole matter over before deciding. It represents an effort to go beyond traditional polling, to get people thinking and talking about issues before giving them a chance to record their views or votes on controversial measures.

A group at the University of Hawaii conducted a televote of citizen views on issues before the Hawaii delegates to their state's 1978 constitutional convention. They picked some issues under discussion at the convention (such as the method for selecting state judges); publicized the issue, providing information about the alternatives (through television, radio, and newspapers); and twice called a random sample of citizens, once to pose the questions and alternatives and then, after all the television and publicity had spoken to the issues, to obtain citizen feedback and "votes."

As the directors of this project readily admit, the technology for two-way teledemocracy is not now available. It is, they say, about ten or twenty years away. The Hawaii project and most like it use television and the media to pose questions and provide information. Then they have to use telephones to obtain citizen feedback. Nonetheless, those who have participated in these experiments favor the idea and like being included—even at these early stages of teledemocracy.[31]

The Warner-Amex "QUBE" interactive television system, tested in the early 1980s in certain neighborhoods in and around Columbus, Ohio, provided cable subscribers with an input device with five buttons permitting multichoice voting. Viewers could watch entertainment or talk shows and provide instant responses—evaluations, preference ratings, or votes. The potential for applying QUBE to direct democracy procedures is obvious. "Interactive systems have a great potential for equalizing access to information, stimulating participatory debate across regions, and encouraging multichoice polling and voting informed by information, discussion, and debate," writes political scientist Benjamin R. Barber. "It suggests ways to overcome the problem of scale and to defeat technological complexity by putting technology to work for popular democratic ends."[32]

Still others believe that the advent of interactive television and new computer technologies, soon to be affordable in most Americans' homes, is likely to transform the public from spectators into participants and offers possibilities for mass referenda on critical issues facing the nation. It may soon be possible to fashion, they claim, a consensus formerly found only in ancient Athens or in the heyday of the New England town meetings.

Clearly, advocates of teledemocracy expect more political interest and political involvement from the average citizen than experience suggests are likely.[33] Most people, most of the time, prefer indirect democracy, or representative government. Just as the populists and the progressives sometimes overstated the degree to which ad hoc groups and average citizens would join together to check and balance or reform state government, so also proponents of teledemocracy risk exaggerating the extent and depth of the average citizen's interest in politics and political issues. Just about every problem that has ever challenged direct democracy devices has been raised anew and probably sharpened by the very idea of video democracy and other two-way inventions proposed for issue voting. The possibilities, the likely deficiencies, and the as-yet-unappreciated consequences of these new technologies are many.[34]

Two possible consequences involve an abdication of responsibility, one by citizens and the other by elected officials. Citizens, precisely because of the existence of these devices, may grow lax in monitoring their legislators and other elected officials. The right to put issues or laws on the ballot for a later public vote or the availability of the recall may encourage an indifference to what goes on in state houses or city halls. So also, legislators and other officials who too often refer issues to the voters may abdicate their responsibility as policymakers and lawmakers. Too frequent a reliance on direct democracy procedures could encourage an atrophying of the legislative function. Neither of these undesirable tendencies has progressed far, but both need to be actively discouraged.

In sum, direct democracy devices have not been a cure-all for most political, social, or economic ills, yet they have been an occasional remedy, and generally a moderate remedy, for legislative lethargy and the misuse and nonuse of legislative power. It was long feared that these devices would dull legislators' sense of responsibility without in fact quickening the people to the exercise of any real control in public affairs. Little evidence exists for those fears today. When popular demands for reasonable change are repeatedly ignored by elected officials and when legislators or other officials ignore valid interests and criticism, the initiative, referendum, and recall can be a means by which the people may protect themselves in the grand tradition of self-government.

CHAPTER 9

▼

Sound and Sensible
Democracy

▼

Referendum and initiative processes divorced from innovative programs for public talk and deliberation fall easy victim to plebiscitary
abuses and the manipulation by money and elites of popular prejudice.

—Benjamin R. Barber, 1984

[The direct democracy] process is now dominated [in California] by
well financed interests, the very groups that the process was intended
to restrict . . . Instead of a system of direct legislation that periodically
permits citizens to set their own political agenda, proponents of initiative measures have recruited professional firms motivated by profit
or political gain.

—Larry L. Berg and
C. B. Holman, 1985

THE American political system
commands praise for its creativity and its improvisation. With the
exception of the Civil War, our political system, based primarily on
the republican principle, has been effective and resilient. Direct democracy, as it has developed during the twentieth century, is no threat
to it. On balance, it has provided for slightly more opportunities for
accountability; and, in those states and localities that provide for them,
the initiative, referendum, and recall have provided a safety valve for
citizens who are upset by controversial policy decisions or unseemly
performance by public officials.

The trade-offs, or side effects, however, are not inconsequential.

This final chapter assesses them comprehensively, outlines procedural safeguards that would help make direct democracy more compatible with representative government, and concludes with some recommendations.

General Effects of Direct Democracy Devices

Has direct democracy enhanced government responsiveness and accountability? The answer is at best a maybe. States that have adopted direct democracy devices are more accountable than they once were. Yet other factors, not limited to states that have the initiative and referendum, also help to account for this change, including better education, vastly increased revenues, professional staffs, and more experience with rule by law. California, Oregon, and Colorado—three notable users of direct democracy—are frequently mentioned by state government experts as pacesetting, trend-starting states. And interviews with people in user states yield the impression that state officials are somewhat more responsive than elsewhere; however, many citizens in those states also think their officials are not responsive enough. Few initiative, referendum, and recall states are known for corruption and discrimination. Still, it is difficult to single them out and argue persuasively that they are decidedly more responsive than those without the initiative, referendum, and recall.

Do direct democracy devices provide an effective safety valve when legislators prove timid, corrupt, or dominated by narrow special interests? Generally, yes. Indeed, the mere circulation of petitions for an initiative, referendum, or recall sometimes "encourages" officials to reconsider what they are doing and how they are doing it.

Do direct democracy devices eventually weaken autocratic bosses and strengthen the policy and political voice of the people? Party bosses have lost power, but this change probably had much more to do with the curtailment of patronage, the institutionalization of the civil service, the advent of the Social Security system, and similar developments, than with the inception of the initiative, referendum, and recall. Partisanship has declined as well. Still, bossism persists in legislatures that retain hierarchical procedures, such as the California Assembly and the Massachusetts House. Moreover, the decline of the traditional turn-of-the-century bosses has not necessarily shifted their power to the common people. Today power appears to be dispersed widely among organized interests, public employee unions or associations, teachers' associations, farmers, real estate developers, and business, manufacturing, and trade associations of all kinds, which regularly wield influence at the state and local levels. Interest groups of all kinds, including those working on behalf of consumers, good government, and working people, are now heard in the councils of government. Public opinion surveys also ensure that legislators and other elected officials hear what the average citizen thinks about public policies. Popular democracy devices have probably lessened the likelihood of boss rule, but so have other developments.

Direct democracy processes have *not* brought about rule by the common people. Government by the people has been a dream for many, but most Americans want their legislators and other elected officials to represent them as best they can and to make the vast bulk of public policy decisions. Direct democracy devices occasionally permit those who are motivated and interested in public policy issues to have a direct personal input by recording their vote, but this is a long way from claiming that direct democracy gives a significant voice to ordinary citizens on a regular basis. That early claim was considerably overstated.

A related claim was that direct democracy devices would lessen the undesirable influences of special interests. These devices may have done this in some respects, but special interests are still present and can still afford highly paid, high-caliber lobbyists at every state legislature. And there are many more lobbyists now than there were in 1900.

On the other hand, direct democracy devices have sometimes allowed less well-represented interests to bring their messages before the public. Environmentalists, for example, have used the initiative process to force legislatures to give greater consideration to conservation and environmental protection issues. Other groups, such as those favoring the death penalty and mandatory sentences, have been able to get their ideas heard and often enacted into law. Ultimately, however, single individuals unwilling to join groups and form coalitions are unable to use direct democracy processes. In the larger states the initiative process has come to be dominated by large organizations, displacing the citizen groups it was once intended to serve. Only in groups and in concert with several groups can a few individuals make these devices work for them. The much-talked-about "common man" is required to become an uncommon joiner and organizer in order to realize the aspirations of the proponents of direct democracy. And it helps to be wealthy and to have access to professional campaign management technologies, especially in California.

Direct democracy was also supposed to stimulate educational debate about important policy issues. It does, yet the debates usually last only five or six weeks. Direct democracy processes do allow debate in public forums well beyond the legislative hearing chambers, and as a result, public officials, newspapers, radio and television stations, and various interest groups often take a stand and trigger at least limited public discussion debate. In a few states voter handbooks, although they are difficult to read on many issues, help individuals to digest complicated information about ballot measures.

The most unfortunate deficiency of this claim, one not adequately anticipated by the early advocates of initiative, referendum, and recall, is that the side with more money too often gets to define the issue and structure the debate in an unbalanced way. Whereas a town meeting gives all sides an equal chance to speak, money and court rulings permitting unlimited spending promote a system in which the better-financed side can, and often does, outspend the other by a dramatic margin.

Direct democracy was also intended to stimulate voter interest in issues and encourage higher election-day turnouts. It often does stir interest and sometimes even polarizes factions. Certainly it heightens interest at election time, although interest in candidate races, especially for top offices such as president, governor, and the U.S. Congress, ordinarily is greater. Interest in any kind of election is in large part a function of the money spent in publicizing and promoting (or fighting against) either the candidate or the issue. A blitz of thirty- or sixty-second spot advertisements in the last weeks of a campaign will almost always stir voter interest—particularly if the issue is one that affects voters personally.

The *New York Times* clearly supported the view that direct democracy is a powerful stimulus to political participation when it editorialized: "People are more likely to vote when issues capture their interest."[1] And public opinion surveys regularly report that nonvoters and unregistered voters say they would be more likely to vote if they could vote on issues as well as candidates. Certain controversial issues—such as the death penalty, abortion, gun control, nuclear power plants, nuclear waste, mandatory bottle deposits, tax increases or cuts, gay rights, AIDS, right-to-work laws, and English-only proposals—undoubtedly bring additional voters to the polls. Civic-minded and informed citizens are already likely to vote; having issues on the ballot probably merely reinforces their customary behavior. Only a few voters probably come solely because of ballot issues. David Schmidt, a journalist and advocate of direct democracy, reports figures showing that turnout is consistently higher, in general, in states with initiatives on the ballot than in states without (see Table 9.1); yet his figures by no means end the debate on this question: in the same year as Schmidt, David Everson of the Illinois Legislative Studies Center compared turnouts in initiative and noninitiative states in the North and West (the South, for historical reasons, has had low turnout rates) and found no difference.[2] At best, having issues on the ballot only slightly increases election-day turnout. Analysts occasionally say too that long lists of issues such as those on California ballots intimidate voters. The implication is that some potential voters may even stay away, scared off by the demands and bewilderment—not to mention the time and energy costs—of having to study complex ballot issues. Others may vote for candidates but not for ballot measures. Both speculations are plausible, yet little evidence exists to confirm either. The 1987 nationwide survey conducted for this book by the Gallup Organization found that virtually no one would be less inclined to vote because issues were on the ballot, and an impressive number of unregistered voters implied that voting on ballot issues was appealing to them. Moreover, common sense suggests that turnout is generally a function of increment—increments among different elements of candidate coalitions, increments from the various levels of races (local, state, federal) and increments from whatever ballot measures (bond

Table 9.1. Relationship between voter turnout and initiatives on ballot, 1978–1984 (%)

| | Turnout of eligible voters | | | |
	1978	1980	1982	1984
States with initiatives on ballot	44.7	59.8	46.8	54.5
States with no initiatives on ballot	39.4	55.0	39.8	51.5

Sources: For 1978–1982: David B. Schmidt, "Ballot Initiatives: History, Research, and Analysis of Recent Initiative and Referendum Campaigns" (Initiative News Service, Washington, D.C., March 1983, Mimeograph), p. 24; for 1984: data from Initiative Resource Center, Washington, D.C.

issues, initiatives, constitutional amendments, and so on) are listed.

The challenge, of course, is to improve the process (through better education, improved debates, increased readability of statements and initiatives) so that larger numbers of citizens will be more competent to vote on ballot issues.

Finally, proponents of direct democracy claimed that their innovations would increase civic pride and trust in government and thereby diminish apathy and alienation. This was a proud boast and a noble aspiration. Trust in or alienation from government is difficult to measure. Americans tend to love their country and to dislike their government. Government reminds them of taxes, regulations, and restrictions. Pride in government is cyclical and is related in part to war or its absence, prosperity or its absence, Olympic successes, bicentennials, and similar events. It would be difficult to prove that Minnesotans or Virginians are less proud or less trusting of their state governments than Coloradans or Californians. Many states without direct democracy devices appear to enjoy as much citizen respect and acceptance as states that have them. In one area civic pride did increase. In states in the West that once were dominated by a few large special interests and often by party bosses—including the Dakotas, Oregon, and California—direct democracy devices doubtless did play a role in encouraging state governments to become more responsive to ordinary citizens. But better education, better and more media, increased competition between the political parties, and other factors also contributed to this same end. Clearly, direct democracy's advocates overstated their claim.

Have the initiative, referendum, and recall undermined representative democracy? Have the devices weakened our legislatures? Although experts still argue about the consequences, most would say that direct democracy has not weakened our regular legislative processes. Even in areas where these devices are used, 98 or 99 percent of the laws remain the responsibility of legislators. Legislatures are more important today than ever, as growing population and growing demands on government force them to assume greater responsibilities. Americans overwhelmingly endorse leaving the job of making laws to their elected representatives and view direct democracy devices almost entirely as a last alternative to the legislative process.

Seats in state legislative bodies today are much valued, sought after, and actively competed for by able citizens. Little evidence exists to suggest that even in the states most frequently using the initiative, referendum, and recall, candidates for the legislatures are harder to find or less motivated to perform effectively. Some legislatures may occasionally refer a few too many controversial topics to the ballot, yet this practice can hardly be said to have undermined representative government. On balance, then, direct democracy has developed as a supplement and not an undermining force in American government.

A second major objection to direct democracy held that it would produce unsound legislation and unwise or bad policy. Unwise legislation does get onto ballots, but the record indicates that voters reject most really unsound ideas. When defective legislation has been approved by direct democracy procedures, it has often been contested later in the courts, resulting in modification or outright invalidation.

Critics say, with some justification, that direct legislation is less well prepared than institutional legislation. Legislators have access to veteran legislative draftsmen, researchers, and counsel—resources that can seldom be matched by interest groups or concerned activists trying to get a measure on the ballot. This problem could be remedied, and safeguards have been adopted in some states, but the number of judicial reversals of initiatives attests to the reality that direct democracy efforts sometimes produce poorly drafted legislation.

A related fear was that minority rights might be sacrificed on the altar of majority rule. However, remarkably few ballot issues of this type have prevailed. When compared with the work of the nation's legislatures, the outcomes of initiative and referendum campaigns can be characterized as equally tolerant of minority rights. In some regions of the country state legislatures, even in the twentieth century, have been notably intolerant of women, minorities, and members of a minority party or even the major opposition political party. Most of these same states do not permit their voters the initiative, referendum, and recall.

Opponents also have long objected to direct democracy on the grounds that the typical voter would not be informed enough to cast an intelligent vote. According to this view, few voters consider all the possible alternatives to and consequences of a single vote; they are asked to render a verdict on a specific point but not on its context. American voters themselves would agree that their votes are often not as informed as they should be. Even people who feel strongly that citizens ought to be able to vote directly on issues admit that many citizens, including themselves, are often not able to cast a well-informed vote. Survey data confirm that as many as one-third to a majority of those voting acknowledge that they felt uncomfortable about voting because they needed more information or more time to discuss the issue or to read the voter pamphlet more carefully, or found that the statement was too hard to read and comprehend. However, most of the perceived flaws of the direct democracy processes are also the flaws of democracy in general. Voters often wish they had more information about the candidates—especially for state and county offices—when they have to choose among them. Delegates at constitutional conventions or national party conventions almost always have similar misgivings when they are forced to render yes-or-no votes on complicated issues. So, too, members of state and national legislatures—especially in those frantic days near the end of a session—yearn for more information about consequences, and more discussion and compromise than time will permit. Despite the misgivings of critics, voters judge reasonably well when faced with initiative, referendum, or recall choices. It is partly a matter of the gap between the ideal and real worlds. In the ideal context, voters would prepare for their votes in a judicious, scholarly, and textbook-citizen fashion. But seldom is the time available. This is also true, but obviously to a lesser extent, for local, state, and national legislators. There too, a gap exists between the textbook legislator and the legislator with a family to raise, campaign funds to collect, a second job to maintain, and party loyalties to sustain.

Few potential voters stay home because they fear initiatives or referenda. Of course some voters are confused. Some are also not sure they have enough information to vote on many or even most of the issues. Still, these would-be voters have the option of voting only for candidates and skipping the ballot issues.

For all potential voters who stay away from the polls because they are intimidated by the issues on the ballot, at least an equal number are motivated to come out and vote precisely because controversial issues are on their ballot. Of course there is an educational bias at work. Better-educated, well-to-do voters are more comfortable and informed when it comes to voting on ballot propositions than are lower-income, less educated citizens. This is a reality—and one that needs to be addressed and remedied, although it will never be entirely remedied.

Critics of direct democracy predicted that special interests would turn these devices to their own advantage. Has this in fact been the case? To get things accomplished, individuals have to join a group with which they share common interest. America has become a nation of interest groups—and this is likely to be even more the case in the future than in the past. These realities confirm some of the fears expressed by Herbert Croly and Richard Hofstadter years ago: that the impulse toward popular democratic rule always ran the risk of losing its meaning when it was divorced from an explicit social movement. Initial achievements or victories were won by the populists and progressives, but the very bosses or interests against whom these devices were aimed soon learned to adapt to the new rules, deflect them, or use them to advance their strategic interests.[3] These critics may have overstated their point, but their argument is compelling, and today's activities in California are another manifestation of the same problem.

In reality special interests and single-issue groups contend with one another regularly both in the legislative processes and in any form of direct democracy. And this is as it should be. "The secret of American politics is the blending of divergent interests into great electoral and governing coalitions," writes Patrick B. McGuigan. "Single issue groups of both the right and the left will not go away, now or ever, and it is much better for them to get involved in direct or representative democracy than to let their frustrations fester and grow."[4] Legislatures, to be sure, are usually the best place to reconcile the divergent interests of a state or nation, but they need not be the only place. Parties, the media, and the processes provided for in direct democracy can sometimes perform the reconciliation and compromising functions we usually assign, and should assign, to our institutionalized legislatures.

The final objection to direct democracy was that it would weaken the political accountability of elected officials. Voters in ballot issue elections seldom have to live with the consequences of their decisions; they seldom understand the longer-term needs and interests of the region; they are likely to think only of the short term and usually of their own self-interest.

These are serious objections. The sharing and checking of powers among elected officials in the three branches of government do provide for greater continuity and consideration of long-range consequences than do the initiative, referendum, and recall. Indeed, one criterion voters use in deciding whom to elect to office is the candidate's ability to comprehend the overall needs of a state or nation. Yet the record suggests that the public can also act responsibly. Indeed, on environmental matters the public appears to be more responsible than most state legislatures. Tax issues in Colorado, Ohio, and Michigan in recent years also suggest that voters can and often will decide on crucial issues on the basis of higher goals, not on that of short-term selfishness. The fear that populist democracy via initiative, referendum, and recall would lead to irresponsible, mercurial, or even bizarre decision making has not been borne out. The outcomes of direct democracy are similar to the outcomes of indirect democratic processes. One reason is that several safeguards regulate the existing forms of direct democracy. Another is that most Americans take their civic responsibilities seriously and have worked hard to make the initiative, referendum, and recall reasonably safe supplements to the traditional Madisonian checks and balances system.

Both proponents and opponents of direct democracy have too often overstated their positions. The existing direct democracy processes have both virtues and liabilities. Further, the American public appreciates this notable paradox: people agree with the central contentions of both the advocates and critics of direct democracy (as Table 9.2 illustrates for New Jersey). Two 1985 polls of Californians confirm that citizens are ambivalent about the initiative in that state: 79 percent said they liked the initiative process, yet 62 percent also told pollster Mervin Field they wanted to see proposed initiatives submitted to the California secretary of state's office for more rigorous review and comment before the petition circulation stage. Field found Californians concerned about the use of initiative by special interest groups in the 1980s. They also said they need more information if they are to cast informed votes in initiative elections.[5] Similarly, a survey by the Institute of Politics and Government at the University of Southern California found that voters generally like the initiative process but also want improvements (see Table 9.3). My 1987 national survey found the same ambivalence—especially with regard to the role of money.

Safeguards for the Initiative and Referendum

Initiatives and referenda are here to stay. Improvements, however, are needed to remedy their abuses and misuses. There are no magic formulas available, and inevitably those who want to can nearly always find inventive strategies to get around or minimize the intent of any regulation. Also, some safeguards will be more appropriate for certain

Table 9.2. Citizen attitudes toward initiative process, New Jersey, 1979 (%)

Issue	Agree	Disagree	Don't know
Benefits of the initiative			
Citizens ought to be able to vote directly on issues.	78	17	5
Government should allow the public to decide when representatives are afraid of offending certain interest groups.	77	14	9
If people could vote on issues, they would become interested in politics and participate in government.	82	14	4
Defects of the initiative			
The job of making laws should be left to elected representatives. They can be voted out of office if they don't do a good job.	64	32	4
Many people will not be able to cast an informed ballot.	76	20	4
Special interests would gain power by spending money to promote only their side of the issue.	63	32	6

Sources: New Jersey Poll no. 38, Eagleton Institute of Politics, Rutgers University, October 1979; adapted from David Magleby, Walt Klein, and Sue Thomas, "The Initiative in the 1980s" (Paper presented at the American Political Science Association annual meeting, Denver, September 1982), p. 8.

states than others. What makes sense for California may not make much sense for Maine. What makes sense for Inkum, Idaho, may not be desirable or workable for Los Angeles. Different jurisdictions have to adjust any safeguards to their own conditions.

Many of the following suggestions have been adopted in various locations. Many have been proposed by interest groups, writers, or legislative committees as ways to help citizen-voters to understand ballot issues better and to exercise the judgment required to make direct democracy live up to its potential. If direct democracy is to work properly, rules of fair play must be established in advance. Our efforts at self-government are never wholly achieved or defeated; every

Table 9.3. Voter attitudes toward initiative process, California, 1985 (%)
(N = 503)

Issue	Agree	Disagree	Don't know
Generally, I like the initiative process, but I would like significant changes in how it works.	71	22	7
All advertisements in initiative campaigns should say what industry or interest group provided money to the campaign organization to pay for the ad.	87	12	1
There should be a limit on the number of initiatives that can be on any ballot.	49	47	3
Increase the number of signatures required in order to qualify an initiative for the ballot.	49	47	4
Prohibit the use of paid signature gatherers for collecting the required signatures.	46	50	4

Source: California public interest poll, conducted by the Institute of Politics and Government, University of Southern California, February 1985; cited in Larry L. Berg and C. B. Holman, "The Initiative Process and Its Declining Agenda Setting Value" (Paper presented at the American Political Science Association annual meeting, New Orleans, August 1985).

generation needs to make improvements and ensure that democratic principles are encouraged.

1. **Sponsorship and filing fee.** A proposed initiative and referendum should have a number of sponsors—between 100 and 200 individuals, depending on the size of a jurisdiction—and there should be a filing fee of between $200 and $1,000, again depending on the population size of the area. These nominal requirements are necessary to discourage frivolous or publicity-seeking petitions.

2. **Drafting advice provided by the attorney general's office.** Advice from a state attorney general need not be accepted, but it should be available, and petitioners should be required to obtain it. Some states now provide for a review board to go over draft language and eliminate

confusing, misleading, or flagrantly unconstitutional wording. Although courts (in advance advisory opinions) could conceivably prejudge the constitutionality of a measure before it goes to court, various officials such as the attorney general and experts in a state's legislative counsel or legislative reference service can offer petitioners some helpful guidance at the drafting stage that may prevent litigation and court intervention at the election or postelection stages.

Some proponents of formal legal review point out that the attorney general at the state level or the city or county attorney may not be the appropriate official to conduct such a preview because of potential conflicts of interest. One group has suggested that legal review be provided free of charge by a voluntary *pro bono* panel of attorneys. "Such a panel could conduct the review in an objective and professional fashion. This service might be provided in the same manner as the Office of the Public Defender, which provides volunteer attorneys to individuals who cannot afford legal assistance."[6] Other combinations of official and unofficial hybrids of these suggestions may work better, depending on the jurisdiction.

3. Mandatory official statement and summary of the petition's contents. After a measure is filed, a state official should be made responsible for giving the measure a title, preparing a concise and readable statement, and providing a slightly longer official summary of the meaning and consequences of the ballot measure. Some jurisdictions already require this, and, obviously, some political problems can arise. Groups who petition often want a glitzier title or a statement. Neutral wording, however, is essential for the integrity of the process and for voter understanding. A worthwhile additional step would be to require state officials to calculate the estimated financial cost of a ballot measure. Although this information must necessarily be approximate, it should be sought at the outset of a campaign.

4. Reasonable signature requirements. It should be neither easy nor nearly impossible to obtain the number of signatures necessary to get measures on the ballot. Six to 8 percent of the last vote for governor seems an appropriate requirement for statutory measures, 8 to 10 percent for constitutional measures.

5. Geographic distribution requirements in certain states. About half of the states permitting the initiative and referendum require some form of geographic distribution for petition signatures. Massachusetts, for example, has a simple stipulation that no more than 25 percent of the signatures may come from any one county, thus ensuring that not all the signatures would be collected in Boston. Arizona requires that 5 percent of signatures come from fifteen different counties. Missouri requires 8 percent to come from two-thirds of its six congressional districts for a constitutional initiative, and 5 percent for a statutory initiative. Geographic requirements are an additional obstacle for those who want to use direct democracy processes. But those who favor these requirements point out it is now possible in California or Colorado to qualify ballot measures by gathering signatures only in the most populous county or two of the state or in only one part of the state. Thus Orange County, California, or Denver, Colorado, could have an undue influence in the initiative process, one far exceeding the locality's representation in the state legislature.

Critics of a geographic distribution requirement dismiss it as an effort to make the initiative and referendum more difficult and more expensive to use. They say no section of a state should be denied access to the process just because it has a proposal of special concern to its region. California's attorney general says a geographic requirement is unnecessary: "If there is something wrong with the measure let the voters vote it down. They've done it before. They'll do it again."[7]

Geographic requirements make sense in states such as New York, Texas, or Hawaii. Surely a petition in New York should include some signatures from localities outside New York City; a petition in Texas should have at least some support in the various regions of that sprawling state; and some percentage of petitions should come from some of the outer islands should Hawaii adopt the initiative and referendum. These requirements should be kept simple—along the lines of the Massachusetts requirement that no more than 25 percent of signatures should come from any one county or that an upstate/downstate or east/west requirement be stipulated—and minimal rather than high.

6. Stiff penalties for deceptive petitioning. The official wording and title of a proposed measure should be visible on all petitions, and signers should be instructed to read the statement beforehand. The message "Be Sure to Read This Statement before You Sign This Petition" should appear prominently at the top of each petition. Groups circulating a measure should be listed on the petition, and all circulators should sign an oath that all petition signatures have been submitted in accordance with the law.

7. **Petition certification requirements.** Secretaries of state or similar appropriate officials should be required to check the validity of signatures by means of standard statistical sampling techniques. A 5 to 10 percent base sample should be sufficient.

8. **Required state legislative hearings.** One way to make direct democracy processes more compatible with representative government would be to require state legislatures to conduct statewide hearings on the merits and drawbacks of a proposed ballot measure once it gets the necessary signatures. In many instances the legislature will have already held hearings on this or similar issues, but the initiative would provide the occasion for proponents and opponents to come together and examine evidence, fiscal estimates, minority rights, and other policy and tax consequences of the measure under consideration. It would allow, and sometimes force, legislators to get involved and make their views known and would allow grass-roots groups as well as leadership elites to offer their views. Press and media coverage should be encouraged in order to educate the general public.

California has made an effort to conduct such hearings in recent years, but these have not lived up to expectations. Most legislators apparently prefer to be back home campaigning for reelection; others prefer to avoid controversial issues. Still others may believe such hearings only give publicity to single-issue groups they would prefer to see get little or no attention. Whatever the reasons, the hearings in California have been cursory at best.

More experimentation with hearings is needed. Possibilities include televised hearings and regional hearings in major population centers. Either would be a way to get legislators involved debating the issues. Legislators should be able to inform and shape public opinion. In the many cases in which the legislatures have decided not to act on these or similar measures, representatives should make it clear to the public why they made that decision.

Mandatory hearings could have undesirable consequences in some states. In California, for example, where it is not unusual for a dozen or more measures to be on the ballot, holding hearings on every issue would be costly. In most states, however, only a few issues are usually on the ballot, and hearings would be far more manageable. It would appear feasible to hold several general "town meeting" style hearings in a few of the major population centers or regional centers in a state, concentrating at least on the most controversial initiatives. In short, what California has tried, if not succeeded with, other states might successfully adapt for their own region.

9. **Voter information pamphlets.** A clearly presented official information pamphlet is essential to enable voters to make wise policy choices. In Massachusetts, Oregon, and Washington such pamphlets are read, used, and often mentioned as a key guide in voting decisions. Properly prepared and designed, they provide each household with the text of an initiative, the basic arguments for and against it, and its projected costs and consequences. Efforts should be made both to simplify the statements and analyses and to provide 100-word "ballot digests," such as are used in some California cities.

A less expensive alternative, and possibly one more likely to reach less well-educated voters, might be for states and localities to print ballot digests in local newspapers or to air them on radio and television. But the real challenge for states remains to provide both readable and informative voter pamphlets.

10. **Mandatory financial disclosure.** States and localities should require that all contributions of $200 or more be disclosed during and after an initiative and referendum campaign. Disclosure satisfies the public's right to know who is supporting and who is opposing a ballot measure. The public deserves to know as much as possible about the way an initiative got on the ballot and how it is being promoted or opposed. The size and source of contributions are often important issues in initiative and referendum campaigns. Grossly excessive contributions from a single source or single industry may well promote backlash among voters, and reasonable full disclosure remains "one of the best guarantees available against the excessive influence of money on election outcomes."[8] To keep reporting and enforcement burdens to a minimum, some figure should be set for the specific disclosure of individual donations. Overall expenditures, however, should also be disclosed. The majority of contributions raised before the election should be reported early enough that the public can appreciate the significance of the information. A final disclosure statement should also be required after the election and upon the termination of the respective campaign committees. States may also want to require im-

mediate public disclosures of notable large contributions (perhaps over $2,500 in large states, or $1,000 in smaller states).

11. **Expenditure floors and public financing.** A fair initiative and referendum campaign should allow both sides to make their case to the public. Although it may not be politically and financially possible to allocate public funds to both sides of every ballot issue campaign, some form of assistance, such as a floor, could be put into effect in one-sided issue campaigns when one side raises more than a specified amount. Such a provision would prevent one group or view from dominating the public debate and the flow of information to prospective voters.[9] Political scientist Austin Ranney makes a persuasive case for this form of regulation:

> The absence of parties and party labels in referendum campaigns means that the voters enter the campaigns with less information and fewer guideposts than in candidate elections. And the campaigns are therefore significantly more important as suppliers of information and arguments that make for interested voters and informed votes. Accordingly, the prime object of government regulation of referendum campaigns should be to ensure that both the proponents and opponents of each proposition should have enough resources to make at least adequate presentations of their cases.[10]

12. **A reinstituted fairness doctrine.** Because most voters get much or most of their information about ballot issue campaigns from radio and television, fair access to media outlets is essential. Broadcasters should hold themselves to tough access standards in initiative and referendum campaigns, precisely because voters need even more information on ballot issues than they do about the candidates for office. If they fail in this obligation, the FCC should again be charged to regulate toward this end.

13. **Stiff penalties for false advertising.** State and local legislatures should pass laws providing for prosecution against false advertising in initiative and referendum campaigns. The integrity of ballot issue elections is too often compromised by misleading claims, phony statistics, and misrepresentations to the voters. Well-publicized fines and penalties for the obvious violators of these laws will go a long way

toward encouraging better-informed debate. Information about the identity of sponsors should be disclosed on the face of all advertisements.

14. **Restriction of statutory and constitutional initiatives to general elections.** Turnout is highest in general elections and considerably lower in primary or special elections. Many voters registered or identifying with neither major political party fail to turn out for primary elections because they are not that interested in intraparty personnel decisions; and in some states only those who are registered with a party affiliation are allowed to vote in primary races. Thus, states should place initiative issues on the ballot only in general elections. Some states already have such a requirement. Although some states would consequently have a long list of issues on the ballot at the general election, this somewhat daunting effect should be offset by two factors: a voter information pamphlet would have to be published only once every two years, and the maximum possible number of voters will be involved in the decisions.

Other Considerations

An *advisory referendum* system, such as that used in some European nations, is sometimes recommended as a better means than our current initiative and referendum to involve the general public yet keep the legislatures in charge of lawmaking. "The advantage of this approach," according to David B. Magleby, "is that the public can indicate its preference for general policy, and the legislature can handle the statutory or constitutional steps necessary for the implementation and administration of policy."[11] Magleby advocates putting simple questions before the public, and sometimes even multiple-response questions, thereby encouraging voters to offer general policy guidance and communicate the direction and intensity of their preferences. The functions of drafting and deciding on specific laws, however, would be left to the legislature.

This alternative to direct democracy would be more than a mere public opinion poll, but much less than advocates of direct democracy would prefer. It would, however, stimulate public debate, attract voter interest, and allow the public to play at least some role beyond selecting the people sent to the state legislatures. Although the results of such elections would be nonbinding, issues that won approval by significant majorities would place the legislature under pressure either to go along or to explain its opposition.

The advisory referendum is an unlikely candidate for adoption in states that now permit regular direct democracy elections; voters in those states would view such a move as a clear diminution of their political rights. On the other hand, if the signature requirements were decidedly less, perhaps just 3 or 4 percent instead of the usual 8 or 10 percent for binding referenda, there would be some merit to viewing the advisory referendum as a complement to rather than a substitute for the regular system. Certainly, the advisory referendum could be a reasonable experimental alternative for states and communities that do not now provide for the initiative and referendum.

Another alternative to the most familiar type of initiative and referendum system is the *indirect initiative*. Whereas under direct initiative a measure automatically goes on the ballot when enough petition signatures are obtained, under the indirect initiative, when enough signatures are filed the proposal first goes to the legislature, which may approve, modify, or reject the measure. Maine, Massachusetts, Michigan, Nevada, and South Dakota, among others, permit some form of indirect initiative. Some of these states allow for modification or amendment; others require the measure to be approved or rejected exactly as it came to the legislature. If rejected or sharply amended, sponsors may force the measure to a vote of the people. Often, however, proponents have to go through the petition process before the measure is certified for the ballot. "The indirect initiative is no panacea," writes Neal R. Peirce, "but there are powerful arguments in its favor." It involves legislators further in the lawmaking process. "It strengthens, rather than weakens, representative democracy for forcing legislators to come to grips with an idea they may have sought to avoid before. It brings into play the forces of moderation, compromise, common sense so often lacking in direct initiatives."[12]

The indirect initiative concept is endorsed by the League of Women Voters and the National Municipal League, but critics see it as just one more obstructionist hurdle raised by those who do not really want direct democracy procedures to be used at all. They claim that where it has been used, state legislatures almost always reject the initiatives, thus protracting an already lengthy process. Critics also point out that a legislature already has the option of passing its own form of legislation addressing the problems raised by petitioners. A responsive legislature would encourage the petitioners to withdraw their ballot measure or undermine their efforts to win petition support for the measure by having acted in a representative fashion.

The indirect initiative does indeed delay legislative change. But it also provides an opportunity for measures to get a formal hearing and to benefit from the experience of veteran legislators and their staffs.[13] It is a sensible option for states not permitting the direct initiative.

A few states have prohibited paying people to circulate and gather signature petitions. Advocates of banning *paid circulators* believe the process should be run by volunteers. They say there is too great a risk that paid circulators will be less candid or even untruthful when gathering signatures. If you have enough money, they argue, you can get just about anything on the ballot. Clearly, the early intentions of direct democracy have been compromised in states such as California, where petition by paid professionals has become a profit-making big business.[14]

Those who favor paying signature gatherers say any restriction against it violates freedom of speech; they note, too, that there is no such restriction on workers in candidate elections. In 1988 the U.S Supreme Court, in *Grant v. Meyer,* struck down a Colorado law that made it illegal to pay people for gathering signatures. Such a law, the Court ruled unanimously, restricts freedom of expression, guaranteed under the First Amendment; it restricts access to the most effective, fundamental, and perhaps economical avenue of political discourse, direct one-on-one communication. Colorado's secretary of state, Natalie Meyer, decried the ruling and predicted it would create a flood of unnecessary and unrepresentative ballot measures. But several conservative groups hailed the decision as one restoring the freedom of all individuals in all states to use their efforts to get initiatives on the ballot.

Each side offers valid points in this debate. Yet the consensus Supreme Court ruling settles the issue, at least for the near future. And as a practical matter, it is necessary anyway to permit paid circulators in the larger states.

A final consideration is whether it will be impossible to *limit large contributions* to initiative and referendum campaigns. Courts have struck down efforts to restrict or limit corporate or individual financial contributions to ballot measure campaigns, but many groups such as Common Cause continue to press for such limits. Large contributions, they say, give an unfair advantage to the side able to attract "big money." Big spenders overwhelm the initiative process and may cause voter apathy. California Common Cause recommends contribution limits on corporations and unions but not on individuals, arguing that corporate, not individual, spending is overwhelming the initiative process in California. The group also believes that courts might eventually be stricter on corporations and unions.

Those who object to limiting contributions contend such a restriction is an infringement of individuals' or organizations' rights to express and support their political preferences; although it is not as severe a limitation as prohibiting them from making any contribution, it is still a significant infringement. If an initiative might significantly damage a group, industry, or individual, surely that group or individual should have the right to contribute any amount desired to defeat it.

We need to determine more accurately the influence, and perhaps the corrupting influence, of "big money" in initiative and referendum campaigns. Valuable preliminary studies have already been done; more will be needed before the courts can be persuaded to allow limits on contributions. Meanwhile, the question of money will best be treated by effective financial disclosure laws and some form of partial public financing or subsidies.

Recommendations for Improving the Recall Process

Recall is in many respects the most controversial of direct democracy practices. Yet it is plainly in the tradition of American concern for keeping public officials accountable. Although existing requirements have limited its use primarily to the local level, it has been used occasionally at the state level in Arizona, California, Idaho, Michigan, and Oregon, and usually with sensible results. Its use to force out of office an insensitive and irresponsible governor in Arizona suggests the positive virtues of the recall at the state level.

Of course the recall has been occasionally misused. In San Francisco, for example, a strident, intense, and irresponsible group used the recall mainly to embarrass Mayor Dianne Feinstein. Some public officials, understandably enough, complain that the presence of the recall in their jurisdiction encourages a zero-risk or overly timid neutrality in elected officials.

On balance, however, the recall has been mainly used to weed out incompetent, arbitrary, or corrupt officials. It is a positive device reminding officials that they are temporary agents of the public they serve.

Perhaps the most bogus of the critics' claims is that the recall discourages able citizens from running for office. There are plenty of factors dissuading thoughtful individuals from running for office, but the recall is far down the list. Able elected officials find that they have considerable latitude to define issues, shape the public policy agenda, educate citizens, and persuade people of their general positions.

As noted in Chapter 6, the recall remains a sometimes mildly helpful but crude safety valve, and its use should be restricted to true emergencies. The essential objective is to encourage recall efforts only in those serious situations when a public official has been inexcusably negligent or has become incompetent. The recall can play an important, if minor, role in our political system, but the possibilities for misuse and abuse are considerable and must be monitored.

Although polls indicate Americans would like to have recall for federal officials, the recall device is not necessary or desirable for members of Congress or for the president. Because of their two-year terms, members of the House of Representatives are already nearly always running for reelection. For a variety of reasons, some of which may not be so healthy, they customarily retain a "candidate's state of mind." U.S. Senators, elected for six-year terms, serve in a chamber that was deliberately designed to take a longer view of the national interest. Recall would alter that view and the federalist principles that justify the existence of the Senate. And presidents can be overridden by Congress, checked by the Supreme Court, or impeached.

The recall is occasionally proposed as a vote of no confidence that would permit the removal of presidents who have lost the ability to govern. But the potential abuses outweigh the potential merits. If, however, presidents were granted six-year terms and House members were allowed four-year terms, some form of recall would become more feasible, and for the same reasons the recall was championed eighty years ago at the state and local levels. "That longer terms of office and a freer range of discretion are conducive to administrative efficiency is everywhere accepted," wrote Charles A. Beard, "and the recall seems to offer to democracy the proper safeguards against usurpation which will warrant the granting of longer terms and larger powers to executive authorities."[15]

Safeguards for the recall device will necessarily vary from place to place, depending on political traditions, and especially between the state and community levels because of the varying populations and time requirements. Still, if we are to permit the recall, these minimal regulations are necessary to ensure its soundness.

1. **Petition statement and identification of petitioners.** A recall petition should contain an explicit statement of the grounds on which the removal of the elected official is sought. The names of the persons or groups sponsoring the petition should appear clearly on the petition, as well as the message "Be Sure to Read This Statement before You Sign This Petition."

2. **High signature requirements.** A large percentage of signatures should be required for recall elections to keep costly elections to a minimum and to discourage sour-grapes and personal, retaliatory efforts. Signatures should be of registered voters—perhaps 25 percent of those voting in the last election for governor, or for the particular office in question, or 20 percent of registered voters in general—or whichever is higher.

3. **No recalls during first six months in office.** No recall petitions should be filed against any officer, state or local, within the first six months of an official's term. This provision would help prevent sour-grapes efforts or the variation of continuous recounts.

4. **No circulation of recall petitions for six months after an unsuccessful recall election.** This limitation would prevent continued harrassment of officials and encourage voters to wait until the next election.

5. **Stiff penalties for making false statements about the petition.** Criminal penalties should exist for misrepresenting or making false statements about the petition to gain signatures, for filing petitions known to contain false signatures, or for using a recall petition as a threat to extort money or special favors and contracts.

6. **Financial disclosure.** Ten days before and a week after a recall election, sponsors should file documents listing any contributions over $200. This information, made available to the local or state media, should allow citizens to discern if one or more single-interest groups were the primary supporters of the recall effort. It would also inhibit persons who have some reason to conceal their interest from investing in the recall campaign. In the absence of other limits or financial restrictions, financial disclosure should be imperative.

7. **Signature verification.** Officials from the secretary of state's office or election clerks at the local level should be authorized to verify recall petitions by using accepted professional statistical sampling techniques.

8. **"Cooling off" period.** Depending on the size of the jurisdiction, there should be a "cooling off" period after signature filings, before the date for the recall election is set. This might be forty or fifty days

at the city level, seventy-five days or more at the state level. It would prevent hasty action in light of a single controversial vote, personnel decision, or budget decision and would allow for emotions to cool and the record and overall performance of the official in question to be appraised. It would also allow for media analysis of the controversy.

9. Public hearings. Depending on the availability of an ethics committee, a campaign fair-practices commission, or some similar relatively neutral and professional body, an open hearing should be scheduled on the merits of the recall. At such time both the petitioners and the targeted official could present their arguments. This discussion and evaluation would make information available to permit citizen-voters to make a more reasoned judgment.

Three Models of Democracy

Ultimately, the debate over direct democracy stems from two clashing perspectives on governance and government. Modern-day disciples of Rousseau, Jefferson, and the populists continue to skirmish with contemporary followers of Burke, Madison, the Federalists, and Whigs. The interplay between these two major schools of thought suggests the development of a third model, one that has in many ways become the operational model for the somewhat amended representative democracy practices in effect today.

The *populist-plebiscitary democracy* model places enormous trust in the people, a trust matched only by its distrust of elected officials and the lobbyists who surround them. Today's populists call for greater opportunities for citizens to participate in public affairs, to assert control over their own lives and the direction of their communities. Freedom has been diminished, they say, by the delegation of too much responsibility to elected officials in remote capitals. Benjamin R. Barber's rousing call for citizen empowerment and strong democracy is built upon the premise that representative government is inadequate, if not antagonistic, to the aspirations of modern-day citizens: "Men and women who are not directly responsible through common deliberation, common decision and common action for the policies that determine their common lives are not really free at all."[16]

Only a few starry-eyed pop sociologists go as far as *Megatrend* author John Naisbitt's claims that representative democracy is now obsolete and that Americans have outlived the historic usefulness of representative institutions.[17] Most champions of the populist-plebiscitary model merely argue that citizen involvement in public affairs is desirable, educational, and important for ensuring continuous accountability in the political system. Trust the people, they urge. Give them their chance to be heard and to participate. They will do no worse than elites, and they will be better for having had the chance.

Direct democracy devices give the people a voice in government decision making and a stake in the political process. "These processes allow them to get their day in court. They may lose and often do, but it is their fellow citizens who tell them that their ideas are acceptable or not," says Patrick B. McGuigan. True, "there is the possibility for distortion, for limiting human rights, or that a bad choice will be made. But the courts and legislators can also make bad decisions and they have. By and large . . . the people make good choices."[18]

An additional case for direct democracy is that it invigorates the political process. People are attracted to politics through these campaigns, and many of them remain active and sometimes even run for office as a result of their involvement. Thus these devices have helped "to open up new pathways for participation, for political communication and even for policy innovation."[19]

The *representative democracy* model, in sharp contrast, dismisses the need for maximum, continuous accountability and stresses the need for informed, responsible decision making. Trust your elected representatives, say its advocates, not the often uninformed or ill-informed general public. The people are not all Athenians. Most issues are complicated.

The framers of the Constitution rejected a system requiring complete consensus because, as practical men, they knew any system would be rife with factions and conflict. The framers knew that face-to-face, Athenian-style direct decision making was impractical for a large nation. They had little experience or knowledge of mass public voting on public policies and would have rejected plebiscitary votes by the people on issues. They were even skeptical of majority rule, for the general public could make wrong decisions about who should be in office. Although they favored the principle of majority rule, the framers chose to refine it by filtering majority impulses through institutional sieves that might screen out the impurities, irrationalities, and passions and "leave a residue of calm, deliberate, seasoned wisdom to be reflected in leaders very much like themselves."[20] Much like themselves, but different. The difference, the founders hoped, would be that elected officials would be wise, informed, and prudent individuals who could weigh competing interests and reconcile the diversity of self-interests with the higher aspirations and common good of the whole nation.

Modern-day Madisonians question most of the claims made by modern-day populists. They prefer to strengthen the capacity of representative institutions to make better policy than to open the system up to various ad hoc participatory ventures. It is not so much that they are pessimists about the capacity of the people to become involved in public affairs, but that they do not believe most people want to spend increased amounts of their leisure time studying issues, debating policy consequences, and making decisions on a large array of complicated policy subjects. Compromise, lengthy hearings, debate, negotiation, and consideration of all sides of an issue are essential—and an effective legislature can perform all these activities. A state senator from Ohio put it this way:

> I'm not crazy about the initiative process, and I'll tell you why. The whole business of governing is a delicate thing. What makes the legislative process such a great institution is that everyone in it is open and candid with one another. We regularly go to our opponents across the aisles and confront them with our ideas and our new proposals, because we have all learned that it's in everybody's interest to give everybody a crack at bill writing.
>
> It's easy to try to do it yourself. But you learn that the strength of the process is that it extends, refines, and helps consider a diversity of viewpoints, especially the views of those people affected by the proposed measure. Sometimes, for example, I think I have come up with some great legislation, but someone whose constituents are adversely affected will come up and say, "Do you realize what you are doing to me?" And I say, "No." Then they may say, "I have some ideas on how you might achieve what you want to do without having to hurt us so much." We can then agree and hammer out some slightly different way to write the legislation. Sure, it's a long process. But with the initiative there is no one to sit down with and talk with about the diverse interests.[21]

Like this Ohio legislator, champions of republican principles dispute that direct democracy will cure the ills of representative democracy. They point to inconsistent ballot measure votes by the people and fail to see how the public interest can be advanced by simple majority voting. They also doubt the claim that direct democracy can reduce alienation, increase voter turnout, and inspire the disaffected. If there are weaknesses in the processes of representative democracy, they say, then institute legislative reforms, not direct democracy. Give legislators the tools and resources to perform their responsibilities more effectively. If they fail, turn them out of office at the end of their terms and elect better representatives in their place.

The chief elements of these two clashing approaches can be summarized as follows:

Popular Democracy	Representative Democracy
Rousseau, Franklin, and Jefferson as godfathers	Burke, Adams, and Madison as godfathers
Maximum and continuous *accountability*	Maximum *responsibility*
Participation of the people	Debate and deliberation among informed elites
Trust the people	Trust the representatives
Permit the people more opportunities for self-government	Strengthen legislative processes
Majority rule translated into procedural democracy	Majority rule balanced against minority rights
Government by the people	Government by democratically chosen leaders

Fortunately, a third model affords a middle way. The model of *sensible democracy* recognizes the cherished values of both the representative and popular models. It also appreciates that most advocates of those clashing perspectives are flexible enough to permit this hybrid perspective. This third mode of thinking in many ways sums up the political values of an increasing number of Americans.

Sensible Democracy

Values representative institutions and wants legislators and other elected officials to make the vast majority of laws

Values majority rule yet understands the need to protect minority rights most of the time

Wants to improve legislative processes

Wants occasionally to vote on public policy issues

Wants safety-valve recall or vote of no confidence procedure as a last resort for inept and irresponsible public officials—but is willing to make these options difficult to use

Wants to improve the access of the common person both to run for office and to use direct democracy procedures

Wants to lessen the influence of secrecy, money, and single-interest groups in public decision-making processes

Trusts representatives most of the time, yet distrusts the concentration of power in any one institution

Trusts the general public's decisions some of the time, yet distrusts majority opinion some of the time

Is indifferent to most initiatives and referenda except when it comes to its own pet initiative issue

Agrees with the central arguments of both the proponents and opponents of populist democracy, hence favors a number of regulating safeguards for direct democracy devices

Is fundamentally ambivalent toward popular democracy—favoring it in theory and holding a more skeptical attitude toward it as it is practiced in states and localities

This mixed model characterizes the views of most Americans who have stopped to think about the current representative processes and their alternatives. It is a healthy way to look at them. Experience, as the Constitution's framers found, is a prudent guide. Representative government has occasional problems, yet most Americans prefer it as a way to govern themselves wisely. They approve of properly regulated direct democracy devices for special circumstances, especially for their own pet causes, but very few Americans express any yearning for routine popular processes and a teledemocratized nation that would permit frequent and binding plebiscites on state and national issues.

The initiative, referendum, and recall have made modest contributions to American democracy. They have become so deeply rooted in the political culture of the many states and cities allowing them that they will undoubtedly continue to be used, and probably used more often, in the future. As in the past, their use will be tied to cycles of citizen impatience and frustration and to periods of social upheaval and economic uncertainty. If these populist devices are to serve us better than they have in the past, they must be subject to the kinds of safeguards outlined in this chapter. Additional states should not adopt these processes without carefully considering the very real abuses detailed in earlier chapters and establishing regulations that will prevent them.

States that have employed these popular democracy practices should continue to do so, with modifications that will improve their integrity. Those states not now allowing the initiative, referendum, and recall should consider them, yet they should prudently weigh their assets and liabilities. Each state and locality will have to decide whether and how these practices would mesh with its own traditions and political culture. The nation has considerable variations and diversity, and no set of uniform policy or structural prescriptions need be imposed on dissimilar states and communities.

These devices should be used only when glaring deficiencies have occurred in basic governmental practices. Thus, recall of public officials should be rare. Initiative petition drives should be launched only when groups have tried to achieve their goals through their regular representative institutions. Legislatures should refer matters to the public reluctantly, understanding that it is primarily their own job to tackle tough policy issues. Too-frequent referrals will undermine the legitimacy of the republican principle. And none of these devices or practices will work well unless voters understand and respect the process and have access to the information necessary to make informed decisions.

Although I favor properly safeguarded initiatives and referenda for states and communities, I continue to oppose the adoption of a national initiative and referendum. The liabilities and deficiencies of these devices can be contained, corrected, or otherwise repaired at the state and local levels better than at the national level. Too many issues at the national level involve national security or international economic relations. The stakes are often very high. The problems of money, deceptive advertisements, ballot access, minority rights, and divisive special campaigns—which already cause problems at the state and local levels—would be greatly multiplied at the national level and could paralyze the nation. Not until these processes can be proved to work with greater integrity at the subnational level should anyone seriously consider amending the Constitution to permit them for the national government.

NOTES

▼

Introduction

1. Woodrow Wilson, address in Kansas City, Mo., May 5, 1911; reprinted in *The Public Papers of Woodrow Wilson*, ed. Ray Standard Baker and William E. Dodd, vol. 2 (New York: Harper and Brothers, 1925), 287.

2. Ibid., pp. 287–288.

3. Governor Thomas Kean, quoted in the *New York Times*, January 15, 1986, p. 84.

4. Richard Gephardt, press release, July 30, 1980 (Mimeograph).

5. Benjamin R. Barber, "Voting Is Not Enough," *Atlantic Monthly*, June 1984, p. 52. See also his *Strong Democracy: Participatory Politics for a New Age* (Berkeley: University of California Press, 1984).

1. To Govern Ourselves Wisely

Epigraph: Alexander Hamilton, speech, June 18, 1787, in *Selected Writings and Speeches of Alexander Hamilton*, ed. Morton J. Frisch (Washington, D.C.: American Enterprise Institute, 1985), pp. 98, 101.

1. Alexander Hamilton, *The Federalist*, no. 22, in *The Federalist Papers*, ed. Jacob E. Cooke (New York: Meridian, 1961), p. 146. All subsequent citations of *The Federalist* are to this edition.

2. James Madison, *The Federalist*, no. 39, p. 251. See also Charles S. Hyneman, "Republican Government in America," in *Founding Principles of American Government: Two Hundred Years of Democracy on Trial*, ed. George J. Graham, Jr., and Scarlett G. Graham (Bloomington: Indiana University Press, 1977), p. 18.

3. See, for example, Barber, *Strong Democracy;* and Patrick B. McGuigan, *The Politics of Direct Democracy in the 1980s: Case Studies in Popular Decision Making* (Washington, D.C.: Institute for Government and Politics, 1985).

4. Richard Hofstadter, *The Age of Reform* (New York: Vintage Books, 1955), p. 16.

5. Harvey C. Mansfield, Jr., and Robert Scigliano, *Representation* (Washington, D.C.: American Political Science Association, 1978), p. 25.

6. Page Smith, *John Adams*, vol. 1: *1735–1784* (Garden City, N.Y.: Doubleday, 1962), 260.

7. John Adams, *Thoughts on Government* (1776), in *The Works of John Adams*, ed. Charles Francis Adams, vol. 4 (Boston: Little, Brown, 1851), 194–195.

8. Donald S. Lutz, "Popular Consent and Popular Control: 1776–1789," in Graham and Graham, *Founding Principles*, p. 64. For a sympathetic interpretation of Adams's theories of leadership, see Bruce Miroff, "John Adams: Merit, Fame, and Political Leadership" (Mimeograph, 1985).

9. "Dissent of Penn. Minority," in John D. Lewis, ed., *Antifederalists versus Federalists: Selected Documents* (San Francisco: Chandler Documents, 1967). See also the views of Patrick Henry and George Mason in Jonathan Elliot, ed., *The Debates in the Several States' Conventions on the Adoption of the Federal Constitution*, vol. 3 (Philadelphia: J. B. Lippincott, 1859).

10. Lutz, "Popular Consent," p. 85. On the suffrage in these early years, see Robert E. Brown, *Middle-Class Democracy and the Revolution in Massachusetts, 1691–1780* (Ithaca: Cornell University Press, 1955); Marchette Chute, *The First Liberty: A History of the Right to Vote in America* (New York: E. P. Dutton, 1971); and Chilton Williamson, *American Suffrage from Property to Democracy, 1760–1860* (Princeton: Princeton University Press, 1968).

11. Lutz, "Popular Consent," p. 93.

12. Hyneman, "Republican Government in America," p. 18.

13. Fisher Ames, quoted in ibid., p. 19.

14. James Madison, speech at the Virginia ratifying convention, June 20, 1788, in *The Writings of James Madison*, ed. Gaillard Hunt, vol. 5 (New York: G. P. Putnam's Sons, 1901), 223.

15. Madison, *The Federalist*, no. 51, p. 349.

16. I draw here upon the analysis of Martin Diamond, in Martin Diamond, Winston Mills Fisk, and Herbert Garfinkel, *The Democratic Republic* (Chicago: Rand McNally, 1966), p. 75.

17. Madison, speech at the Virginia ratifying convention, June 11, 1788, in Hunt, *Writings of Madison*, 5: 158.

18. Thomas Paine, *The Rights of Man*, in *The Writings of Thomas Paine* (Albany, N.Y.: Charles R. and George Webster, 1792).

19. For a discussion of city administrative decentralization, see Joseph F. Zimmerman, *Participatory Democracy: Populism Revised* (New York: Praeger, 1986), chaps. 6 and 7. For a discussion of employee participation and workplace democracy, see Robert A. Dahl, *A Preface to Economic Democracy* (Berkeley: University of California Press, 1985); and for a discussion of new types of grassroots citizen involvement, see Harry C. Boyte, *The Backyard Revolution: Understanding the New Citizen Movement* (Philadelphia: Temple University Press, 1980).

2. Representative Democracy

Epigraphs: Walter Lippmann, *The Public Philosophy* (New York: New American Library, 1955), p. 19; George F. Will, opinion column, *Washington Post*, July 28, 1977.

1. Gordon S. Wood, *Representation in the American Revolution* (Charlottesville: University of Virginia Press, 1969), p. 3.

2. Robert E. Brown, *Middle-Class Democracy and the Revolution in Massachusetts, 1691–1780* (Ithaca: Cornell University Press, 1955), p. 401.

3. Ibid., pp. 402–403.

4. Thomas Hartley, *Annals of Congress,* 1st Cong., 1st sess., August 15, 1789, 761.

5. Clement Eaton, "Southern Senators and the Right of Instruction, 1789–1860," *Journal of Southern History,* 18 (August 1952), 316.

6. Ibid., p. 319.

7. Hanna F. Pitkin, "The Concept of Representation," in *Representation* (New York: Atherton Press, 1969), pp. 19–20.

8. Edmund Burke, speech to Bristol constituents, in *Burke's Works,* ed. James Prior, vol. 1 (London: Bell and Daldy, 1871), 446.

9. Heinz Eulau, "Changing Views of Representation," in *The Politics of Representation,* ed. Heinz Eulau and John C. Wahlke (Beverly Hills, Calif.: Sage, 1978), p. 50.

10. James Madison, *The Federalist,* no. 10, p. 64.

11. Martin Diamond, in Martin Diamond, Winston Mills Fisk, and Herbert Garfinkel, *The Democratic Republic* (Chicago: Rand McNally, 1966), p. 75.

12. Madison, *The Federalist,* no. 63, p. 427.

13. These principles have their roots in *The Federalist,* nos. 62 (Madison) and 63 (Madison). See also John Adams, *Defense of the Constitution,* in *The Works of John Adams,* ed. Charles Francis Adams (Boston: Little, Brown, 1851).

14. James Wilson, in *The Works of James Wilson,* ed. Robert G. McCloskey, vol. 1 (Cambridge, Mass.: The Belknap Press of Harvard University Press, 1967), 291–292.

15. Madison, *The Federalist,* no. 62, p. 418.

16. Ibid.

17. Governor George H. Hodges, message to the Kansas legislature, March 10, 1913, in Legislative Reference Department, Kansas State Library, *Legislative Systems* (Topeka: Kansas State Printing Office, 1914), p. 3.

18. George W. Norris, *Fighting Liberal: The Autobiography of George W. Norris* (New York: Macmillan, 1961), p. 343. A standard work on the subject is Alvin W. Johnson, *The Unicameral Legislature* (Minneapolis: University of Minnesota Press, 1938).

19. Benjamin I. Page, "Cooling the Legislative Tea," in *American Politics and Public Policy,* ed. Walter Dean Burnham and Martha Wagner Weinberg (Cambridge, Mass.: MIT Press, 1978), p. 185. Although this essay speculates about the national legislature, much of it is of use in assessing bicameralism in general. For additional studies on bicameralism, see Lawrence D. Longley, "Why Bicameralism?" *Legislative Studies Newsletter,* November–December 1985, pp. 83–89; and Lawrence D. Longley and Walter J. Oleszek, *Bicameral Politics* (New Haven: Yale University Press, 1986). A May 11–14, 1987, *New York Times/CBS News Poll* of a national sample of 1,254 adults asked the question: "Do we need to have both a House of Representatives and a Senate, or would one legislative body be enough?" Seventy-two percent responded that both are needed, 21 percent said one is enough, and 7 percent didn't know or had no answer.

20. For additional studies on the politics of unicameralism, see John P. Senning, *The One-House Legislature* (New York: McGraw-Hill, 1937); and Daniel B. Carroll, *The Unicameral Legislature in Vermont* (Montpelier: Vermont Historical Society, 1933).

21. I have drawn upon Philippa Strum, *The Supreme Court and "Political Questions": A Study in Judicial Evasion* (Tuscaloosa: University of Alabama Press, 1974), pp. 29–30; and W. A. Coutts, "Is a Provision for the Initiative and Referendum Inconsistent with the Constitution of the United States?" *Michigan Law Review*, February 1908, pp. 304–317.

22. Kadderly v. Portland, 44 Or. 118 (1903). See also Straw v. Harris, 54 Or. 424 (1910); and Kiernan v. Portland, 43 Or. (1910).

23. Coutts, "Is a Provision Inconsistent?" p. 307.

24. On this point see Joseph Schumpeter, *Capitalism, Socialism, and Democracy* (New York: Harper and Brothers, 1942), p. 296. See also William Riker, *Liberalism against Populism* (San Francisco: W. H. Freeman, 1982).

25. Nicholas M. Butler, *True and False Democracy* (New York: Macmillan, 1907), p. 18. See also Henry Fairlie, "The Unfiltered Voice," *New Republic*, June 24, 1978, pp. 16–17.

26. Herbert McClosky and Alida Brill, *Dimensions of Tolerance: What Americans Believe about Civil Liberties* (New York: Russell Sage Foundation, 1983), p. 437.

27. See, for example, Daniel C. Kramer, *Participatory Democracy* (Cambridge, Mass.: Schenkman, 1972); Laura Tallian, *Direct Democracy* (Los Angeles: People's Lobby, 1977); Benjamin R. Barber, *Strong Democracy: Participatory Politics for a New Age* (Berkeley: University of California Press, 1984); and Patrick B. McGuigan, *The Politics of Direct Democracy in the 1980s: Case Studies in Popular Decision Making* (Washington, D.C.: Institute for Government and Politics, 1985).

3. Direct Democracy

Epigraph: Woodrow Wilson, quoted in Burton J. Hendrick, "The Initiative and Referendum and How Oregon Got Them," *McClure's Magazine*, July 1911, p. 235.

1. See G. E. Atlmer, ed., *The Levellers in the English Revolution* (Ithaca: Cornell University Press, 1975).

2. Ernest Barker, ed., *Social Contract: Locke, Hume and Rousseau* (New York: Oxford University Press, 1962). See also Richard Fralin, *Rousseau and Representation* (New York: Columbia University Press, 1978); and Sheldon S. Wolin, *Politics and Vision* (Boston: Little, Brown, 1960), pp. 368–376.

3. Thomas Jefferson to James Madison, December 20, 1787, in *The Writings of Thomas Jefferson*, ed. Andrew A. Lipscomb, 11 vols. (Washington, D.C.: Thomas Jefferson Memorial Association, 1903), 6:391.

4. Jefferson, ibid., 10:4.

5. Jefferson's maxims come from Saul K. Padover, ed., *Thomas Jefferson on Democracy* (New York: New American Library, 1939). I have also drawn on Padover's introductory essay.

6. John H. Bass, "The Initiative and Referendum in Oklahoma," *Southwestern Political Science Quarterly*, 1 (September 1920), 126. See also Charles S. Lobinger, *The People's Law, or Popular Participation in Law Making* (New York: Macmillan, 1909).

7. Luther Martin, in *The Records of the Federal Convention of 1787*, ed.

Max Farrand, vol. 3 (New Haven: Yale University Press, 1911), 194 (the emphasis is Martin's).

8. Quoted in Norman Pollack, ed., *The Populist Mind* (Bloomington: Indiana University Press, 1967), p. 22.

9. Ray Billington, *Westward Expansion* (New York: Macmillan, 1949), p. 741. The standard works on the populist movement are John D. Hicks, *The Populist Revolt* (Minneapolis: University of Minnesota Press, 1931); and Lawrence Goodwyn, *Democratic Promise: The Populist Movement in America* (New York: Oxford University Press, 1976).

10. For a few particularly helpful analyses of farmers' alliances and state populism, see James R. Green, *Grass Roots Socialism: Radical Movements in the Southwest, 1895–1943* (Baton Rouge: Louisiana State University Press, 1978); Norman Pollack, *The Populist Response to Industrial America: Midwestern Populist Thought* (Cambridge, Mass.: Harvard University Press, 1962); and James E. Wright, *The Politics of Populism: Dissent in Colorado* (New Haven: Yale University Press, 1974), p. 74.

11. George McKenna, ed., *American Populism* (New York: G.P. Putnam's Sons, 1974), p. 94.

12. Lars A. Ueland, quoted in Raymond V. Anderson, "Adoption and Operation of Initiative and Referendum in North Dakota" (Ph.D. diss., University of Minnesota, 1962), p. 38.

13. Nathan Cree, *Direct Legislation by the People* (Chicago: A.C. McClurg, 1892), p. 16.

14. J. W. Sullivan, *Direct Legislation by the Citizenship through the Initiative and Referendum* (New York: True Nationalist Publishing, 1893), p. 5.

15. Ibid., p. 93.

16. Ibid., p. 71. Other books and treatises being read at the time contributed to the general fund of alternatives. See, for example, Charles Borgeaud, *Adoption and Amendment of Constitutions in Europe and America* (New York: Macmillan, 1895); and James Bryce, *The American Commonwealth*, vol. 1 (London: Macmillan, 1888).

17. William S. U'Ren, quoted in Lincoln Steffens, *Upbuilders* (Garden City, N.Y.: Doubleday, 1909), p. 288.

18. U'Ren, quoted in Scott W. Reed, "W. S. U'Ren and the Oregon System" (Senior honors thesis, Princeton University, 1950), p. 18. This thesis is available in the Oregon Historical Library, Salem, Oregon.

19. H. G. Fisher, quoted in *Rocky Mountain News*, December 20, 1909.

20. Anderson, "Adoption of Initiative in North Dakota."

21. Anson E. Van Eaton, "The Initiative and Referendum in Missouri" (Ph.D. diss., University of Missouri, 1955).

22. Robert C. Benedict, "Some Aspects of the Direct Legislation Process in Washington State: Theory and Practice, 1914–1973" (Ph.D. diss., University of Washington, 1975).

23. Charles F. Todd, "The Initiative and Referendum in Arizona" (M.A., Jr., thesis, University of Arizona, 1931); and Russell B. Roush, "The Initiative and Referendum in Arizona: 1912–1978" (Ph.D. diss., Arizona State University, 1979).

24. Editorial, *Los Angeles Times,* September 10, 1911; quoted in V. O. Key, Jr., and Winston W. Crouch, *The Initiative and Referendum in California* (Berkeley: University of California Press, 1939), p. 437.

25. Editorial, *Arizona Daily Star,* September 10, 1910, p. 8.

26. John F. Shafroth, quoted in *Rocky Mountain News,* February 2, 1910.

27. Editorial, *Denver Republican,* October 4, 1910; quoted in Paul D. Starr, "The Initiative and Referendum in Colorado" (M.A. thesis, University of Colorado, 1958), pp. 16–17.

28. These excellent and often entertaining debates at the Massachusetts convention consume 1,086 pages: "The Initiative and Referendum," in *Debates in the Massachusetts Constitutional Convention,* vol. 2 (Boston: Wright and Potter, 1918). A short summary of the opposing views presented can be found in Commonwealth of Massachusetts, Legislative Research Council, *Report Relative to Revising Statewide Initiative and Referendum Provisions of the Massachusetts Constitutions,* House no. 5435, February 4, 1975, pp. 67–77.

29. Woodrow Wilson, "Issues of Reform," prepared from an essay he wrote in 1910 and an address he gave in 1911, quoted in *The Initiative, Referendum, and Recall,* ed. William B. Munro (New York: D. Appleton, 1912), p. 87.

30. Bryce, *The American Commonwealth,* chap. 44.

31. Speech by Edwin L. Godkin, *Unforeseen Tendencies in Democracy* (Boston: Houghton Mifflin, 1898), p. 117.

32. Ibid., p. 118.

33. Theodore Roosevelt, *The Outlook,* January 21, 1911; reprinted in Munro, *Initiative, Referendum, and Recall,* p. 60.

34. Speech by Robert La Follette, quoted in Carl Resek, ed., *The Progressives* (Indianapolis: Bobbs-Merrill, 1967), p. 269.

35. Hiram Johnson, quoted in Eugene C. Lee and Larry L. Berg, *The Challenge of California,* 2d ed. (Boston: Little, Brown, 1976), p. 98.

36. Richard Hofstadter, *The Age of Reform* (New York: Vintage Books, 1955), p. 261. But see Norman Pollack, "Hofstadter on Populism: A Critique of 'The Age of Reform,' " *Journal of Southern History,* 26 (November 1960), 478–500.

37. A. Lawrence Lowell, *Public Opinion and Popular Government* (New York: Longmans, Green, 1913), pp. 141, 142.

38. Nicholas M. Butler, *True and False Democracy* (New York: Macmillan, 1907), pp. 35–36. This is also, in part, the view expressed in Henry J. Ford, *Representative Government* (New York: Henry Holt, 1924).

39. Pollack, "Hofstadter on Populism," p. 500.

4. The Question of Voter Competence

Epigraphs: Alexander Hamilton, speech, June 18, 1787, in *Selected Writings and Speeches of Alexander Hamilton,* ed. Morton J. Frisch (Washington, D.C.: American Enterprise Institute, 1985), p. 108; Benjamin R. Barber, testimony in U.S. Congress, Senate, *Voter Initiative Constitutional Amendment: Hearings before the Subcommittee on the Constitution of the Committee on the Judiciary, on S.J. Resolution 67,* 95th Cong., 1st sess., December 1977 (Washington, D.C.: U.S. Government Printing Office, 1978), p. 195.

1. Hermann Lieb, *The Initiative and Referendum* (Chicago: H. Lieb, Jr., 1902), p. 168. See also Eltweed Pomeroy et al., *By the People: Arguments and Authorities for Direct Legislation* (Newark, N.J.: Direct Legislation League, 1900); also published as U.S. Congress, Senate, Committee on the Judiciary, *Direct Legislation, Etc.*, Senate Document no. 340, 55th Cong., 2d sess. (Washington, D.C.: U.S. Government Printing Office, 1898).

2. Chip Dent, testimony in New York State Legislature, *Public Hearings of the Subcommittee on Initiative and Referendum* (Albany: State of New York, 1979), p. 102.

3. Carol Carlton, testimony, ibid., p. 165.

4. Howard Jarvis, testimony, ibid., p. 26.

5. Harold F. Gosnell, *Democracy: The Threshold of Freedom* (New York: Ronald Press, 1948), p. 258.

6. Robert McCarney, interview with author, Bismarck, N.D., September 12, 1979. McCarney's role in North Dakota direct democracy campaigns is discussed in Theodore Pedeliski, Robert W. Kweit, Mary G. Kweit, and Lloyd Omdahl, "Cleavages on Recent Ballot Measures: The Two States of North Dakota?" (Paper presented at the American Political Science Association annual meeting, Chicago, September 1987).

7. Raymond V. Anderson, "Adoption and Operation of Initiative and Referendum in North Dakota" (Ph.D. diss., University of Minnesota, 1962), p. 217.

8. Ed Koupal, interview, *California Journal*, 6 (March 1975), 83.

9. Ibid.

10. Maureen S. Fitzgerald, "Computer Democracy," *California Journal*, special report, June 1980, p. 13. These same fears are raised by Larry L. Berg and C. B. Holman, "Losing the Initiative: The Impact of Rising Costs on the Initiative Process," *Western City*, June 1987, pp. 27–30, 44.

11. Raymond E. Wolfinger and Steven J. Rosenstone, *Who Votes?* (New Haven: Yale University Press, 1980), p. 102.

12. See, for partial evidence, Arthur Hadley *The Empty Voting Booth* (Englewood Cliffs, N.J.: Prentice-Hall, 1978).

13. Keith Ian Polakoff, "In California, the Elite Take the Initiative," *Los Angeles Times*, June 5, 1980, pt. 2, p. 7. See also Robert Kuttner, "Why Americans Don't Vote," *New Republic*, September 7, 1987, pp. 19–21.

14. David D. Schmidt, *Initiative News Report*, December 24, 1980, p. 6.

15. John S. Shockley, *The Initiative Process in Colorado Politics: An Assessment* (Boulder: Bureau of Governmental Research and Service, University of Colorado, 1980), p. 2.

16. Ibid., p. 4.

17. Barbara Hinckley, "The American Voter in Congressional Elections," *American Political Science Review*, 14 (September 1980), 644.

18. James K. Pollock, *The Initiative and Referendum in Michigan* (Ann Arbor: University of Michigan Press, 1940), p. 46.

19. Henry M. Bain, Jr., and Donald S. Hecock, *Ballot Position and Voter's Choice* (Westport, Conn.: Greenwood Press, 1973).

20. Anderson, "Adoption of Initiative in North Dakota," p. 427.

21. Joseph G. LaPalombara, *The Initiative and Referendum in Oregon: 1938–1948* (Corvallis: Oregon State College, 1950), p. 97.

22. Paul D. Starr, "The Initiative and Referendum in Colorado" (M.A. thesis, University of Colorado, 1958), p. 55.

23. Russell B. Roush, "The Initiative and Referendum in Arizona: 1912–1978" (Ph.D. diss., Arizona State University, 1979), pp. 213, 215; and Robert C. Benedict, "Some Aspects of the Direct Legislation Process in Washington State: Theory and Practice, 1914–1973" (Ph.D. diss., University of Washington, 1975), p. 221. Similar findings are reported in Betty H. Zisk, *Money, Media, and the Grass Roots: State Ballot Issues and the Electoral Process* (Newbury Park, Calif.: Sage, 1987), chap. 3.

24. Secretary of state survey, election day poll (Mimeograph, Boston, 1976).

25. James A. Meader, "Voter Rationality and Initiatives: The Case of the Dakota Proposition" (Paper presented at the Western Political Science Association annual meeting, Denver, March 1981), p. 18. For similar points see Dennis M. Anderson, "Instrumental Rationality in Referenda Voting: An Empirical Test and Analysis of the Limits of Voter Rationality," *Politics and Policy*, 5 (1985), 12–22.

26. Hugh A. Bone, "The Initiative in Washington, 1914–1974," in *Washington Public Policy Notes* (Seattle: Institute of Governmental Research, University of Washington, 1974), p. 4. See also Robert O. Simmons, Jr., "Rationality and Representatives in the American Referendum Electorate" (Mimeograph, August 1980, provided by the author).

27. New York State Senate, *Report of the Subcommittee on Initiative and Referendum to the Majority Leader of the New York State Senate* (Albany: State of New York, May 1980), pp. 43–44.

28. Deborah R. Hensler and Carl P. Hensler, *Evaluating Nuclear Power: Voter Choice on the California Nuclear Energy Initiative* (Santa Monica, Calif.: Rand Corporation, 1979), p. 106.

29. David B. Magleby, *Direct Legislation: Voting on Ballot Propositions in the United States* (Baltimore: Johns Hopkins University Press, 1984), p. 144.

30. Robert C. Benedict and Lauren H. Holland, "Initiatives and Referenda in the Western United States, 1976–1980: Some Implications for a National Initiative?" (Paper presented at the American Political Science Association annual meeting, Washington, D.C., August 1980), pp. 36–37.

31. Magleby, *Direct Legislation*, p. 117.

32. Ibid., p. 121.

33. Simmons, "Rationality and Representativeness," pp. 8 and 9.

34. See, for example, a survey of potential Massachusetts voters conducted by the *Boston Globe* (Mimeograph, October 1976); Benedict and Holland, "Initiatives and Referenda in the Western United States," p. 13; and Dennis M. Anderson, "Referenda Exit Interviews: What Do Referendum Voters Know?" (Paper presented at the American Political Science Association annual meeting, New Orleans, August 1985), p. 19.

35. Howard D. Hamilton, "Direct Legislation: Some Implications of Open Housing Referenda," *American Political Science Review*, 64 (March 1970), 137.

36. California Opinion Index, *Initiative Process* (San Francisco: Field Institute, 1983), p. 2.

37. Gallup Organization, "The Gallup Study of Public Opinion regarding Direct Democracy Devices," conducted for Thomas E. Cronin (Princeton, N.J., September 1987).

38. Deputy director, Legislative Counsel's Office, interview with author, Colorado State House, Denver, 1980.

39. Rosemarie Rose, Montana Secretary of State's Office, telephone interview with author, June 11, 1981.

40. Donald G. Balmer, *State Election Services in Oregon, 1972* (Princeton, N.J.: Citizens' Research Foundation, 1972), p. 56.

41. Bone, "The Initiative in Washington, 1914–1974," p. 5.

42. Personal interviews by author.

43. Magleby, *Direct Legislation*, p. 136.

44. Shockley, *Initiative Process in Colorado Politics*, pp. 41–42.

45. State administrator, interview with author, Bismarck, N.D., September 11, 1979.

46. Mervin Field, quoted in Eugene C. Lee, "The Initiative and Referendum: How California Has Fared," *National Civic Review*, February 1979, p. 74.

47. Shockley, *Initiative Process in Colorado Politics*, p. 43.

48. See Pollock, *Initiative and Referendum in Michigan;* LaPalombara, *Initiative and Referendum in Oregon;* and John Gillespie, "Direct Legislation in Oklahoma" (M.A. thesis, University of Oklahoma, 1949), p. 83. See also David D. Schmidt, "United States Direct Democracy in Perspective" (Paper presented at the annual meeting of the Direct Democracy Research Group, American Political Science Association, Washington, D.C., September 1986).

49. Anderson, "Adoption of Initiative in North Dakota," p. 423.

50. Richard Lucier, "The Oregon Tax Substitution Referendum: The Prediction of Voting Behavior," *National Tax Journal*, 24 (March 1971), 87–90.

51. Lou Cannon, "Poll Shows Californians Support Controversial Initiatives," *Washington Post*, September 20, 1978, p. A2.

52. Mervin Field, "Sending A Message: Californians Strike Back," *Public Opinion*, July/August 1978, p. 5.

53. Zisk, *Money, Media, and Grass Roots*, p. 192.

54. Joseph G. LaPalombara and Charles B. Hagan, "Direct Legislation: An Appraisal and a Suggestion," *American Political Science Review*, 45 (June 1951), 414. More recent defenses of direct democracy can be found in Benjamin R. Barber, *Strong Democracy: Participatory Politics for a New Age* (Berkeley: University of California Press, 1984); Patrick B. McGuigan, *The Politics of Direct Democracy in the 1980s: Case Studies in Popular Decision Making* (Washington, D.C.: Institute for Government and Politics, 1985); and Joseph F. Zimmerman, *Participatory Democracy: Populism Revised* (New York: Praeger, 1986).

5. Minority Rights, Money, and the Media

Epigraphs: Kenneth T. Walsh, *Denver Post*, November 30, 1980, p. 29; John S. Shockley, "Direct Democracy, Campaign Finance, and the Courts: Can Corruption, Undue Influence, and Declining Voter Confidence Be Found?" *University of Miami Law Review*, 39 (May 1985), 427–428.

1. John Adams, *Defense of the Constitutions of Government of the United States of America* (1786).

2. Alexander Hamilton, *The Federalist*, no. 51, pp. 351, 352.

3. Henry Steele Commager, *Majority Rule and Minority Rights* (Gloucester, Mass.: Peter Smith, 1958), p. 65.

4. Lee Cruce, quoted in William S. Harmon, "Oklahoma's Constitutional Amendments: A Study of the Use of the Initiative and Referendum" (Ph.D. diss., University of Oklahoma, 1951), p. 6.

5. V. O. Key, Jr., and Winston W. Crouch, *The Initiative and Referendum in California* (Berkeley: University of California Press, 1939), p. 474.

6. Derrick A. Bell, Jr., "The Referendum: Democracy's Barrier to Racial Equality," *Washington Law Review,* 54 (1978), 20–21.

7. Philip Hager, "San Jose Area Voters Reject Two Gay Rights Ordinances," *Los Angeles Times,* June 5, 1980, p. 21.

8. See John W. Soule and Paul J. Strand, "Public Attitudes toward Homosexuality: The Proposition 6 Case in California" (Paper presented at the Western Political Science Association annual meeting, Portland, Or., 1979). See also Lou Cannon, "After Low-Key Campaign, Comeback Is Seen for Gay Rights," *Washington Post,* October 27, 1978, p. A5.

9. Richard Mersereau, "California Elections Go as Planned," *Initiative and Referendum Report,* December 1986/January 1987, p. 16.

10. Ibid.

11. Patrick B. McGuigan, "When in Doubt, Vote No" (Paper presented at the annual meeting of the Direct Democracy Research Group, American Political Science Association, Washington, D.C., August 1986), p. 3.

12. Ibid., p. 15.

13. David D. Schmidt, "United States Direct Democracy in Perspective" (Paper presented at the annual meeting of the Direct Democracy Research Group, American Political Science Association, Washington, D.C., August 1980), sec. 2, p. 25.

14. Eugene Lee, "California," in *Referendum,* ed. David Butler and Austin Ranney (Washington, D.C.: American Enterprise Institute, 1978), p. 104.

15. Ronald J. Allen, "The National Initiative Proposal: A Preliminary Analysis," *Nebraska Law Review,* 38 (1979), 1033.

16. Schmidt, "Direct Democracy in Perspective," sec. 2, p. 25.

17. Ibid.

18. Robert Woodford, vice-president, New Jersey Business and Industry Association, statement delivered at a hearing held by the Assembly State Government Committee in Freehold, N.J., May 31, 1986 (Mimeograph handout), p. 2.

19. First National Bank of Boston et al. v. Bellotti, 435 U.S. 765 (1978).

20. Both of the following summaries draw upon Steven D. Lydenberg, *Bankrolling Ballots: The Role of Business in Financing Ballot Question Campaigns* (New York: Council on Economic Priorities, 1979), pp. 14–15 and 15–16.

21. Herbert Schmertz, vice-president for public affairs, Mobil Oil Corporation, testimony in U.S. Congress, House of Representatives, *IRS Administration of Tax Laws Relating to Lobbying: Hearings before a Subcommittee of the Committee on Governmental Operations,* 95th Cong., 2d. sess., May and July 1978, p. 286.

22. John S. Shockley, "Corporate Spending in the Wake of the Bellotti Decision" (Paper presented at the American Political Science Association annual meeting, New York, September 1978), p. 4.

23. Daniel H. Lowenstein, "Campaign Spending and Ballot Propositions: Recent Experience, Public Choice Theory, and the First Amendment," *UCLA Law Review,* 29 (February 1982), 608.

24. See, for example, the editorial in the *Washington Post,* May 2, 1970, p. A18; and Gary Hart and William Shore, "Corporate Spending on State and Local Referendums: First National Bank of Boston v. Bellotti," *Case Western Reserve Law Review,* 29 (Summer 1979), 808–829.

25. Fred Wertheimer, senior vice-president of Common Cause, news release statement, Washington, D.C., April 26, 1978.

26. Citizens against Rent Control v. City of Berkeley, 454 U.S. 290 (1981).

27. Stephen Wermiel, "Justices Invalidate Ordinance Limiting Campaign Gifts Made to Sway Referenda," *Wall Street Journal,* December 15, 1981, p. 11.

28. See the preliminary findings in David B. Magleby, "Campaign Spending in Ballot Proposition and Candidate Election" (Paper presented at the American Political Science Association annual meeting, Washington, D.C., August 1986).

29. My own review of financial disclosure records in the 1970s and 1980s is supported by several other studies. See especially Betty H. Zisk, *Money, Media, and the Grass Roots: State Ballot Issues and the Electoral Process* (Newbury Park, Calif.: Sage, 1987), chaps. 4 and 8; Lydenberg, *Bankrolling Ballots;* Lowenstein, "Campaign Spending and Ballot Propositions"; John S. Shockley, *The Initiative Process in Colorado Politics: An Assessment* (Boulder: Bureau of Governmental Research and Service, University of Colorado, 1980).

30. John S. Shockley, "Initiatives Go Up in Smoke When Attacked by Big Money," *Denver Post,* November 2, 1980, p. 30. See also idem, *Initiative Process in Colorado.*

31. John S. Shockley, testimony in House Committee on Government Operations, *IRS Administration of Tax Laws,* p. 265.

32. Ibid., p. 256.

33. Steven D. Lydenberg, *Bankrolling Ballots, Update 1980: The Role of Business in Financing Ballot Question Campaigns* (New York: Council on Economic Priorities, 1981), pp. 17–18.

34. Ibid., pp. 1–5.

35. Randy M. Mastro, Deborah C. Costlow, and Heidi P. Sanchez, *Taking the Initiative* (Washington, D.C.: Media Access Project, 1980), p. 4.

36. Zisk, *Money, Media, and Grass Roots,* pp. 90–137 and 245.

37. Lowenstein, "Campaign Spending and Ballot Propositions," p. 513.

38. Ibid., p. 546.

39. Lydenberg, *Bankrolling Ballots,* p. 110. Much of the information in the paragraph above is drawn from this study.

40. Allen, "The National Voter Initiative Proposal," p. 1031.

41. Doris A. Graber, *Mass Media and American Politics* (Washington, D.C.: Congressional Quarterly Press, 1980), p. 189. This study generalizes from analysis of the role of the media in candidate elections.

42. Mastro, Costlow, and Sanchez, *Taking the Initiative,* p. 3.

43. Harvey Shulman, testimony in House Committee on Government Operations, *IRS Administration of Tax Laws,* p. 58.

44. Shockley, testimony, ibid., p. 270.

45. Gail S. Hand, "A Critique of the *Grand Forks Herald*'s Coverage of Initiative Measure Number Four, The Health Care Issue of 1978" (Honors thesis, University of North Dakota, 1979), p. 38.

46. Zisk, *Money, Media, and Grass Roots,* p. 247.

47. Quoted in J. Kent Marlor and A. Robert Inama, "The 1986 Right-to-

Work Campaign in Idaho: An Evaluation of Direct Democracy in Action" (Paper presented at the American Political Science Association annual meeting, Chicago, September 1987), p. 20.

48. Ibid., pp. 19–20.

49. Zisk, *Money, Media, and Grass Roots,* pp. 98–103.

50. Ibid., p. 136.

51. Shockley, testimony in House Committee on Government Operations, *IRS Administration of Tax Laws,* pp. 271–272.

52. Red Lion Broadcasting v. FCC, 395 U.S. 367 (1969). See also Benno C. Schmidt, Jr., *Freedom of the Press vs. Public Access* (New York: Praeger, 1976), chap. 11; and a more critical view of this case in Lucas A. Powe, Jr., *American Broadcasting and the First Amendment* (Berkeley: University of California Press, 1987), chap. 7.

53. Mastro, Costlow, and Sanchez, *Taking the Initiative,* p. 19.

54. Edwin M. Yoder, Jr., "Broadcasters Have More to Worry About than 'Fairness,' " *Washington Post National Weekly Edition,* August 31, 1987, p. 28. Yoder's view was echoed in most editorial reactions to the FCC's decision to abandon the fairness doctrine. See "The Blandness Doctrine," *Wall Street Journal,* June 23, 1987, p. 30; " 'Fairness' Calls for a Veto," *Washington Post,* June 10, 1987, p. A16; " 'Fairness' Forced on TV Didn't Create Fairness on TV," *Denver Post,* August 13, 1987, p. 10B; and "President Was Right to Veto 'Fairness' Bill," *USA Today,* June 25, 1987, p. 12a.

55. Christopher Swan, "Veto of 'Fairness Doctrine' Settles Issues Once— but Not for All," *Christian Science Monitor,* July 2, 1987, p. 27.

6. The Recall Device

Epigraphs: William Howard Taft, *Popular Government: Its Essence, Its Permanence, and Its Perils* (New Haven: Yale University Press, 1913), p. 83; Herbert Croly, *Progressive Democracy* (New York: Macmillan, 1914), pp. 325–326.

1. Delos F. Wilcox, *Government by All the People* (New York: Macmillan, 1912), p. 171.

2. Hiram Johnson, quoted in George E. Mowry, *The California Progressives* (Berkeley: University of California Press, 1951), p. 148.

3. Three political science professors at the University of Southern California advocated a national recall both for presidents and for other federal officeholders. For the recall of a president, they proposed a signature requirement of 8 percent of the number who voted in the last presidential election, and for members of Congress a 10 percent signature requirement; Larry L. Berg, Harlan Hahn, and John R. Schmidhauser, *Corruption in the American Political System* (Morristown, N.J.: General Learning Press, 1976), pp. 192–193. See also Larry Berg, "Recall Is Needed Nationwide," *Los Angeles Times,* August 25, 1974, pt. 8, p. 2. (In a 1987 telephone interview Berg informed me he no longer advocates a national recall.) For an earlier, unconvincing discussion advocating the recall for federal officials, including judges, see Wilcox, *Government by All the People,* pp. 305–312.

4. Advisory recall is a process in which elected officeholders or aspirants for office may or must file a statement declaring a willingness to abide by the outcome of a future recall vote. If the candidate agrees to submit to such a vote,

the ballot would state under the official's name "pledged to recall." If the official refuses to agree, the name is accompanied by the words "silent as to recall." Only Arizona provided for advisory recalls, and its impact there was reduced by a 1973 statute eliminating the printing of statements on the ballot indicating candidates' willingness to abide by a recall election verdict.

5. See Theodore Roosevelt, "Charter of Democracy," *Outlook*, February 24, 1912, pp. 390–402; idem, "Right of the People to Rule: Address at Carnegie Hall," *Outlook*, March 23, 1912, pp. 618–626. See also William L. Ransom, *Majority Rule and the Judiciary* (New York: Da Capo Press, 1971).

6. Wilcox, *Government by All the People*, pp. 170–171.

7. Frank A. Munsey, quoted in Edith M. Phelps, ed., *The Recall*, 2d ed. (New York: H.W. Wilson, 1915), p. 33.

8. Taft, *Popular Government*, p. 83.

9. A. Lawrence Lowell, *Public Opinion and Popular Government* (New York: Longmans, Green, 1913), p. 147.

10. Massachusetts House of Representatives, Legislative Research Council, *Report Relative to Recall of Local Officials*, Document 5690 (Boston, 1979), p. 15.

11. Taft, *Popular Government*, pp. 84–85.

12. See Jerry B. Briscoe, "Just and Unjust Recall Elections: California Experience" (Mimeograph, University of the Pacific, Stockton, Calif., 1977). I have drawn on this paper and several of the author's case studies in my discussion.

13. Tony Quinn, "The Proliferation of Recalls in One Single-Issue Society," *California Journal*, 10 (November 1979), 400–401.

14. Michigan Constitution, Article 11, section 8.

15. Dianne Feinstein, "Argument against the Recall," *San Francisco Voter Information Pamphlet* (April 26, 1983), p. 10.

16. Editorial, *San Francisco Examiner*, April 28, 1983, p. B2.

17. David R. Lipson, "California Law of Recall," in *The Law of Politics*, ed. Palmer Brown Madden and Curtis C. Sproul (Berkeley: California Continuing Education of the Bar, 1977), p. 381.

18. Charles M. Price, "Don't Forget the Recall," *Citizen Participation*, July/August 1980, p. 15. See also his useful "Recalls at the Local Level: Dimensions and Implications," *National Civic Review*, April 1983, pp. 199–206.

19. Judith Boggs, Jonathan S. Fuhrman, and Fred Register, Jr., "A History of Recall: Its Origins and Use in the City of Los Angeles" (Mimeograph, Foothills Research Associates, Pasadena, Calif., May 21, 1979), pp. 14, 39.

20. Ronald J. Busch, "Polls, Public Opinion, and Politics in a Recall Election: The Case of Cleveland" (Mimeograph, 1979), p. 8.

21. Interview with author, Colorado Springs, Colorado, 1983.

22. See James A. Kelley, Jr., "Conflict Resolution and California School Board Recall Elections" (Ph.D. diss., Stanford University, 1967), p. 103.

23. Howard Miller, interview with author, Los Angeles, October 17, 1980.

24. Charles Hanlon, interview with author, Portland, Ore., April 30, 1980.

25. John Houser, "The Historical Development and Use of the Recall" (Mimeograph, Legislative Council Staff, Salem, Ore., October 31, 1976), p. 11.

26. Executive director, National Municipal League, interview with author, New York City, 1980.

27. Interview with author, Manitou Springs, Colo., 1981.

28. Austin F. MacDonald, *American State Government and Administration,* 3d ed. (New York: Crowell, 1948), p. 141.

29. Croly, *Progressive Democracy,* pp. 326–327.

30. Editorial, *Denver Post,* January 22, 1988, p. 10C.

31. Frederick L. Bird and Frances M. Ryan, *The Recall of Public Officials: A Study of the Operation of the Recall in California* (New York: Macmillan, 1930), pp. 172–173.

32. Massachusetts House of Representatives, *Report Relative to Recall of Local Officials,* p. 41.

33. Editorial, *Oregon Statesman,* October 19, 1979, p. 6A.

34. Charles M. Price, "Recalls at the Local Level," p. 206.

35. Ibid.

7. A National Initiative and Referendum?

Epigraphs: U.S. Senator Mark Hatfield (R.–Ore.), *Citizen Participation,* November/December 1979, p. 5; Arthur D. Laffer, "A Modest Proposal," *New Management,* Spring 1983, p. 42.

1. George Gallup, Sr., interview, January 10, 1984; quoted in David D. Schmidt, "United States Direct Democracy in Perspective: The Case for Initiative and Referendum" (Paper presented at the annual meeting of the Direct Democracy Study Group, American Political Science Association, Washington, D.C., September 1986), p. 9.

2. These two proposals are outlined in Matt Shermer, *The Sense of the People or the Next Development in American Democracy* (New York: American Referendum Association, 1969), app. B.

3. Sarah Wambaugh, *Plebiscites since the World War,* vol. 1 (Washington, D.C.: Carnegie Endowment for International Peace, 1933), 487–488.

4. Jean-Francois Aubert, "Switzerland," in *Referendums: A Comparative Study of Practice and Theory,* ed. David Butler and Austin Ranney (Washington, D.C.: American Enterprise Institute, 1978), p. 66.

5. Philip Goodhart, *Referendum* (London: Tom Stacey, 1971), p. 98.

6. Adapted from Butler and Ranney, *Referendums,* pp. 224, 225, and 226.

7. Thomas Jefferson to William Charles Jarvis, September 28, 1820, quoted in Dumas Malone, *Jefferson and His Time: The Sage of Monticello* (Boston: Little, Brown, 1981), p. 353.

8. Nathan Cree, *Direct Legislation by the People* (Chicago: A.C. McClurg, 1892), p. 86.

9. Ibid., p. 102. At virtually the same time, a prominent labor editor and social reformer, J. W. Sullivan, published a similar manifesto praising the Swiss system and advocating the initiative and referendum for the United States: *Direct Legislation by the Citizenship through the Initiative and Referendum* (New York: True Nationalist Publishing, 1893). He had been making this case in labor journals even earlier. His theme was that direct legislative action was already very American: "It exists here in town meetings, labor unions, state constitutional changes and so on. In fact, the vast United States seems to have seen as much of the Referendum as little Switzerland" (p. 85).

10. This questionnaire and its response are discussed in Richard G. Jones,

"Organized Labor and the Initiative and Referendum Movement: 1885–1920" (M.A. thesis, University of Washington, 1963), pp. 61–62.

11. John Foster, *A Sermon Preached before the Ancient and Honourable Artillery Company, in Boston, June 5, 1809* (Boston: Monroe, Francis and Parker, 1809), pp. 4–20.

12. See Robert E. Beasley, *A Plan to Stop the Present and Prevent the Future Wars* (Rio Vista, Calif., privately published, 1864).

13. Allan L. Benson, "Appeal to Reason," September 19, 1914; in Benson, *A Way to Prevent War* (Girard, Kans., privately published, 1915).

14. Robert M. La Follette, Editorial, *La Follette's Magazine*, May 1916, p. 1.

15. See Ernest C. Bolt, Jr., *Ballots before Bullets: The War Referendum Approach to Peace in America, 1914–1941* (Charlottesville: University of Virginia Press, 1977).

16. *Congressional Record*, January 16, 1935, p. 514.

17. Speech by Louis Ludlow, reprinted in *Congressional Digest*, 17, no. 2. (February 1938), p. 45.

18. Ibid., p. 46.

19. Hadley Cantril and Mildred Strunk, *Public Opinion—1935 to 1946* (Princeton: Princeton University Press, 1954), p. 1025.

20. *New York Times*, December 22, 1937.

21. *Congressional Digest*, 17, no. 2 (February 1938), p. 41.

22. Helpful discussions of these events are found in: Bolt, *Ballots before Bullets;* Harold W. Holtzclaw, "The American War Referendum Movement, 1914–1941" (Ph.D. diss., University of Denver, 1965); and Richard Dean Burns and W. Addams Dixon, "Foreign Policy and 'The Democratic Myth': The Debate on the Ludlow Amendment," *Mid-America*, 47 (October 1965), 288–306.

23. This and the Nader quote above come from a handout, "Progressive Support for the Voter Initiative," put out by the group Initiative America in the early 1980s.

24. Roger J. Diamond, legal counsel, People's Lobby, testimony in U.S. Congress, Senate, *Voter Initiative Constitutional Amendment: Hearings before the Subcommittee on the Constitution of the Committee on the Judiciary, on S.J. Resolution 67*, 95th Cong., 1st sess., December 1977 (Washington, D.C.: U.S. Government Printing Office, 1978), p. 147.

25. Congressman Jack Kemp, direct mass mailing addressed to "Fellow American" from Washington, D.C., 1978.

26. Patrick J. Buchanan, "Letting the Voters Become Lawgivers," *Chicago Tribune*, December 20, 1977.

27. Laffer, "A Modest Proposal," p. 44.

28. James Jones, quoted in Senate Subcommittee on the Constitution, *Voter Initiative Constitutional Amendment*, p. 20.

29. Henry Abraham, in ibid., pp. 66–69. Abraham reiterated his support for these devices in a short interview with the author in 1987.

30. See Benjamin R. Barber, *Strong Democracy: Participatory Politics for a New Age* (Berkeley: University of California Press, 1984); and Larry L. Berg, Harlan Hahn, and John R. Schmidhauser, *Corruption in the American Political System* (Morristown, N.J.: General Learning Press, 1976), chap. 7.

31. See Ronald J. Allen, "The National Initiative Proposal: A Preliminary Analysis," *Nebraska Law Review,* 58 (1979), 965–1052. For the views of Miller and Bezold, see Senate Subcommittee on the Constitution, *Voter Initiative Constitutional Amendment.* Lowenstein served on the national advisory board of Initiative America.

32. Quoted in *Initiative News Report,* June 15, 1981, p. 7.

33. Proposition B, Los Angeles County ballot, June 6, 1978.

34. See Don F. Hadwiger and Rose B. Talbot, *Pressures and Protests: The Kennedy Farm Program and the Wheat Referendum of 1963* (San Francisco: Chandler Publishing, 1965).

35. Congressman Richard Gephardt, press release, July 30, 1980.

36. Tom Ryan, "The National Advisory Referendum," *Citizen Participation,* January/February 1981, p. 17.

37. Ellis P. Oberholtzer, *The Referendum in America* (New York: Charles Scribner's Sons, 1911), p. 420.

38. See, for example, Ralph M. Goldman, "The Advisory Referendum in America," *Public Opinion Quarterly,* 14 (Summer 1950), 301–315; Matt Shermer, *The Sense of the People* (New York: American Referendum Association, 1969); and George Gallup, Jr., "The Public Opinion Referendum," *Public Opinion Quarterly,* 35 (Summer 1971), 220–227.

39. George Gallup, Sr., interview, January 10, 1984; quoted in Schmidt, "Direct Democracy in Perspective," pp. 8–9.

40. National Center for Initiative Review, direct mass mailing addressed to "Dear Friend" from Englewood, Colo. (about 1982 or 1983).

41. Austin Ranney, *Public Opinion,* February/March 1981, p. 41.

42. See a report from *Initiative News Report,* reprinted in *Today,* October 8, 1982, p. 13.

43. Joel D. Sherman, "A Comparative Study of Referendum Voting Behavior in Oregon, Ohio, and Switzerland" (Ph.D. diss., Columbia University, 1977), pp. 287 and 289. See also Dennis M. Anderson, "Instrumental Rationality in Referenda Voting: An Empirical Test and Analysis of the Limits of Voter Rationality," *Politics and Policy,* 5 (1985), 12–22.

44. Roger Teleschow, telephone interview with author, December 21, 1983.

45. Gallup Organization, "The Gallup Study of Public Opinion regarding Direct Democracy Devices," conducted for Thomas E. Cronin (Princeton, N.J., September 1987). Forty-eight percent of registered voters said they too would be more likely to turn out and vote. Only one percent said they would be less likely to vote, and 48 percent said it would make no difference.

46. Gary E. Gammon, "Direct Democracy Nationwide? An Assessment of the National Statutory Initiative Proposal" (Paper presented at the Southwestern Political Science Association annual meeting, Houston, April 1980), pp. 7–8.

47. Daniel H. Lowenstein, "Campaign Spending and Ballot Propositions: Recent Experience, Public Choice Theory, and the First Amendment," *UCLA Law Review,* 29 (February 1982), 608.

48. John S. Shockley, "Direct Democracy, Campaign Finance, and the Courts: Can Corruption, Undue Influence, and Declining Voter Confidence Be Found?" *University of Miami Law Review,* 39 (May 1985), 427–428.

49. Gallup Organization, "Gallup Study of Direct Democracy Devices."

50. Butler and Ranney, *Referendums*, p. 200.

51. Ronald J. Allen, "The National Initiative Proposal: A Preliminary Analysis," *Nebraska Law Review*, 58 (1979), 1045.

52. Benjamin R. Barber, testimony in Senate Subcommittee on the Constitution, *Voter Initiative Constitutional Amendment*, p. 195.

8. Direct Democracy and Its Problems

Epigraph: David B. Magleby, *Direct Legislation: Voting on Ballot Propositions in the United States* (Baltimore: Johns Hopkins University Press, 1984), pp. 183–184.

1. Herbert McClosky and Alida Brill, *Dimensions of Tolerance* (New York: Russell Sage Foundation, 1983), pp. 415–416.

2. David D. Schmidt, "Ballot Initiatives," *Today*, September 16, 1983, p. 5.

3. Patrick B. McGuigan, interview with author, Washington, D.C., November 1984. This theme is expanded in his *The Politics of Direct Democracy in the 1980s: Case Studies in Popular Decision Making* (Washington, D.C.: Institute for Government and Politics, 1985).

4. David D. Schmidt, "Ballot Initiative: History, Research, and Analysis of Recent Initiative and Referendum Campaigns (Mimeograph, Initiative News Service, Washington, D.C., March 1983), p. 52.

5. David D. Schmidt, *Initiative News Report*, November 30, 1984, p. 1.

6. Austin Ranney, "Initiatives 1986," *Public Opinion*, January/February 1987, p. 45.

7. Quoted in Robert Lindsey, "Rise of Voter-Initiated Referendums: The Right Hones a Tool of Liberals," *New York Times*, July 24, 1984, p. 9. See also on this same theme Jay Mathews, "Initiatives: America's Direct Democracy Binge," *Washington Post Weekly Review*, July 16, 1984, pp. 6–8.

8. Sue Thomas, "Lawmakers as Petitioners: An Analysis," *Initiative Quarterly*, Third Quarter 1984, p. 3.

9. Adapted from ibid., p. 4.

10. Over 80 percent of New Jersey citizens say they like the initiative idea of voting directly on issues. Over 80 percent of California voters told that state's leading pollster they thought statewide proposition elections were "a good thing." Over 85 percent told a statewide Hawaii survey in 1978 that they liked the initiative and referendum. Over 75 percent of the citizens in New York State (which does not allow the initiative, referendum, and recall) responded favorably to the idea of amending New York's constitution to authorize the initiative and referendum. In a survey I conducted in 1980, Colorado voters said they believed people who had a chance to vote on issues would "become more interested and participate more in government and politics." See also the results of state senate members' questionnaires in fourteen senate districts, summarized in New York State Senate, *Report of the Subcommittee on Initiative and Referendum to the Majority Leader of the New York State Senate* (Albany: State of New York, May 1980), p. 67.

11. Thomas, "Lawmakers as Petitioners," p. 5.

12. William Cassella, quoted in *Initiative Quarterly*, First Quarter 1983, p. 10.

13. League of Women Voters of California, *Initiative and Referendum in California: A Legacy Lost? A Study of Direct Legislation in California from Progressive Hopes to Present Reality* (Sacramento, 1984).

14. Patrick B. McGuigan, telephone interview with author, January 1987.

15. Neal R. Peirce, "Citizen Initiatives Can Reap Grim Harvest," *County News*, October 22, 1984, p. 11. But see also Patrick B. McGuigan's commentary on the Michigan tax revolt, *Initiative and Referendum Report*, January 1985, p. 2.

16. Coro Foundation, *Local Initiative: A Study of the Use of Municipal Initiatives in the San Francisco Bay Area* (San Francisco, 1984), pp. 23–24.

17. Schmidt, *Initiative News Report*, November 30, 1984, p. 12.

18. Ibid.

19. From the argument in favor of Proposition 38, *California Ballot Pamphlet*, 1984 general election (Sacramento: California State Government, 1984), p. 52.

20. Betty H. Zisk, *Money, Media, and the Grass Roots: State Ballot Issues and the Electoral Process* (Newbury Park, Calif.: Sage, 1987), p. 245.

21. John S. Shockley, "Direct Democracy, Campaign Finance, and the Courts: Can Corruption, Undue Influence, and Declining Voter Confidence Be Found?" *University of Miami Law Review*, 39 (May 1985). See also Zisk, *Money, Media, and Grass Roots*, p. 263.

22. Paul K. Grant et al. v. Natalie Meyer, Civil Action No. 84-JM-1207, U.S. District Court, Denver, July 3, 1984. See also *Initiative Quarterly*, Third Quarter 1984, p. 5.

23. League of Women Voters of California, *Initiative and Referendum*, p. 65.

24. Larry L. Berg and C. B. Holman, "Losing the Initiative: The Impact of Rising Costs on the Initiative Process," *Western City*, June 1987, p. 29.

25. William K. Shireman, executive director of Californians against Waste, testimony to the California State Assembly Committee on Elections and Reapportionment, December 7, 1983 (Mimeograph).

26. Ibid.

27. John Van de Kamp, California attorney general, speech to Symposium on Initiative and Referendum Reform, Center for the Study of Law and Politics, San Francisco, December 7, 1984 (Mimeograph), p. 120.

28. Patrick B. McGuigan, statement of August 28, 1984. McGuigan is editor of *Initiative and Referendum Report,* published by the Free Congress Research and Education Foundation, Washington, D.C.

29. "The Courts and the Ballot," *Initiative Quarterly*, Third Quarter 1984, p. 4.

30. See, for example, Richard Hollander, *Video Democracy: The Vote-from-the-Home-Revolution* (Mt. Airy, Md.: Lomand, 1985).

31. See, for example, Ted Becker and Christa Slaton, "Hawaii Televote: Measuring Public Opinion on Complex Policy Issues" (Paper presented at the American Political Science Association annual meeting, Washington, D.C., 1980); and Theodore Becker, "Teledemocracy," *The Futurist*, December 1981.

32. Benjamin R. Barber, *Strong Democracy: Participatory Politics for a New Age* (Berkeley: University of California Press, 1984), p. 276.

33. See Hollander, *Video Democracy;* Starr Roxanne Hiltz and Murray Tur-

off, *The Network Nation: Human Communication via Computer* (Reading, Mass.: Addison-Wesley, 1978), p. 198; and A. J. Bahn, *Computocracy: Our New Political Philosophy—Its Time Has Come* (Albuquerque, N.M.: World Books, 1986).

34. See David Broder, "Electronic Democracy Is a Nice Idea, but It Won't Work," *Denver Post*, August 31, 1987, p. 48; and F. Christopher Arterton, *Teledemocracy: Can Technology Protect Democracy?* (Newbury Park, Calif.: Sage, 1987), chaps. 6–9.

9. Sound and Sensible Democracy

Epigraphs: Benjamin R. Barber, *Strong Democracy: Participatory Politics for a New Age* (Berkeley: University of California Press, 1984), p. 263; Larry L. Berg and C. B. Holman, "The Initiative Process and Its Declining Agenda Setting Value" (Paper presented at the American Political Science Association annual meeting, New Orleans, August 1985), pp. 31–32.

1. Editorial, *New York Times*, November 27, 1978, p. A18.

2. David Everson, *Initiative Quarterly*, First Quarter 1983, p. 10. See also David B. Magleby, *Direct Legislation: Voting on Ballot Propositions in the United States* (Baltimore: Johns Hopkins University Press, 1984), chap. 5.

3. Richard Hofstadter, *The Age of Reform* (New York: Vintage Books, 1955), pp. 266–267. See also Herbert Croly, *Progressive Democracy* (New York: Macmillan, 1914), chaps. 11–13.

4. Patrick B. McGuigan, *Initiative and Referendum Report*, August 1984, p. 16.

5. Mervin Field, "While California Public Likes Initiative System, Amenable to some Proposed Changes," *California Poll*, June 5, 1985.

6. Coro Foundation, *Local Initiative: A Study of the Use of Municipal Initiatives in the San Francisco Bay Area* (San Francisco, 1984), p. 47.

7. John K. Van de Kamp, California attorney general, speech to Symposium on Initiative and Referendum Reform, Center for the Study of Law and Politics, San Francisco, December 7, 1984 (Mimeograph), p. 7.

8. Austin Ranney, "Regulating the Referendum," in *The Referendum Device* (Washington, D.C.: American Enterprise Institute, 1981), p. 92.

9. See Daniel H. Lowenstein, "Campaign Spending and Ballot Propositions: Recent Experience, Public Choice Theory, and the First Amendment," *UCLA Law Review*, 29 (February 1982), 578–582.

10. Ranney, "Regulating the Referendum," p. 95.

11. Magleby, *Direct Legislation*, p. 195.

12. Neal R. Peirce, "The Indirect Way for Americans to Take the Initiative," *Sacramento Bee*, February 12, 1979, p. B11.

13. Nick Brestoff outlines one of the best variations on the indirect initiative in "The California Initiative Process: A Suggestion for Reform," *Southern California Law Review*, 48 (1975), 922–958.

14. Larry L. Berg and C. B. Holman, "Losing the Initiative: The Impact of Rising Costs on the Initiative Process," *Western City*, June 1987, p. 44.

15. Charles A. Beard, Introduction to Charles A. Beard and Birl E. Shultz, eds., *Documents on the State-Wide Initiative, Referendum, and Recall* (New York: Macmillan, 1912), p. 69. See also Croly, *Progressive Democracy*, pp. 324–327.

16. Barber, *Strong Democracy*, pp. 145–146.

17. John Naisbitt, *Megatrends* (New York: Warner Books, 1982).

18. Patrick B. McGuigan, interview with author, Washington, D.C., November 1984. For similarly optimistic views of the people's ability to vote responsibly, see Laura Tallian, *Direct Democracy* (Los Angeles: People's Lobby, 1977); Larry L. Berg, Harlan Hahn, and John R. Schmidhauser, *Corruption in the American Political System* (Morristown, N.J.: General Learning Press, 1976); and Mike A. Males, *Be It Enacted by the People: A Citizens' Guide to Initiatives* (Helena, Mont.: Northern Rockies Action Group, 1981).

19. Betty H. Zisk, *Money, Media, and the Grass Roots: State Ballot Issues and the Electoral Process* (Newbury Park, Calif.: Sage, 1987), p. 268.

20. James MacGregor Burns, *The Power to Lead* (New York: Simon and Schuster, 1984), p. 106.

21. Interview with author, Columbus, Ohio, 1980.

SELECTED BIBLIOGRAPHY

▼

Abbott, Frank Frost. *A History and Description of Roman Political Institutions.* 3d ed. Boston: Ginn, 1911.

Adams, Charles Francis, ed. *The Works of John Adams.* Boston: Little, Brown, 1851.

Anderson, Raymond V. "Adoption and Operation of Initiative and Referendum in North Dakota." Ph.D. diss., University of Minnesota, 1962.

Arterton, F. Christopher. *Teledemocracy: Can Technology Protect Democracy?* Newbury Park, Calif.: Sage Publications, 1987.

Bacon, Edwin, M., and Morrill Wyman. *Direct Election and Law Making by Popular Vote.* Boston: Houghton Mifflin, 1912.

Balmer, Donald G. *State Election Services in Oregon, 1972.* Princeton, N.J.: Citizens' Research Foundation, 1972.

Bandza, Alfred. "An Analysis of the Electoral Response to the Initiative and Referendum in North Dakota, 1918–1960." M.A. thesis, University of North Dakota, 1963.

Barber, Benjamin R. *Strong Democracy: Participatory Politics for a New Age.* Berkeley: University of California Press, 1984.

Barker, Ernest, ed. *Social Contract: Locke, Hume and Rousseau.* New York: Oxford University Press, 1962.

Barnett, James D. *The Operation of the Initiative, Referendum and Recall in Oregon.* New York: Macmillan, 1915.

Beard, Charles A. *The Republic.* New York: Viking Press, 1943.

Beard, Charles A., and Birl E. Shultz, eds. *Documents on the State-Wide Initiative, Referendum and Recall.* New York: Macmillan, 1912.

Benedict, Robert C. "Some Aspects of the Direct Legislation Process in Washington State: Theory and Practice, 1914–1973." Ph.D. diss., University of Washington, 1975.

Benello, C. George. *The Case for Participatory Democracy.* New York: Grossman, 1971.

Berg, Larry L., Harlan Hahn, and John R. Schmidhauser. *Corruption in the American Political System.* Morristown, N.J.: General Learning Press, 1976.

Best, Wallace. "The Initiative and Referendum Politics in California, 1912–1952." Ph.D. diss., University of Southern California, 1958.

Birch, A. H. *Representation.* New York: Praeger, 1971.

Bird, Frederick, L., and Frances M. Ryan. *The Recall of Public Officials: A Study of the Operation of the Recall in California*. New York: Macmillan, 1930.

Blackorby, Edward C. *Prairie Rebel: The Public Life of William Lemke*. Lincoln: University of Nebraska Press, 1963.

Borgeaud, Charles. *Adoption and Amendment of Constitutions in Europe and America*. New York: Macmillan, 1895.

Boyte, Harry C. *Community Is Possible*. New York: Harper & Row, 1984.

Breckenridge, Adam C. *One House for Two: Nebraska's Unicameral Legislature*. Washington, D.C.: Public Affairs Press, 1957.

Brown, Robert E. *Middle-Class Democracy and the Revolution in Massachusetts, 1691–1780*. Ithaca: Cornell University Press, 1955.

Brown, W. Jethro. *The New Democracy: A Political Study*. London: Macmillan, 1899.

Bryce, James. *The American Commonwealth*. London: Macmillan, 1888.

Burnheim, John. *Is Democracy Possible?* Berkeley: University of California Press, 1985.

Butler, Nicholas M. *True and False Democracy*. New York: Macmillan, 1907.

Carter, April. *Direct Action and Liberal Democracy*. New York: Harper & Row, 1973.

Civic Federation of Chicago. *Dangers of the Initiative and Referendum*. Chicago, 1912.

Codding, George A., Jr. *The Federal Government of Switzerland*. Boston: Houghton Mifflin, 1961.

Cohen, Carl. *Democracy*. Athens: University of Georgia Press, 1971.

Commager, Henry Steele. *Majority Rule and Minority Rights*. Gloucester, Mass.: Peter Smith, 1958.

Cooper, John R. "Institutional Factors Affecting the Outcome of School Board Referenda." Ph.D. diss., University of Virginia, 1967.

Corry, J. A., and Henry J. Abraham. *Elements of Democratic Government*. 4th ed. New York: Oxford University Press, 1964.

Cree, Nathan. *Direct Legislation by the People*. Chicago: A.C. McClurg, 1892.

Croly, Herbert. *Progressive Democracy*. New York: Macmillan, 1914.

Crotty, William J. *Political Reform and the American Experiment*. New York: Crowell, 1977.

Culbertson, Paul I. "A History of the Initiative and Referendum in Oregon." Ph.D. diss., University of Oregon, 1941.

Cunningham, R. J., ed. *The Populists in Historical Perspective*. Boston: D.C. Heath, 1968.

Dahl, Robert A. *After the Revolution*. New Haven: Yale University Press, 1970.

———*A Preface to Democratic Theory*. Chicago: University of Chicago Press, 1956.

———*Who Governs?* New Haven: Yale University Press, 1961.

De Grazia, Alfred. *Public and Republic: Political Representation in America*. New York: Alfred A. Knopf, 1951.

Delmatier, Royce D., Clarence F. McIntosh, and Earl G. Waters, eds. *The Rumble of California Politics: 1848–1970*. New York: John Wiley and Sons, 1970.

De Witt, Benjamin Parke. *The Progressive Movement.* New York: Macmillan, 1915.

Diamond, Martin, Winston Mills Fisk, and Herbert Garfinkel. *The Democratic Republic.* Chicago: Rand McNally, 1966.

Dixon, Robert G. *Democratic Representation: Reapportionment in Law and Politics.* New York: Oxford University Press, 1968.

Dodds, Gordon B. *Oregon: A History.* New York: Morton, 1977.

Eaton, Allen H. *The Oregon System: The Story of Direct Election in Oregon.* Chicago: A.C. McClurg, 1912.

Ekirch, Arthur A., Jr. *Progressivism in America.* New York: New Viewpoints, 1974.

Eulau, Heinz, and John C. Wahlke. *The Politics of Representation.* Beverly Hills, Calif.: Sage Publications, 1978.

Evans, Sara M., and Harry C. Boyte. *Free Spaces: The Sources of Democratic Change in America.* New York: Harper & Row, 1986.

Flower, B. O. *Progressive Men, Women, and Movements of the Past Twenty-five Years.* 1914; reprint, Westport, Conn.: Hyperion Press, 1975.

Ford, Henry Jones. *Representative Government.* New York: Henry Holt, 1924.

——————*The Rise and Growth of American Politics.* New York: Macmillan, 1898.

Fraker, Elmer L. "The Spread of Populism into Oklahoma Territory." M.A. thesis, University of Oklahoma, 1938.

Galbreath, C. B., ed. *Initiative and Referendum.* Columbus, Ohio: F.J. Heer, 1912.

Gillespie, John. "Direct Legislation in Oklahoma." M.A. thesis, University of Oklahoma, 1949.

Goodhart, Philip. *Full-Hearted Consent: The Story of the Referendum Campaign and the Campaign for the Referendum.* London: Davis-Poynter, 1976.

——————*Referendum.* London: Tom Stacey, 1971.

Gosnell, Harold F. *Democracy: The Threshold of Freedom.* New York: Ronald Press, 1948.

Graham, George J., Jr., and Scarlett G. Graham, eds. *Founding Principles of American Government: Two Hundred Years of Democracy on Trial.* Bloomington: Indiana University Press, 1977.

Green, James R. *Grass-Roots Socialism: Radical Movements in the Southwest, 1895–1943.* Baton Rouge: Louisiana State University Press, 1978.

Green, Philip. *Retrieving Democracy: In Search of Civic Equality.* Totowa, N.J.: Rowman and Allanheld, 1985.

Hackney, Sheldon, ed. *Populism: The Culture Issues.* Boston: Little, Brown, 1971.

Hahn, Harlan, and Sheldon Kamieniecki, *Referendum Voting: Social Status and Policy Preferences.* Westport, Conn.: Greenwood Press, 1987.

Hamilton, Howard D., and Sylvan H. Cohen. *Policymaking by Plebiscite: School Referenda.* Lexington, Mass.: D.C. Heath, 1974.

Hanson, Russell L. *The Democratic Imagination in America: Conversations with Our Past.* Princeton: Princeton University Press, 1985.

Harmon, William S. "Oklahoma's Constitutional Amendments: A Study of the Use of the Initiative and Referendum." Ph.D. diss., University of Oklahoma, 1951.

Hattersley, Alan F. *A Short History of Democracy*. Cambridge: University Press, 1930.

Headlam, James W. *Election by Lot at Athens*. 2d ed. Cambridge: University Press, 1933.

Hedges, Gilbert L. *Where the People Rule*. San Francisco: Bender-Moss, 1914.

Hicks, John D. *The Populist Revolt*. Minneapolis: University of Minnesota Press, 1931.

Hofstadter, Richard. *The Age of Reform*. New York: Vintage Books, 1955.

Hollander, Richard. *Video Democracy: The Vote-from-the-Home Revolution*. Mt. Airy, Md.: Lomand, 1985.

Holtzelaw, Harold W. "The American War Referendum Movement, 1914–1941." Ph.D. diss., University of Denver, 1965.

Honey, Samuel Robertson. *The Referendum among the English*. London: Macmillan, 1912.

Hubbard, Benjamin V. *Making America Safe for Democracy: The Referendum— An Instrument of Government*. Chicago: Chicago Legal News, 1926.

Huntington, Samuel P. *American Politics: The Promise of Disharmony*. Cambridge, Mass.: Belknap Press of Harvard University Press, 1981.

Jarvis, Howard, with Robert Pack. *I'm Mad as Hell*. New York: Times Books, 1979.

Johnsen, Julia E., ed. *Selected Articles on the Recall*. Minneapolis: H.W. Wilson, 1911.

Johnson, Walter. *William Allen White's America*. New York: Henry Holt, 1947.

Jones, A. H. M. *Athenian Democracy*. Baltimore: Johns Hopkins University Press, 1986.

Jones, Henry W. *Safe and Unsafe Democracies*. New York: Crowell, 1918.

Jones, Richard G. "Organized Labor and the Initiative and Referendum Movement, 1885–1920." M.A. thesis, University of Washington, 1963.

Kales, Albert M. *Unpopular Government in the United States*. Chicago: University of Chicago Press, 1978.

Kelly, James A., Jr. "Conflict Resolution and California School Board Recall Elections." Ph.D. diss., Stanford University, 1967.

Kelso, William A. *American Democratic Theory*. Westport, Conn.: Greenwood Press, 1978.

Kirkpatrick, Samuel A. *The Legislative Process in Oklahoma*. Norman: University of Oklahoma Press, 1914.

Kirkpatrick, Samuel A., David R. Morgan, and Thomas G. Kielhorn. *The Oklahoma Voter: Politics, Elections, and Parties in the Sooner State*. Norman: University of Oklahoma Press, 1977.

Kotter, Milton. *Neighborhood Government*. Indianapolis: Bobbs-Merrill, 1967.

LaPalombara, Joseph G. *The Initiative and Referendum in Oregon: 1938–1948*. Corvallis: Oregon State College, 1950.

League of Women Voters of California. *Initiative and Referendum in California: A Legacy Lost? A Study of Direct Legislation in California from Progressive Hopes to Present Reality*. Sacramento, 1984.

Legislative Reference Department, Kansas State Library. *Legislative Systems*. Topeka: Kansas State Printing Office, 1914.

Lieb, Hermann. *The Initiative and Referendum.* Chicago: H. Lieb, Jr., 1902.

Lindsay, A. D. *The Essentials of Democracy.* 2d ed. London: Oxford University Press, 1942.

Lippmann, Walter. *The Public Philosophy.* New York: New American Library, 1955.

Lobinger, Charles S. *The People's Law, or Popular Participation in Law Making.* New York: Macmillan, 1909.

Lockridge, Kenneth A. *A New England Town: The First Hundred Years.* New York: W. W. Norton, 1970.

Lowell, A. Lawrence. *Public Opinion and Popular Government.* New York: Longmans, Green, 1913.

Lowenstein, Daniel H. "Campaign Spending and Ballot Propositions: Recent Experience, Public Choice Theory, and the First Amendment." *UCLA Law Review,* 29 (February 1982), 505–641.

MacPherson, C. B. *The Life and Times of Liberal Democracy.* New York: Oxford University Press, 1977.

Magid, Fay Armand. "The Recall Election of School Board Members in California, 1945–1965." Ed.D. diss., Stanford University, 1967.

Magleby, David B. *Direct Legislation: Voting on Ballot Propositions in the United States.* Baltimore: Johns Hopkins University Press, 1984.

Maisel, Louis, and Joseph Cooper, eds. *The Impact of the Electoral System.* Newbury Park, Calif.: Sage Publications, 1977.

Mansbridge, Jane J. *Beyond Adversarial Democracy.* New York: Basic Books, 1980.

Margolis, Michael. *Viable Democracy.* New York: Penguin Books, 1979.

Maynard, David M. "The Operation of the Referendum in Chicago." Ph.D. diss., University of Chicago, 1930.

McClosky, Herbert, and John Zaller. *The American Ethos.* Cambridge, Mass.: Harvard University Press, 1984.

McGuigan, Patrick B. *The Politics of Direct Democracy in the 1980s: Case Studies in Popular Decision Making.* Washington, D.C.: Institute for Government and Politics, 1985.

McKenna, George, ed. *American Populism.* New York: G.P. Putnam's Sons, 1974.

Meyer, C. Kenneth. "A Longitudinal Analysis of State Question Voting Patterns in Oklahoma: 1907–1972." Ph.D. diss., University of Oklahoma, 1979.

Munro, William B., ed. *The Initiative, Referendum, and Recall.* New York: D. Appleton, 1912.

Munroe, Edwin B. *Direct Election and Law Making by Popular Vote.* Boston: Houghton Mifflin, 1912.

Neuman, W. Russell. *The Paradox of Mass Politics.* Cambridge, Mass.: Harvard University Press, 1986.

Norris, George W. *Fighting Liberal: The Autobiography of George W. Norris.* New York: Macmillan, 1945.

Nugent, Walter T. K. *The Tolerant Populists: Kansas Populism and Nativism.* Chicago: University of Chicago Press, 1963.

Nye, Russell B. *Midwestern Progressive Politics: A Historical Study of Its Origins and Development, 1870–1958.* East Lansing: Michigan State University Press, 1959.

Oberholtzer, Ellis Paxson. *The Referendum in America*. New York: Charles Scribner's Sons, 1911.

Olson, Laura L. K. "Power, Public Policy, and the Environment: The Defeat of the 1976 Winter Olympics in Colorado." Ph.D. diss., University of Colorado, 1974.

Osbun, Lee Ann. *The Problem of Participation*. Lanham, Md.: University Press of America, 1985.

Parsons, Stanley B. *The Populist Context: Rural versus Urban Power on a Great Plains Frontier*. Westport, Conn.: Greenwood Press, 1973.

Pateman, Carole. *Participation and Democratic Theory*. New York: Cambridge University Press, 1980.

Phelps, Edith M., ed. *Selected Articles on the Recall*. 2d ed., rev. New York: H.W. Wilson, 1915.

Piele, Philip K., and John S. Hale. *Budgets, Bonds, and Ballots: Voting Behavior in School Finance Elections*. New York: Lexington Books, 1973.

Pitkin, Hanna F., ed. *Representation*. New York: Atherton Press, 1969.

Pollack, Norman. *The Populist Response to Industrial America: Midwestern Populist Thought*. Cambridge, Mass.: Harvard University Press, 1962.

Pollock, James K. *The Initiative and Referendum in Michigan*. Ann Arbor: University of Michigan Press, 1940.

Pomeroy, Eltweed, et al. *By the People: Arguments and Authorities for Direct Legislation*. Newark, N.J.: Direct Legislation League, 1900. Also published as U.S. Senate, Committee on the Judiciary. *Direct Legislation, Etc.* Senate Document no. 340. 55th Cong., 2d sess. Washington, D.C.: U.S. Government Printing Office, 1898.

Powe, Lucas A., Jr. *American Broadcasting and the First Amendment*. Berkeley: University of California Press, 1987.

Randall, John Herman. *The Essence of Democracy*. New York: Dodge, 1919.

Ransom, William L. *Majority Rule and the Judiciary*. New York: Da Capo Press, 1971.

Reed, Scott W. "W. S. U'Ren and the Oregon System." Senior honors thesis, Princeton University, 1950.

Robbins, James W. "A Consideration and Analysis of Initiated and Referred Legislation Submitted to the Electorate of North Dakota from 1940 to 1958." M.A. thesis, University of North Dakota, 1959.

Roosevelt, Theodore. *Progressive Principles*. New York: Progressive National Service, 1913.

Roush, Russell B. "The Initiative and Referendum in Arizona: 1912–1978." Ph.D. diss., Arizona State University, 1979.

Scales, James R. "Political History of Oklahoma, 1907–1949." Ph.D. diss., University of Oklahoma, 1949.

Schaffner, Margaret A. *The Recall*. Madison: Wisconsin Library Commission, 1907.

Schmidt, Benno C., Jr. *Freedom of the Press vs. Public Access*. New York: Praeger, 1976.

Schmidt, David D. "Ballot Initiative: History, Research, and Analysis of Recent Initiative and Referendum Campaigns." Mimeograph. Initiative News Service, Washington, D.C., March 1983.

———*National Referendum '87–'88: Ballots vs. the Arms Race*. Washington, D.C.: Initiative Resource Center, 1987.

Senning, John P. *The One-House Legislature*. New York: McGraw-Hill, 1937.

Sharp, Clifford D. *The Case against the Referendum*. Fabian Tract no. 155. London: Fabian Society, 1911.

Shockley, John S. "Direct Democracy, Campaign Finance, and the Courts: Can Corruption, Undue Influence, and Declining Voter Confidence Be Found?" *University of Miami Law Review*, 39 (May 1985), 377–428.

———*The Initiative Process in Colorado Politics: An Assessment*. Boulder: Bureau of Governmental Research and Service, University of Colorado, 1980.

Smith, David G. *The Convention and the Constitution*. New York: St. Martin's Press, 1965.

Smith, J. Allen. *The Spirit of American Government*. New York: Macmillan, 1907.

Spitz, Elaine. *Majority Rule*. Chatham, N.J.: Chatham House, 1984.

Starr, Paul D. "The Initiative and Referendum in Colorado." M.A. thesis, University of Colorado, 1958.

Steffens, Lincoln. *Upbuilders*. Garden City, N.Y.: Doubleday, 1909.

Strum, Philippa. *The Supreme Court and "Political Questions": A Study in Judicial Evasion*. Tuscaloosa: University of Alabama Press, 1974.

Sullivan, J. W. *Direct Legislation by the Citizenship through the Initiative and Referendum*. New York: True Nationalist Publishing, 1893.

Taft, William Howard. *Popular Government: Its Essence, Its Permanence, and Its Perils*. New Haven: Yale University Press, 1913.

Tallian, Laura. *Direct Democracy*. Los Angeles: People's Lobby, 1977.

Thompson, C. J. "The Origins of Direct Legislation in Oregon." M.A. thesis, University of Oregon, 1929.

Thompson, Dennis F. *John Stuart Mill and Representative Government*. Princeton: Princeton University Press, 1976.

Tindall, George B., ed. *A Populist Reader: Selections from the Works of American Populist Leaders*. New York: Harper & Row, 1966.

Todd, Charles F. "The Initiative and Referendum in Arizona." M.A. thesis, University of Arizona, 1931.

U.S. Congress. Senate. *Voter Initiative Constitutional Amendment. Hearings before the Subcommittee on the Constitution of the Committee on the Judiciary, on S.J. Resolution 67*. 95th Cong. 1st sess. December 1977. Washington, D.C.: U.S. Government Printing Office, 1978.

Van Eaton, Anson E. "The Initiative and Referendum in Missouri." Ph.D. diss., University of Missouri, 1955.

Weinstein, Esther G. "William Simon U'Ren: A Study of Persistence in Political Reform." D.S.Sc. diss., Syracuse University, 1967.

Weyl, Walter L. *The New Democracy*. New York: Macmillan, 1912.

Wilcox, Delos F. *Government by All the People*. New York: Macmillan, 1912.

Wright, James E. *The Politics of Populism: Dissent in Colorado*. New Haven: Yale University Press, 1974.

Zeittlin, Josephine Ver Brugge. *Recall: A Bibliography*. Los Angeles: John Randolph Haynes and Dora Haynes Foundation, 1940.

Zimmerman, Joseph F. *The Massachusetts Town Meeting: A Tenacious Insti-*

tution. Albany: Graduate School of Public Affairs, State University of New York, 1967.

———*Participatory Democracy: Populism Revised*. New York: Praeger, 1986.

Zisk, Betty H. *Money, Media, and the Grass Roots: State Ballot Issues and the Electoral Process*. Newbury Park, Calif.: Sage Publications, 1987.

Zurcher, Arnold J. "The Hitler Referenda." *American Political Science Review*, 29 (February 1935), 91–99.

Index

▼